CROSSBOW HUNTING

CROSSBOW HUNTING

William Hovey Smith

STACKPOLE
BOOKS

Published by
STACKPOLE BOOKS
5067 Ritter Road
Mechanicsburg, PA 17055
www.stackpolebooks.com

Printed in the United States

First edition

10 9 8 7 6 5 4 3 2 1

Cover design by Caroline Stover
Cover photo courtesy Excalibur, Inc.

Library of Congress Cataloging-in-Publication Data

Smith, William Hovey.
  Crossbow hunting / William Hovey Smith.
      p. cm.
  Includes index.
  ISBN-13: 978-0-8117-3311-3 (alk. paper)
  ISBN-10: 0-8117-3311-4 (alk. paper)
  1. Crossbow hunting. I. Title.

SK36.15.S65 2006
799.20285—dc22

                                                    2006003654

CONTENTS

PREFACE

The crossbow, that ingenious combination of bow, supporting stave, and trigger, has played a part in human history as a hunting and military weapon for more than 2,000 years. It predated the invention of gunpowder by at least a millennium, and yet was an interesting enough hunting tool to be continuously made from its long-lost date of invention to the twenty-first century. Crossbows of both antique and modern styles are still available from individual craftsmen working out of their homes, from shops, and from multinational companies that sell their products worldwide.

Why is this age-old weapon still popular? Because it meets the needs of many kinds of crossbow users. In the right hands, the crossbow with its carefully matched arrows, points, and sights is capable of extreme precision. This characteristic, by itself, appeals to those crossbow users with competitive instincts. In Europe, crossbow-shooting contests have been held for hundreds of years. Man's drive for perfection led to the development of many features such as adjustable sights and set triggers, which were later adapted to firearms. Striving to register a series of perfect shots on a target creates an itch that the competitive-minded shooter just has to scratch.

Another subset of crossbow users love technology and prefer to experience technological developments firsthand, rather than vicariously through celluloid or digital representations. Even among this group, two distinct camps exist: The first uses replicas of medieval and Renaissance crossbows; the second wants to try the latest modern designs of compound, recurve, and reverse-draw crossbows. Bagging record heads of big game does not interest these shooters. This group prefers to prove that this anciently derived technology still works and that the user can develop sufficient skills to use the crossbow effectively. Most likely,

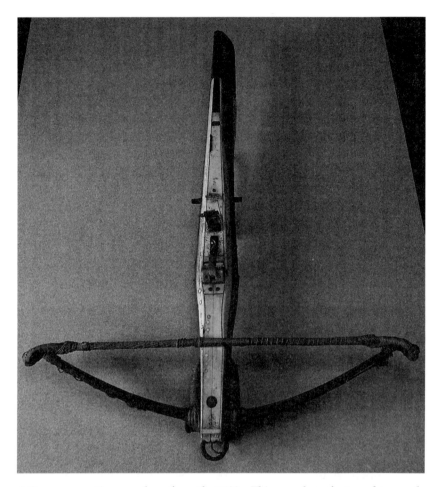

A German sporting crossbow from the 1400s. This crossbow features bone and ivory components and an adjustable rear sight and was originally used with a spanner. The pull weight on this crossbow was probably on the order of 300 pounds.

members in this category also hunt with muzzleloaders, conventional bows, handguns, black-powder cartridge rifles, spears, and other off-beat hunting methods. And yes, in case you were wondering, I fall into this grouping.

By far, the largest population of crossbow users consists of hunters who seek deer, hogs, bear, and larger game with crossbows. These hunters also have several different reasons for taking up the crossbow. Many crossbow hunters want to expand their hunting opportunities by participating in archery seasons, and the crossbow appears to be an easier and commonly less expensive tool to master than the compound bow. Unfortunately, many former gun hunters have unrealistic expectations of a crossbow's capabilities, and they seriously underestimate the time it takes to master their new hunting implements.

Bow hunters also are taking up the crossbow, often because age, injury, loss of vision, or other physical ailments prevent them from shooting their beloved bows any longer. Just as a crossbow keeps a young bow hunter from having to sit out an entire season because an injury prevents him from using his traditional bow, older hunters can extend their archery hunting by twenty or even thirty years by using a crossbow. At 63, I am on the cusp of this. I still shoot bows, both recurve and compounds, but the improved sighting, provided by a scope or red-dot sights, enables me to see the target better and make more precise hits. In the final analysis, a hunter's ability to place a first hit in the right place is more important than what hunting tool is used. Crossbows can make those precise shot placements.

I know from firsthand experience the limitations of wheelchair confinement, stumbling around with a walker, and not being able to fully use my limbs. Because the crossbow provides low recoil, easy cocking, and excellent sights, thousands of physically challenged hunters may use a piece of archery equipment to reliably kill game, allowing crossbows to be justifiably embraced by such groups as Wheelin' Sportsmen.

Another growing category of crossbow hunters includes young people of both genders and women who don't have the physical strength to draw the powerful traditional bows used to reliably kill big-game animals. Crossbows also allow supervised children to learn more about hunting during archery season. To successfully take game with a crossbow, children must learn how to scout animals; pick a spot for a blind; watch wind directions; and employ proper camouflage as well as scent, noise, and insect control. Most important of all, children learn the importance of sitting still, being vigilant, and not giving up, useful lessons for any young hunter to learn. Even if no game is taken during archery season, the young hunter will be much better prepared for his or her first gun season and for all hunts that follow.

If necessity is the mother of invention, then need is the mother of book writing. At the moment, the most commonly circulated book on the crossbow is *The Crossbow* by Sir Ralph Payne-Gallwey. This book was first published in 1903, republished in 1958, and has had more recent printings. In 1978, George M. Stevens published *Crossbows: From 35 Years with the Weapon*, which covered the history and technological aspects of crossbows but provided little information about hunting. Robert Combs's

Sheila Foulkrod spanning a crossbow. Crossbows enable women, the young, and the disabled to enjoy archery hunting, an experience that traditional bows, which require strength to pull, may deny them. Many crossbow hunters were one-time bowhunters until age and infirmities prevented them from using their bows any longer.

1987 release of *Crossbows* detailed both the modern and traditional aspects of target shooting with crossbows. He also touched on the slowly emerging hunting possibilities offered by crossbows. Since the crossbow has experienced more technological developments in the past twenty years than during the previous two thousand, I believed the time was ripe for an update, which would focus on the hunting potential of the modern crossbow. I began approaching publishers about such a book in 1999.

Because publishers hate risks, a well-developed pack instinct often applies to books. If someone has a successful self-help book on body building, every publisher wants such a title. Many publishers seemed to think, "If no one else has a crossbow book, then obviously crossbow books don't sell and there is no need for one." However, my experience revealed an increasing demand for a comprehensive book on crossbows, which would talk realistically about what is available today.

I also could find almost nothing written about crossbows in popular magazines. Bowhunting magazines, as a group, do not accept articles about crossbows. I have been able to sell on-line pieces about crossbows to Sportsman's Guide and Cabela's, and occasionally I have featured crossbows in articles about hunts for urban deer. One of the more consistent publishers of materials about crossbows is the magazine *Horizontal Bowhunter,* the official publication of the American Crossbow Federation. Editor and owner Daniel James Hendricks and I became correspondents and friends. Our conversations covered many topics, and we both agreed on the need for a comprehensive book on modern crossbows.

Ultimately, I approached Stackpole, a long-time publisher of outdoor books, about a book on the modern hunting crossbow. I received an expression of interest, but it took the publication of another of my books, *Practical Bowfishing* in 2004, to demonstrate that I could write a prize-winning book about an outdoor subject to achieve a commitment for publication.

Rapid technological advances, the very thing that compelled this book's writing in the first place, are a double-edged sword. Books take a year to write and publish, yet each year crossbow makers bring out new models and make improvements to old ones. Any book that attempts to be a catalogue quickly becomes obsolete. Recognizing this reality, I will show a lot of crossbows in this book but make no attempt to include all crossbows or to quote exact prices, as both are subject to change.

What I try to do is to include examples of different crossbows from several makers, covering a range of prices and options. Although you may not find every new "MegaStrike Quadlimbed SuperCross" (to use a made-up name) in the pages of this book, you will find discussions of each type of crossbow and what each maker is attempting to achieve with its crossbows.

Often, higher-priced crossbows get most of the attention in advertising, marketing, and whatever little is written about crossbows. Because many new users buy lower-priced crossbows, I have purposely taken several crossbows in the $100 to $150 range on hunts to see what they could do. Although low-cost crossbows are typically more difficult to shoot and often come with little or no instructive materials, they can effectively take game when used within their limitations. Paradoxically, experienced shooters are more likely than novice hunters to have success with these low-priced crossbows. Competition is strong in the crossbow market, and the prices of today's crossbows honestly reflect added value in design, materials, accuracy, effectiveness, and ease of use. The more expensive bows are more accurate, easier to shoot, and more effective killers of big game than their bargain-basement cousins. If a user buys the better products, he or she will have better results and likely be more satisfied with crossbows in general.

Putting all of this together is my challenge as a writer. All of the crossbow makers cited in this book have been helpful in arranging for me to visit their factories, shoot their products, and even, on occasion, hunt with them. Photos, anecdotes, and the hunts described in these pages, in many cases, have been derived from the experiences of others who agreed with me that a book on the modern crossbow was long overdue. To all, my heartfelt thanks. I have enjoyed the writing, and I hope you will enjoy the read. Welcome to the world of the crossbow.

Wm. Hovey Smith
Sandersville, Georgia

1

HISTORY OF THE CROSSBOW

Rather than spending much time exploring the largely conjectural early history of the crossbow, I would like to refer interested readers to Sir Ralph Payne-Gallwey's 328-page book *The Crossbow: Medieval and Modern Military and Sporting*, which was first published in 1903 and has undergone frequent reprintings. An inexpensive paperbacked version has been reissued by Dover Publications. Payne-Gallwey reasoned that the crossbow probably originated in China some two to three thousand years ago and spread westward into the Middle East, Africa, and Europe. Early derivations were used by the Greeks and Romans and more refined versions by the Crusaders. Modernized target and sport crossbows were still being made when he was writing early in the twentieth century.

Several unproven and unprovable theories have emerged to explain how the original vertically held bow became transformed into a horizontal component fixed in a stock and fired by a trigger. A common theory is that the crossbow's progenitor was an early type of trap where a bow was held at full draw by a stick to which was tied a string attached to bait. When the bait was pulled away, the restraining stick moved, allowing the bowstring to fire an arrow at the animal. Proponents of this theory claim that this early design could easily evolve into a weapon with a permanent stock to hold the bow and a more sensitive trigger device to discharge the string. The trigger could be as simple as a round stick poking through a flat plank to hold the string. By running the string around a handy root or branch, a downward force would be exerted to pull down the rod, release the string, and fire the arrow.

In this manner, crossbow traps and crossbows could be made without metallic components using wood, cord, and a bit of stone, bone, or sharpened bamboo for a point. Only in bogs, deserts, or arctic environments

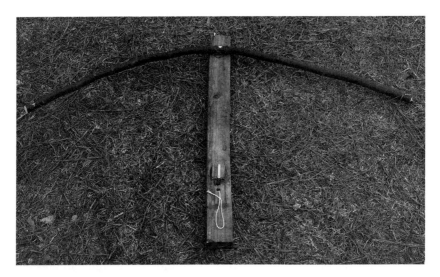

Primitive crossbow trap made with only wood and string. This type of mechanism, which may have been the crossbow's ancestor, could have been used shortly after the invention of the bow thousands of years ago.

would traces of such an implement be preserved. Because this technology would have been within the reach of earliest man, the precursor to the crossbow could have been made not two or three thousand years ago, but as long as five to ten thousand years ago, shortly after the bow was developed.

Another line of thought, although I have not seen it in print, is that the crossbow was first developed from the foot bow, a powerful device that is bent using the legs rather than the relatively weak arms. To use it, the bowman lies on his back, holds the bowstring, and pushes his legs forward to apply pressure to the middle of the bow. When the arrow is fully drawn, it is launched at the target. Foot bows were used for elephant hunting in Asia and Africa, and the Assyrians employed more refined versions as a sort of long-range artillery.

Because mechanical objects are typically substituted for human limbs in the evolution of machines, a wooden handle would have been affixed to an ax to take the place of a hand holding a sharp stone. This would have resulted in less wear on the hand and increasing leverage and force of the blow. Just as shorter and longer handles were affixed to blades to make knives and spears, it is not too much of a technological leap to attach a handle to a foot bow and use it instead of the legs to hold an arrow at full draw. Add a leather or cord stirrup, which would allow a bow (now crossbow) to be drawn while standing, and all of the supporting components of the crossbow are in place. All that remains are the drilling of a hole and the use of a pin to restrain the string, and you have a functional crossbow.

Darwinism has trained modern westerners to look for a single point of origin for an invention and then follow its dispersion and evolution through time and space. To conform to this theory, the crossbow could well have originated, in say, China, and its use could have spread throughout Asia, the Middle East, and Africa, before finally making its way to Europe and the New World. Along the way each country, indeed almost each maker, would have modified the basic crossbow to better use the materials at hand and to make it more effective.

A supporting argument in favor of this straight-line distribution is that although native societies in the Americas had a high degree of technological evolution in some fields, they apparently did not know or use the crossbow, or the wheel for that matter, until these items were introduced by Europeans. Apparently some event in the Asian-African-European experience prompting the invention of the crossbow did not take place in the Americas. Perhaps the absence of huge game animals such as the elephant in the Americas did not prompt the invention of powerful foot-drawn bows.

In reality, crossbow evolution appears to be more along the lines of invention, dispersion, development, discontinuance, rediscovery, evolution, and the coexistence of both primitive and more modern forms.

Although of uncertain origin, this crossbow is reputed to be Vietnamese. It employs several leaf springs to power the bow, peg sights, and a simple trigger.

Rather than undergoing a progressive evolutionary process, the crossbow has experienced a lot of stops and starts along the way. Once the concept was known, it did not take long for enterprising minds to reinvent the crossbow and produce it from whatever materials, primitive or modern, that the then-existing technology allowed.

THE HOW AND WHY OF THE MODERN CROSSBOW
If not for the persistence of crossbow target shooting in Europe, the activities of a few pioneering individuals, and the release of a couple of movies, today's most common crossbows would likely be low-powered children's toys shooting foam arrows. In 1975, the popular Peter Sellers's movie *Return of the Pink Panther* showed actor Catherine Schell using a skeletal all-metal crossbow with a built-in cocking device to steal the fabulous Pink Panther diamond. This crossbow was built for Pinewoods Studio by Bernard Horton.

Crossbows showed up again in the 1981 James Bond movie *For Your Eyes Only* when Melina Havelock (Carole Bouquet) used two different crossbows to dispatch the villainous characters who had killed her parents. Just as Clint Eastwood's *Dirty Harry* boosted the sales of Smith and Wesson's .44-Magnum revolver, the appearance of crossbows in several popular movies sparked interest in modernized versions of the ancient crossbow.

In tracing the evolution of the modern hunting crossbow, it seems only appropriate to look at the history of several makers of crossbows and see how they have helped the modern crossbow evolve to what it is today.

Horton Crossbow Company
As a 12-year-old rabbit stalker in the English countryside, Bernard Horton first became interested in crossbows in 1956. He found that he could crawl close enough to his prey to take it with his homemade bow, but when he rose to shoot, the rabbit would spot him and run. The crossbow appealed to him because he could shoot it while prone, and he would not have to reveal himself to his game. When he saw the poor, weak quality of the crossbows and kits that he could afford, Horton thought that he could make a better version.

But instead of making a crossbow just for himself, he designed a more powerful hunting crossbow that could be commercially produced. At 19, he started the Horton Crossbow Company and began manufacturing crossbows near his home in South Wales. In 1977, Horton relocated his crossbow manufacturing facility to Scotland, where he also

These two English-made Horton crossbows illustrate the use of both wood and metal as the principal structural components of the crossbow. As good wood became more expensive to use, wood stocks were progressively replaced with metal. In recent years wood stocks have made a comeback in the form of laminated varieties sold by Parker, Fred Bear, and other makers.

began making custom hunting guns. An avid hunter, Horton believed that he could make an efficient modern crossbow that could reliably take game.

Horton's first crossbow stocks were made of wood and used steel prods. These early crossbows carried a circular nameplate in the stock inscribed "Horton Crossbows Merthry Tydfil S. Wales." Soon after his wood-stocked version was introduced, he made a rugged aluminum crossbow for hunters. When he was called upon to design a "sexy" crossbow for the *Return of the Pink Panther*, Horton made a crossbow with a built-in cocking device, which, although an interesting design, offered no performance advantage over conventionally cocked crossbows. He never produced it commercially. Another company, Barnett, later sold a version of this crossbow as its "Commando" crossbow.

Wanting to improve the performance and ruggedness of his crossbows, Horton introduced the Safari Magnum crossbow in 1975. This crossbow, which featured a polypropylene stock, his new Dial-A-Range sight adjustment feature, a 150-pound draw, and a rawhide-thong foot stirrup, was aimed at U.S. hunters, whom Horton saw as a major market. The wooden-stocked LS Express was simultaneously offered with compound fiberglass limbs. Due to the increasing price of quality wood

Detail of stock medallion on an early Horton crossbow. Horton, who relocated his factory from Wales to Scotland, produced medallioned stocks for only a few years.

An argument can be made that the Horton Safari Magnum with its fiberglass stock was the first truly modern crossbow.

and its dimensional instability, wooden-stocked crossbows would be replaced by the fiberglass-filled polypropylene-stocked Safari Express within a few years.

The Express series is the precursor to Horton's present line of compound crossbows, which now includes the 200-pound draw weight Hunter XS and Fire Hawk, the 175-pound draw weight Legend SK, and the 150-pound draw Hawk and Yukon. The SteelForce, offered with both 80- and 150-pound draw weights, still uses a steel prod. Common to all modern Horton crossbows is the use of synthetic stocks and the Dial-A-Range sighting system.

Because the bulk of its sales were in North America and the company found it more economical to produce crossbows in the United States than in the United Kingdom, Horton moved its entire operations in 1987 to Akron, Ohio, where its factory and research facilities are now located. Horton's current crossbows can be viewed on-line at www.crossbow.com.

Barnett International
Barnett, a crossbow company that also has its roots in the United Kingdom, has produced more models of crossbows than any modern maker and very likely holds the record for selling the largest number of crossbows. In recent years, Barnett has sought to cover the entire crossbow

Horton's Safari Express was originally offered with a wood stock and was among the first crossbows to feature compound limbs. Within a few years, the Express also featured a fiberglass stock and became the ancestor to the present line of Horton crossbows.

Barnett's crossbows cover the lower and intermediate range of the crossbow market. The Panzer recurve crossbow, although a technologically more advanced version of the lightweight Ranger, is targeted toward users who want to try a crossbow but are unwilling, or unable, to make a large cash investment.

market, and its offerings encompass toy crossbows, inexpensive hunting and target crossbows, and midrange-priced models intended for serious big-game hunters.

This attempt to be "everyman's crossbow maker" has unfortunately resulted in some of its lower-priced crossbows, while functional, not having particularly good performance characteristics or durability. Some Barnett crossbows may be purchased for less than $150, a price that cannot be expected to maintain the same quality standards as crossbows costing four or five times that amount.

Among the older crossbows produced by Barnett, the Wildcat has the best reputation for efficiently delivering crossbow arrows into big game. The mechanically interesting "self-cocking" Commando may also be used to take game, but it is not as efficient as a similar pull weight Wildcat. The Commando also has the problem of being rough on strings, particularly if, as is often the case, the protective plastic caps have been lost off the hooks of the cocking arm.

Also among Barnett's commercial offerings, crossbow pistols, as a class, are weakly powered, difficult to shoot well, and do not develop sufficient energy to be effective against anything but the smallest of game. The tiny arrows are best used for indoor target practice at ranges of from 5 to 10 yards.

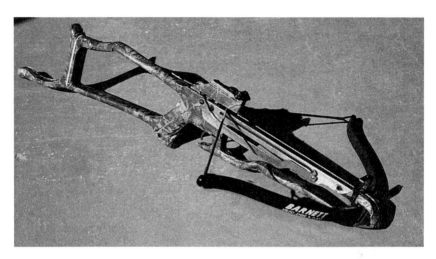

This Barnett Commando crossbow was missing almost a third of its original black-crackle finish when it was purchased used. The remainder of the finish was removed, and the cast-aluminum frame was then covered with camo tape.

In looking at Barnett options for $500 or less, the Barnett Revolution XS with 160-pound draw limbs is the current highest quality crossbow. Next, at about $400, is the Barnett Revolution with split fiberglass limbs and a 150-pound pull. The Quad 300, a 150-pound crossbow with a 15 1/4-inch power stroke to increase velocity and down-range energy, costs about $300, and the various Ranger crossbows at the low end of the market range from about $200 to occasionally less than $150 from discount houses. Even these Rangers will effectively take deer at close range, as I have done with an older model that only produced a velocity of 205 feet per second (fps) (see table on page 85) and 32 foot-pounds of energy (see table on page 87). The most recent Ranger design is the RC-150, which has recurve limbs and a higher velocity. Barnett's most recent recurve crossbow, the $150 Panzer, features a full-size stock in contrast to the skeletal stocks of the Ranger series.

Barnett International has sales operations in both the United Kingdom and the United States. Its current U.S. operations are based in Odessa, Florida. A complete line of Barnett products may be viewed at the company's website at www.barnettcrossbows.com.

Robertson Crossbows
Sometime in the 1950s, Hank Robertson of Longmont, Colorado, designed a crossbow featuring a cast metal frame, plastic panels for the stock, and fore end and steel prods. The recurve prod with its longer steel stave

The author shooting a Barnett Ranger crossbow. Not too long after this photograph was taken, the author harvested his first crossbow deer with this inexpensive crossbow and a simple red-dot sight. Even though relatively low powered and using a heavy arrow-point combination, this crossbow cleanly took an 80-pound doe with a double-lung shot.

gave a base pull weight of about 80 pounds. To upgrade its power level to 150 and perhaps even 170 pounds, supplemental shorter staves could be ordered with the crossbow and placed in back of the main prod to provide added resistance and energy storage.

The Robertson shot fairly well and had a smooth trigger pull. It was also compact, but its all-metal construction made it very heavy for its size. Although a used crossbow can occasionally be found, Robertson crossbows have not been produced for decades.

Jennings–Fred Bear
When Tom Jennings designed his 1986 Devastator crossbow, he employed several not-then-conventional approaches. By modern standards, the Devastator was huge and ugly, but it worked. Prior to the Devastator, Jennings's 1976 compound crossbow Arrowstar had narrow limbs and aluminum grips. For the Devastator, a hollow magnesium riser was set between the limbs to allow the arrow to pass between rather than over the top of the limbs as was done with a conventional crossbow. Because an arrow in the Devastator is supported, bow fashion, by the nock in the string and by an arrow rest located in the cylindrical riser, it does not sit on the deck of the crossbow, thus eliminating a source of friction and fletching impact.

The American-made Robertson crossbow with its heavy all-metal frame has a unique sighting system etched on a sliding glass sight. Its pull is adjustable by installing or removing steel strips to strengthen the prod. The uppermost bow is a typical wood-stock Swiss target crossbow made by W. Glaser. Because of their heritage, the Swiss have a warm place in their hearts for the crossbow and use them regularly in target competitions.

Other hunter-friendly features of the Devastator were a 150-pound pull weight, automatic safety, redesigned trigger, and adjustable peep and pin sights. But its bulk and weight made the Devastator cumbersome to carry and use. It also looked more like a military weapon than a civilian hunting crossbow.

In 1994, Fred Bear decided to produce a new Lightning Strike crossbow, which retained the trackless design of the Devastator but lightened the weight and reduced the width. The Lightning came with a camo finish and a unique forearm that slid on a round member that connected the buttstock to the limbs. An optional scope rail permitted the use of either long- or short-eye-relief scopes.

The Devastator made one more appearance as the QuadPoint Crossbow, which had split limbs and round wheels and retained the three-point arrow support system used on the later-model Devastators. Although still a large crossbow, the QuadPoint's new limbs slimmed the crossbow's width by several inches.

Still seeking a model that would appeal to hunters, Bear made the Buckmaster MaxPoint crossbow by incorporating the barrel stock and

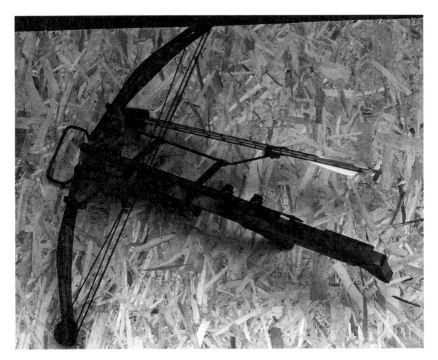

The Jennings-Bear Devastator crossbow, although huge, ugly, and heavy, is a functional crossbow that could reliably kill deer. This design, which used an air-deck and supported the arrow on the nocked bowstring, employs an arrow rest that was similar to other bows of that same period.

trigger from Excalibur and adding its riser and split limbs. The results were 150- and 175-pound draw pull weight crossbows, which weighed between 6 and 7 pounds compared to the nearly 10-pound weight of the original Devastator. The new tracked crossbows were stronger, lighter, and easier to shoot.

Currently Fred Bear crossbows are almost entirely made in Gainesville, Florida. The limbs, riser, cams, and frames are produced in-house and coupled with the stock, trigger, and a few other parts obtained from outside sources. Bear also does its own camo-dipping on the current F300, F325, and F340 crossbows. The new crossbows feature full-size buttstocks, 2.5-pound two-stage triggers, and no-let-off cams that provide more thrust on the arrow at the beginning of its travel to produce more velocity and striking energy.

A new development for Bear has been the licensing of Reverse Draw Technology from its inventor, Sam Collora. Instead of locating the crossbow riser and limbs on the front of the bow, Bear places the riser at the rear with the limbs extending forward like a U. The string is drawn

Sam Collora's reverse-draw crossbow prototype, held here by Henry Gallops of Fred Bear. In this unique design, the bow is reversed and bends toward the front instead of toward the rear. The developmental prototype was used for testing prior to the crossbow's commercial release.

rearward, as in a conventional crossbow, and restrained by a trigger-released catch. Limb tension is transferred by the string through the use of large cam wheels located on the ends of the split limbs. The result is a crossbow that can propel an arrow at a higher velocity but does not require the heavy draw weights needed by conventional designs. Consult www.fredbear.com to view current offerings.

PSE Crossbows

PSE, Precision Shooting Equipment, began as a traditional bow maker and decided to take a stab at the crossbow market. Its entries included several models, such as the Crossfire, Flashfire, Foxfire, Spitfire, Sport-fire, and Starfire. All were compound crossbows with glass-graphite limbs and trackless designs that shot arrows with conventional nocks and supported them near the cocking stirrup with a V-shaped bridge. Touching at only two points, this design offered minimal friction. Depending on the model, the pull weight on the crossbows was 50, 80, or 125 pounds. All of the PSE crossbows, with the exception of the wooden-stocked Crossfire, featured skeletal stocks with aluminum barrels. Peep-and-pin sights were standard, but an optional rail allowed a scope to be mounted on the crossbow.

Two crossbows, the PSE Maxim and Deerslayer, were introduced in 2004 and were retained for only a year. These bought-in designs featured composite, thumbhole stocks, aluminum barrels, and split limbs. The Maxim was rated at 165 pounds and the Deerslayer at 150.

PSE's present offering is the Viper Copperhead Crossbow, which has an aluminum barrel, fiberglass limbs, composite thumbhole stock, and 150-pound draw. With the trackless features and skeletal metal of the older designs eliminated, this crossbow has a much more conventional, contemporary look with a full-size buttstock. Introduced in 2005 at a price of $250, this crossbow is one of the better values in today's market. Additional information is found at www.pse-archery.com/2005.

The PSE Foxfire is a large but inefficient crossbow with a military look to it. As might be expected from a company that made bows, this crossbow employed an air deck and used conventionally nocked and shafted arrows.

Excalibur

Bill Throubridge, co-founder and president of Excalibur Crossbows, first experienced crossbows when he purchased a Daco Hornet in the early 1970s. He described this crossbow's most memorable features as a "poor

Bill Throubridge holding a new camo stock for his Excalibur crossbow. Stocks on crossbows must be weather resistant, strong, stable, lightweight, and comfortable to hold, and must be able to support all of the working mechanisms of the crossbow in their proper positions. A camo-clad stock is less obvious to game.

design and lousy quality" compounded by a lack of technical service. He decided to use a Daco prod to build a better crossbow, and three years later he had done just that. He called his prototype "heavy, absurdly complex . . . and so ugly that its mother would have abandoned it." Nonetheless, it shot well, and in 1983 he killed his first black bear with one.

By 1983, the Throubridges decided to go into the crossbow-making business. A slimmed-down, more refined design called the Relayer was prepared for the sportsmen's show in hopes that it would generate enough orders to start production. It did. His first one hundred Relayers were handmade, and Throubridge reports that he sold sixty-five of them. It helped that not only did the Relayers look considerably better than his prototype, but they had won the U.S. National Hunter Division crossbow-shooting contest for several years running. After 1985, Throubridge's Relayers had aluminum deck plates on their wooden stocks to improve arrow speed and accuracy.

Then, a pair of seemingly fatal blows came in rapid succession. First, a large contract for Relayers was canceled because compound crossbows were believed to dominate the market to the exclusion of recurve

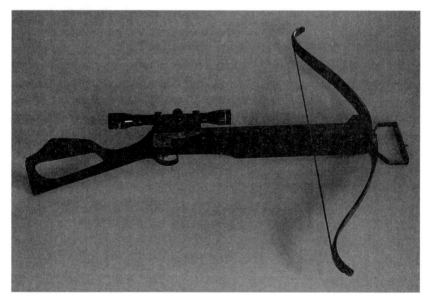

A 1979 version of the Excalibur crossbow, which, although ugly and primitive, shot better than anything that maker Bill Throubridge could buy. Throubridge, who had already built muzzleloading rifles for himself and his wife, was prompted to make a crossbow because his wife could not pull a conventional bow.

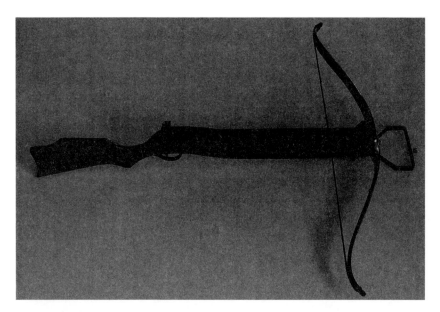

The Excalibur Relayer that won a national competition in 1983 and established the company as a serious contender. After orders for the new crossbow flooded in, the Throubridges had to scramble to develop production facilities that would keep pace with demand.

designs. Second, Daco, the company that had been supplying Excalibur's crossbow limbs, went bankrupt. Excalibur was forced to make its own fiberglass limbs and to refit the Relayers already in inventory with the new limbs.

The company introduced a second model, the Wolverine, which resembled the old Relayer, except that it was fitted with the new limbs. Manufacturing was moved into a factory building in Kitchener, Ontario, which allowed production to reach about a thousand units a year.

By 1991, inconsistencies of wood and its increasing price prompted the redesign of Excalibur crossbows around a polymer stock. The polymer was combined with an extruded aluminum barrel and the company's fiberglass limbs to make the new Exo series, which now includes the 150-pound draw weight Vixen, the 175- and 200-pound Exocets, and the 225 draw weight ExoMax.

Combining its own fiberglass limb-making technology with other advances, such as Fast-Flight strings, has allowed Excalibur to achieve higher draw weights and speeds in lightweight crossbows with recurve prods. Excalibur crossbows and accessories may be viewed at www.excaliburcrossbows.com.

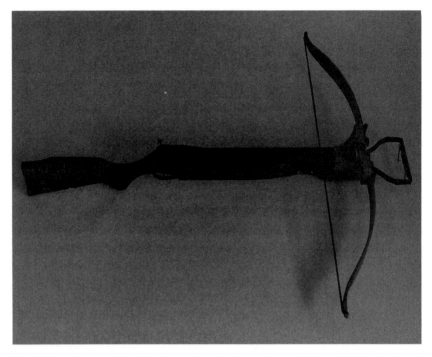

The Wolverine was Excalibur's modernized crossbow with synthetic stock and fiberglass recurve prod. After a supplier of fiberglass prods went bankrupt, Excalibur had to expand its production facility to make its own prods. What seemed a setback at the time was actually a blessing, because now the company controls all aspects of crossbow production in-house.

TenPoint

Although a comparatively new company that produced its first crossbows in 1994, TenPoint has brought new technology, new manufacturing methods, and new features to the crossbow. This company aims to make the best available crossbow using the most up-to-date features. If that crossbow must sell at $1,200, so be it. Optimum design is considered more important than price or obtaining the highest possible arrow velocities.

TenPoint crossbows are unique in that they offer built-in cocking mechanisms, dry-fire inhibitors, a thumb safety to prevent finger strikes, and a detachable monopod. A string or wind-up cocker, which may be installed in the stock, makes this crossbow particularly useful for disabled individuals who cannot draw a conventional bow. Any person who does not have the flexibility to easily do the reaching and bending necessary to install, use, and stow away a separate cocking mechanism will

TenPoint's variable draw Slider crossbow held by sales manager Randy Wood.

appreciate the built-in cockers. The new monopod also helps support the crossbow in a ground blind, another useful feature for those who must shoot from wheelchairs.

Starting at about $500 without the built-in cocking accessories and other extras, the 165-pound pull Titan TL-4 is TenPoint's entry level bow. It was rated as *Inside Archery*'s best buy for 2004. The Hybrid Lite is a 175-pound draw crossbow with a 1-inch shorter stock and 2-inch shorter barrel intended for use by smaller-statured individuals. Stepping up to a 180-pound draw weight, the Elite QX-4 is available with all of the accessories and includes TenPoint's DropTine Foot Stirrup as standard.

Are all these expensive gadgets and accessories really necessary? Maybe not for many shooters, but they are nice to have if you need them. A robust individual will find the TL-4 lightweight and easy to shoot with sufficient power to handle ninety percent of the world's big game. His cousin, who might not have been so fortunate to possess a whole and perfectly functional body, will find that TenPoint's accessories allow him to hunt with a greater degree of self-sufficiency than would otherwise be possible. More about TenPoint's crossbows may be found at www.tenpointcrossbows.com.

2

TODAY'S CROSSBOWS

oday's crossbows feature stocks with synthetic composite or laminated components, a fiberglass or laminated single or multiple-staved prod, the ability to accept a variety of sighting options, low pull-weight triggers, and the availability of one or more types of cocking aids. Notably missing from this list is a mention of compound-limb technology as being "modern" compared to recurve limbs. While most modern crossbow makers have embraced compound limbs, recurve-bow technology has undergone a parallel evolution, and modern, effective recurve crossbows are available today. This issue is discussed more fully in the following chapter.

I have argued in print that crossbow technology has advanced more in the past twenty years than the previous two thousand. Modern materials and components have made the crossbow easier to use and a more effective hunting tool than crossbows made centuries, or even decades, ago. During the 1950s, most crossbows were monotonously similar: The majority had all-wood gun-style stocks and steel prods. Some departures from this tradition came when Horton, Barnett, and others introduced all-metal stocks. Barnett made an aluminum-stocked crossbow called the Commando. This crossbow, which originally had a 170-pound pull, was cocked by bending a hinged stock that allowed brass cocking arms to rise and hook the string and transport it along the barrel to the locking mechanism (a so-called self-cocking mechanism). This design required a metal frame to resist cocking pressures. One problem with the bow was that the brass hooks tended to abrade the strings, particularly after the protective pads wore away. The Commando was made until the 1970s, when it was replaced by polymer-stocked crossbows without the cocking feature.

Today's crossbows cannot be called more powerful, since ancient crossbows were often made with stronger limbs, but the modern crossbow

A. W. Glaser Sporthouse European target crossbow with wood stock and steel prod. This target crossbow has a relatively short draw length for shooting bolts. With a typical draw weight of only about 80 pounds, the crossbow developed too little energy to use except against small game.

does pack more punch in a lighter-weight package. Much of the force expended by old crossbows was consumed in accelerating heavy limbs and huge strings, whereas modern crossbow limbs store their energy in a much lighter-weight limb package and deliver a higher percentage of this energy to the arrow.

Improvements in arrows and points also resulted in more efficient use of the power generated by the new composite limbs. Lighter, stiffer arrows could be thrown at greater speeds, resulting in flatter trajectories and deeper penetration at close range.

Does this mean that today's crossbows can kill at longer distances than yesteryear's models? Not really. Although lighter arrows and faster speeds have increased the point-blank range out to about 20 yards, rapid arrow drop—20 inches or so at 40 yards—limits the effective range of the crossbow for humane use on big game. Within this range, the lightweight crossbow arrows kill efficiently, but beyond it the heavier arrows thrown by a compound bow or heavy draw weight crossbows are better killers. The best way for a crossbow hunter to ensure proper shot placement on

Modern crossbow arrows are made of aluminum and carbon fibers. Not only are they lighter, faster, and more effective than traditional wooden arrows and bolts, they do not warp when wet and their plastic fletching remains usable even during a heavy rain.

game is to invest in a rangefinder. This instrument will tell the hunter, without question, if his deer is at 35 yards, rather than 20, and this 15-yard difference can result in a bad hit or miss.

When compared to the universe of crossbows, past and present, today's crossbows are lightweight, medium-powered hunting bows. Much bigger, more powerful crossbows were made in ancient and medieval times and mounted on ships, walls, and carts or used as artillery and for long-range sniping. A heavy steel-shod arrow from the largest of these, the Roman arcabalistas, could break through the hull of

Today's crossbows, such as this Cabela's Outfitter made by Fred Bear, are medium powered. The laminated wood stock employed by the outfitter not only feels good, but makes an extremely attractive and naturally camouflaged crossbow.

Vital equipment for a crossbow hunter includes arrows, an optical rangefinder, and a hunting bag. Inside the bag, place a snack, a small pruning saw, hunting knives, and anything else you may need to pass a quiet morning or afternoon in the woods.

a ship. Different styles of points were designed to cut rigging, tear sails, and even disable banks of oars. Any individual who got in the way of such a missile would be impaled like a bug on a pin.

Howard L. Blackmore in his book *Hunting Weapons* cites an account of two feuding brothers who lived in nearby castles in the Tyrol. Hans of Frundsberg killed his brother Ulrich with a crossbow shot at a range of about 500 yards when his brother exposed himself in a window. Most likely, the weapon used in this case was a wall-mounted crossbow of heavy pull weight. No doubt, Hans had secretly practiced with his long-range crossbow until he was confident that he could make this shot with a high probability of success.

Maximilian I, the Holy Roman emperor who battled with France, the Netherlands, and Germany for control of central Europe as he simultaneously fought off the Turks, was among the most avid hunters of his day. He had the money to invest in fine hunting implements, many of which survived to today and are in museums where they are regarded as works of fine art. He experimented with all hunting technologies, killing boars with swords and shooting chamois and other game with crossbows. After a steel-prod crossbow he was using flew apart, knocked off his hat, and injured a bystander, he came to prefer the composite horn crossbow. Nonetheless, it was with a steel crossbow that he reportedly took a chamois at 200 yards. His observations on hunting were recorded in *Geheimes Jagdbuch*, which he wrote to instruct his young relations. This book and other works, which contained illustrations commissioned by Emperor Maximilian, remain some of the most commonly viewed depictions of sixteenth-century hunts.

If Emperor Maximilian could shoot an animal as small as a chamois 200 yards away, why can't we with our significantly better equipment do the same? The crossbow arrow will certainly cast that far, but its extreme amount of drop and wind deflection reduce the probability of obtaining a hit. Also quite possibly, the emperor exaggerated the range by a considerable margin. If he said the distance was 200 yards, none of his retainers were likely to disagree. A crossbow shooter can hit targets hundreds of yards away, but this effort requires much practice. The amount of deliverable energy at that range is also significantly diminished, making a killing shot less likely. If we struck a shoulder blade on our prey at that distance, the crossbow arrow would probably not penetrate the vitals of the animal. If that occurred during his reign, Maximilian would have no problem calling out an army to comb the Alps to recover his game, but we common folk do not have an army at our disposal, and thus we need to take careful close-range shots.

MODERN CROSSBOW DESIGN

David Choma, vice president of design and engineering at Horton Crossbow, has been a part of the company since he graduated from college in 1988 with an engineering degree. In a discussion about crossbow design, he used Horton's new Talon Trigger to describe how innovation and development occur with the modern crossbow.

For years, Horton has received customer feedback telling it that hunters love the company's crossbow, but that the trigger needed to be improved. "The basic problem with the crossbow trigger design is that it is holding a lot more weight than the shotgun or rifle trigger," Choma said. "Rather than a harsh, long or mushy trigger, our customers wanted a crisp trigger more like their rifles and shotguns. An added complication was that this trigger had to fit inside the space used for our present trigger so that we did not have to make new molds for the stocks."

Among the first things that Choma did was to consult with existing parts suppliers to find the best technology for producing the complex pieces used for the trigger. The company selected metal-injection molding, a technique in which a steel powder and polymer carrier are forced

Horton's new Talon triggers resulted in improved performance for this company's crossbows.

into a hot mold under high pressure. When the polymer evaporates, the resulting part is produced. These parts exit the molds requiring much less finishing than investment castings produced by the hot-wax process.

"Once we had chosen the method, we could experiment with different configurations of parts on the CAD (computer-assisted design) machine until we were confident enough that we could produce a prototype and install it in a crossbow," Choma continued. "Different triggers were tested until we achieved what we wanted—a new design with a safe 4.5- to 5-pound pull. Each trigger assembly we put together is tried to make sure that it conforms to specs."

Choma went on to explain that Horton could have made a lighter trigger, but the company believed that the majority of its customers would want a trigger pull like those on the guns they owned. For this reason, Horton reduced its customers' learning curve by using a heavier trigger pull.

LIGHTWEIGHT AND GENERIC CROSSBOWS

Small crossbows with minimal weight are useful for several groups of hunters. Anyone who has lost an arm can support and shoot a 5-pound crossbow, like the Barnett Ranger, with one arm, whereas a 7- to 11-pound crossbow would be too heavy. No doubt, those hunting in brushy

Barnett Ranger shown here with the author's first crossbow deer.

country, as I often do, appreciate the smaller profile of lightweight crossbows because they are less trouble to snake through the alders and briers. Finally, anyone who is backpacking can easily pack a light crossbow with a half-dozen arrows.

A Taiwanese Brand X crossbow with a replacement red-dot sight. The crossbow had limited power and about 6 inches of arrow drop between 10 and 20 yards, which severely limited its effective range, but the replacement sight permitted this crossbow to be used for close-range deer hunting.

Modern polymer stocks, particularly when skeletonized, make for a handy crossbow, as is the case with the Barnett's Ranger-series crossbows. This crossbow was sold with an inexpensive red-dot sight for about $130. Its fiberglass prod was advertised to have a 150-pound pull, but I suspect that it is somewhat less. Notwithstanding, this little crossbow with a Barnett shaft and Muzzy 125-grain point cleanly killed a deer for me at 20 yards with a pass-through double-lung shot. The crossbow had a reasonable—if not the best—trigger, could be readily cocked by hand, and had short limbs that handled well in a tree stand. With all of these advantages, why do people use bigger crossbows?

Like their gun counterparts, lightweight crossbows are more difficult to shoot accurately, particularly from off-hand. These crossbows work best if shot from a rest or when firmly braced. My friend Larry Wheishund describes handgun hunting as "spending half the time hunting and half the time looking for a rest." The person using a lightweight crossbow has to take the same approach to minimize wobble and partly negate having a less-than-perfect trigger.

Some of these lightweight crossbows are manufactured by makers of questionable ability. I recently saw an ad in a Sportsman's Guide catalogue for what was described as an Eagle-I Crossbow with BEC red-dot sight for $98.97. This crossbow featured folding limbs that collapsed against the body of the bow, 180 pounds of draw weight, fiberglass limbs, auto safety, and an aluminum flight rail, and it came with two 14-inch aluminum arrows and a 105-grain field point.

The crossbow appealed to both my tight-fisted Scotch nature and the techno-geek aspects of my personality. I had an Alaska hunt planned for black-tailed deer on Kodiak Island. What better way to hike up through the alders than with a lightweight crossbow with collapsible limbs? The crossbow arrived and it was as advertised, but absolutely nothing more. It came with no attachable quiver, no video, no instruction booklet, no name on the crossbow, and absolutely no information on how to get replacement parts or repairs. The only thing stamped on it was, "Made in Taiwan." I also saw an obvious need for more than two arrows.

The crossbow's adjustable sights, general stock design, style of reinforcing steel backing plates, and safety mechanism were visually identical to the same components on a Barnett crossbow. The significant new feature was that the prod was in two pieces, which were hinged and connected to the body of the crossbow by a single, threaded bolt. The only instructions about assembly and shooting were printed on the outside of the box, but these said nothing about lubricating the string or the shooting rail, which is vital maintenance if one intends to shoot the crossbow more than a few times.

Would this "Brand X" crossbow shoot? There was only one way to find out. I had some 17$\frac{1}{2}$-inch Lightning Strike 7 shafts with half-moon nocks that appeared to be of appropriate length and spline. After waxing the string and lubricating the rail, I hand-cocked the crossbow. It felt more like a 150-pound pull than the advertised 175-pound pull, but even the lesser pull weight would work fine for deer.

Using iron sights, I had the first few arrows with their 100-grain field points walk into the bull on the 10-yard target. The trigger pull was a little mushy but shootable. However, the stock was so short that I had to hold my head in an uncomfortably rearward position to obtain a sharp focus on the rear sight. I removed the iron sights and installed the BEC Miradot scope. The red dot was quite faint even at its highest power setting. After a dozen shots and three batteries, I gave up on it. I had to grind away a vertical steel pin on the aluminum sight base, but after that a BSA red-dot sight went on smoothly. Because of the short stock, I moved the red-dot sight as far forward as possible to prevent cutting my nose. This lightweight crossbow had recoil, which made me appreciate the ancient expression about crossbows having "teeth."

The vital stress points on the crossbow were the welds attaching the barrel of the hinged limbs to the frame, the plastic tips on the fiberglass limbs, and the string. If any of these failed, I had no way of replacing them. This was a crossbow that I would sight in, record the drop information, and not use again until it was time for it to take game. I knew that at some point these components would fail. It may be on the fifth shot, the fiftieth, or the five hundredth, but the less it was shot before I took it on a hunt, the greater the possibility that it would hold together long enough for me to take game with it.

After about 20 shots, I noted that the crossbow was dropping its arrows lower on the target, indicating that it was developing less velocity. I also heard a disconcerting "pop" from the front end of the crossbow when it was spanned. When I checked, screws on both the side-plate and limb-retaining assembly had loosened, so I retightened them. Prior to any hunt, I would have to check the tension on all the front-end fastenings. Tightening up everything restored the crossbow to full strength. I also noted that paint was coming off the welded joints, indicating that they were flexing slightly each time the crossbow was fired.

The final decision on taking the Brand X crossbow on my Kodiak Island hunt was made when chronographing revealed that the bow only developed a velocity of 161 feet per second (fps) at 10 yards. My old Barnett Ranger was not only a pound lighter, but with a speed of 205 fps with the same arrow, it shot significantly faster. The Ranger also had an attached quiver, which the folding-limb crossbow lacked, and fewer mechanical components. After considering all the factors, I knew the Ranger was a better choice for a tough hunt. I could put better sights on it and use more effective carbon arrows and mechanical points. The Ranger might, indeed, ride again.

ENTRY-LEVEL CROSSBOWS

Horton's entry-level crossbow, the SteelForce, is among the last, if not *the* last, steel-prod crossbow available from a major manufacturer. This economy product, with its nylon strap for a cocking stirrup, relatively high-friction arrow rail, and hard trigger pull, is available with both 80- and 150-pound prods and comes with Horton's Dial-A-Range sighting system. The SteelForce, which usually sells for about $200 but is frequently discounted, may be purchased at Wal-Mart and, if for no reason other than availability, is commonly sold.

This crossbow is popular with hunters who want to try crossbows but are not quite ready to make the commitment for higher-grade, higher-priced equipment. It may be successfully used, but the user

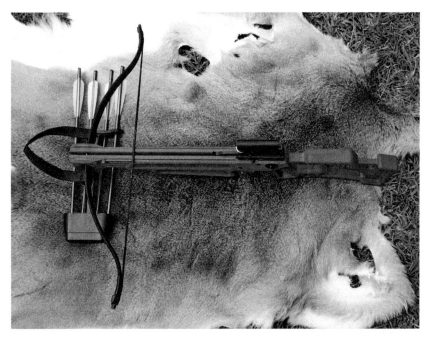

The SteelForce is Horton's entry-level crossbow. Although inexpensive, commonly available, and often used, this model has a hard trigger pull, which makes it difficult to shoot. Thus, this crossbow is often more suited to the experienced crossbowman, rather than a beginner.

must accept an added challenge: cocking. The nylon strap has to be symmetrically placed on the prod so that the force is equally applied to both limbs. When the string is pulled up to lock in the cocked position, the user must make sure that the string is not off center, or the arrow will deflect to the left or right.

To symmetrically cock this bow, hold your thumbs next to the stock of the crossbow and use them as guides, or build a simple string cocker from a length of nylon rope and a couple of carabiners.

Horton recommends using the LS7 Lite, a 17-inch aluminum arrow, with the SteelForce. I used the veined arrows shipped with the crossbow with a Muzzy 75-grain three-bladed broadhead and found that the 75-grainers shot significantly better than 100- or 125-grain Muzzys.

I hunted several times with the SteelForce, but I never had a shot. My biggest concern was the crossbow's long, hard trigger, but this smooths up a bit with shooting. Because I wanted to adapt a crossbow for bowfishing, I cut some fiberglass bowfishing arrows to appropriate lengths. The first time out, after perhaps fifty shots with the bow, a plastic tip broke off the end of the prod, and I lost the string into the water. The bowfishing arrow was discharged but did not develop full energy. I had previously had success sighting in the crossbow with the fiberglass shaft, so I suspect that losing the string was the result of brittle failure of the plastic component, rather than having anything to do with the fiberglass arrow.

If I had been hunting in some distant place, breaking the tip and losing the string would have ended the hunt. However, I always take a spare set of bowfishing gear with me, so I was able to continue, minus the crossbow. The next time I cut some fiberglass bowfishing arrows, I used a Dremel tool to shape the back into a half-moon nock. This bowfishing trip also taught me that red-dot sights are not good under the bright-light conditions typical of daytime bowfishing. A scope or even iron sights would have been more effective.

As it turns out, failure of the tip of a recurve crossbow is among the most common problems of the recurve design, particularly with steel-prod crossbows. If you are going to use one, make sure you carry spare tips as well as an extra string.

INTERMEDIATE-PRICED CROSSBOWS

When you move up in quality, price, and technology, you usually get a crossbow with solid fiberglass limbs, compound wheels, a better trigger mechanism, adjustable iron or red-dot sights, a range of models, generic camo coating, markedly superior instructional materials, and a better overall fit and finish. The crossbow I own in this category is the Horton Hawk SL. It originally came with a peep-and-pin sighting system, but I have added a sight base to allow the use of either red-dot or scope sights.

This class of crossbows usually has pull weights of about 150 pounds, which is fine for close-range shots at deer-size game. Lower pull weights keep the price of these crossbows hundreds of dollars less than their high-end cousins, which use more expensive technology to obtain higher speeds. Intermediate-priced crossbows, which are presently in the $300 to $400 range, are easy to shoot, effective, and generally trouble free. When their features are compared to game-killing ability, they often represent "best buys." A beginner who selects a first crossbow in this class will have a faster learning curve and more gratifying results than starting with the lowest-priced crossbows.

Crossbows in this class include the Horton Explorer XL 150, Barnett Rhino, Bear F-300, and PSE Copperhead, all of which are offered with factory-installed accessory packages that include quivers. Some makers also offer premounted scopes or red-dot sights at a considerable savings over add-on prices.

One crossbow in this class that I have shot is the Horton Hawk SL. At 6 pounds 8 ounces, the Hawk is 1 pound 3 ounces heavier than the SteelForce. Its massive fiberglass limbs provide distinctly more weight in the front of the crossbow. This weight-forward balance was particularly noticeable in the tree stand, and I had to take care to ensure that the crossbow did not pitch out the stand. With target points, the cross-

Horton's Hawk with a 150-pound compound fiberglass prod is a simple, solid, and reliable crossbow that will accept a variety of cocking accessories. Although not as fast as other Horton models, it is effective when used on deer-size game.

bow was very accurate, and I had to shoot only one arrow at a time at the target to keep from ruining the shafts. Although I tried several fixed points with this bow, the best flight conditions came from 100-grain mechanical broadheads and Horton's Lightning Strike 2 shafts with plastic veins.

I shot a number of squirrels with the Hawk and experimented with different shafts and points. Through it all, the crossbow performed well and gave me no trouble. I would rate the trigger on this particular crossbow as good, but Horton has since upgraded its triggers, and more recent versions come with Horton's improved Talon triggers.

Presently priced at about $400, the Vixen is Excalibur's entry-level crossbow. Although less powerful than the company's present Exocet (200-pound draw, an increase over this model's original 175 pounds) and ExoMax (225-pound draw) models, the Vixen is certainly adequate for deer-size game and is more convenient to use because it can be hand-cocked by most individuals. The ExoMax might be considered the .375 Holland and Holland Magnum of the crossbow world because it is most useful on very large game such as bison, buffalo, and even elephant.

The Vixen, Excalibur's entry-level crossbow, has the typical Excalibur stock, rails, and prod but is limited to a 150-pound draw. This crossbow is ideal for women and slightly built men. When disassembled, the Vixen can be packed easily in a suitcase.

I found the Vixen easy to shoot. It felt good at the shoulder, was stable enough to offer excellent control with off-hand shots, and was quite accurate even when used with the 100-grain Wasp broadheads shipped with the bow. Excalibur uses a flat-backed arrow that is screw threaded to allow arrow pullers to extract the shafts from Styrofoam targets without bending the shafts.

MID-RANGED-PRICED CROSSBOWS

At this price level, a crossbow will include some expensive add-ons, such as higher pull weights, laminated limbs, vibration-dampening systems, excellent triggers, and brand-name camouflage coatings. Parker's and TenPoint's lowest-priced crossbows start at about $500 with additional charges for scopes and cocking mechanisms. These companies take the position that this is what it takes to produce a quality crossbow in North America today. Yes, they could make a less expensive bow by using simpler designs, paying less attention to quality, and not relying on premium-quality materials, but their aim is to make a best-quality crossbow and they must charge accordingly.

Models of Fred Bear crossbows fall in this price range with a number of different models currently listed at between $450 and $700. The company is currently making a radically different reverse draw crossbow with the riser located at the rear and the limbs pointing forward rather than back, a design that promises to give higher velocities for a given pull weight.

Excalibur's entry into this price bracket is the Phoenix, which has 175-pound recurve limbs and a 14-inch power stroke that shorter-armed individuals will find easier to cock.

Parker takes a different approach by offering 150-pound pull weight crossbows, which are advertised to yield 320 fps, as much velocity as provided by other makers' 200-pound pull weight bows. This added velocity is achieved, as is the case of Fred Bear's F340, by increasing the power stroke, which makes the crossbows more difficult to cock by shorter-armed individuals. Hunters who are 6-feet and taller can comfortably cock these longer power-stroke bows, but anyone 5 feet 10 inches or so would have to strain a bit, even when using rope-cocking mechanisms.

TOP-OF-THE-LINE CROSSBOWS

At twice the price of the previous category, crossbows in the $1,000 range include the highest-powered commercial models presently available with pull weights of 185 to 225 pounds, high-velocity cams and limbs, cam-

A TenPoint crossbow with Acudraw winder, thumb safety, footpiece, and red-dot sight. Among the most expensive of American-made crossbows, TenPoint's models are noted for their accuracy and variety of built-in accessories. Many disabled hunters enjoy this crossbow's features, which now include a drop-down monopod for additional stability.

ouflage, and scope sights. Several of these are the "big-game hunters" among crossbows and have taken huge beasts such as the Asiatic water buffalo and large African species. These high-powered crossbows require the use of some type of cocking aid, although even the heaviest crossbow may be cocked by strong individuals using a rope cocker.

Just as it is not necessary to use a .375 Holland and Holland Magnum to shoot American whitetails and African impalas, a typically heavier and more difficult-to-use maximum-velocity-producing crossbow is not needed for the smaller species of big game.

Once you get these crossbows cocked, they are easier to shoot and easier to learn how to shoot and will almost invariably provide satisfactory results. They come with excellent manuals, often videos, and explicit instructions on care and use, and they are the best supported for accessories, add-ons, and extra features. What little appears in the popular press about crossbows most often features these top-of-the-line products, which return more profit to the manufacturers. In the "speed game," each maker attempts to eke a few more feet per second out of these high-end crossbows than their competitors. However, the speed of the crossbow is only one factor that should influence a potential buyer; ease of use, weight, maneuverability, balance for off-hand shots, trigger pulls, and sighting systems are also important.

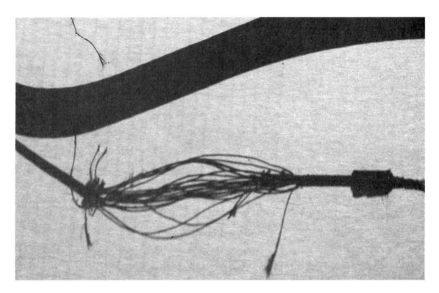

Components on crossbows will sometimes break. The owner of this Barnett Commando crossbow had ample warning that the multistrand string was going to fail when the individual strands started to part. This self-cocking crossbow is notorious for chewing through strings with its cocking hooks.

Now that the technological aspects of the modern crossbow are fairly well understood, the feel-good aspects of the weapon are receiving more attention. In Fred Bear's new line of crossbows, for example, the rear of the crossbow has been purposefully weighted to give the crossbow more the feel and balance of a gun, rather than the usual prod-heaviness typical of many less-expensive crossbows with heavy, solid fiberglass limbs. To make their crossbows more user friendly, more makers are incorporating such features as adjustable stocks (Barnett), easier-to-use attached winder mechanisms (TenPoint and Barnett), better foot stirrups (TenPoint), and anti-dry-fire mechanisms (TenPoint and PSE).

It is possible to build crossbows with significantly higher pull weights more akin to the old wall-mounted crossbows of medieval times. With this increase come the liabilities of more weight, size, and complexity, and the additional strain put on the crossbow's components increases the chances of potentially dangerous catastrophic failures. In addition, the faster the arrow, the more sensitive the crossbow is to the arrows and points that it will shoot well. New arrows would have to be designed to handle the faster velocities generated by crossbows with 300- or 500-pound pull weights. The present shafts, which were originally intended for bows, are not up to the task. Can it be technically done? Yes, it can.

With only 5 to 7 pounds of pressure, the winder in the stock of this TenPoint crossbow can cock a prod with a 175-pound pull weight. Disabled shooters will find the winder contained in the stock to be a great convenience.

Would such powerful crossbows serve a useful purpose for today's hunters? I have my doubts.

I have seen winder mechanisms fall to pieces, strings break, limbtips fail, and experienced shooters dry fire their crossbows. I do not want to think of what the consequences might have been had they been using 300- or 500-pound pull weight crossbows. It is sometimes difficult for modern man to accept, but all mechanical things will ultimately fail. Any mechanical system will experience wear on parts and stress on components. The more power contained in the system, the more wear and stress. Crossbows with 200-pound pull weights have sufficient power for hunters to do whatever they need to do with a handheld crossbow.

My most frequent advice to first-time crossbow buyers is to purchase the best-feeling and easiest-to-use 150-pound pull weight bow that they can afford. Hunt your deer and take them at under 30 yards. If you want to move up to bigger game, then get a more powerful version of the same crossbow. This is an easier and much more reliable path to success with a crossbow than starting out with the "baddest crossbow on the block."

THE ANCIENT WAY

Can the modern hunter step back in time and use the same type of cross-bow that Maximilian I used in the 1500s? The answer is, somewhat surprisingly, yes. Individual craftsmen in the United States and Europe still will make replicas of medieval crossbows. For years, they quietly have been making replica crossbows for museums, period movies, and reenactors. As in the more commonly seen replica muzzleloaders, the more exacting the copy, the more expensive it is to make.

F. S. Schroter Antique Arms of Costa Mesa, California, offers among his selection a Swiss-made crossbow with a 125-pound forged-steel prod inlaid with bone decorations. This late-style crossbow has a cheek piece and trigger guard and is a "call for price" item. None was quoted.

David R. Watson of New World Arbalest in Austin, Texas, presently catalogues eleven different styles of medieval and Renaissance crossbows, ranging from Spanish to Finnish to Central European styles with pull weights of 125 to 170 pounds. All of these crossbows are functional instruments and are available with either primitive or adjustable sights. Although true to the spirit of the crossbows of the period, some modifications have been made to decrease costs. Watson will build an exacting replica of an historic crossbow, if desired, but it will cost extra, depending on the availability of materials and the degree of work desired. The price range of his regular models runs from about $300 to $700, not including optional extras. For additional information, Watson may be contacted at info@crossbows.net.

My Watson crossbow is a slim Northern European design with a ball end fitted with a 150-pound draw steel prod made by Jim Knoch of Alchem, Ohio, who also makes the crossbow irons. The total length of my crossbow is 2 feet 8$^1/2$ inches, and when strung at the rest position, its width is about 2 feet 4 inches. The crossbow weighs almost exactly 6 pounds, making it relatively lightweight.

An intermediate and composite design, technologically speaking, this crossbow has a foot stirrup, which is absent from very early crossbows, and a steel prod, which became popular in Europe in the 1400s. Crossbow irons began to appear on crossbows produced in the late 1500s, near the end of common crossbow use in Europe. The long tiller and thin, long stock were also fairly late developments. One nontraditional element on this crossbow is a turning-bolt safety fitted over the tickler. A traditional safety employed a device that looks something like half a wing nut protruding from the bottom of the crossbow.

My Watson crossbow also uses a blend of ancient and modern materials. The nut, which retains the spring, is made from moose horn; the

David Watson inletting the trigger of a replica crossbow. A decades-long student of the crossbow, Watson is one of the few craftsmen in North America who still builds traditional crossbows for reenactments and hunting.

stock is straight-grained walnut; and the metal components are hand-forged steel. The deck of the crossbow has an inlaid macarta top instead of bone, and the string is fifty strands of twisted Dacron served in the center and ends to reduce wear. Watson described the string as thicker than necessary, but he thought thin strings looked bad on period cross-bows. Even so, his $1/4$-inch-diameter strings are half as thick as the original flax and hemp strings.

The arrows furnished with the replica crossbow were 14 inches long and $3/8$ inch in diameter and came with field points. Since I wanted to shoot a deer with this replica crossbow, I also received two-bladed hunting points. Once home, I set up a Styrofoam target block on my back porch, waxed the string and deck, and shot some of Watson's arrows. From off-hand, the first three holes shot at 10 yards were almost touching and made a group slightly smaller than 1 inch measured center to center. The first shaft penetrated in virgin material to a depth of 9 inches, the second slightly more, and the third buried itself out of sight. The entire group was 12 inches high of the point of aim, which was difficult to adjust since the crossbow doesn't have any sights.

As it turns out, the fat arrow shaft is its own front and rear sight. Just as a trap shooter aligns his shotgun by using the elevated rib, a hunter using this crossbow relies on the long arrow shaft as a sight. The only fault I found with shooting the crossbow was its soft, but very long trigger pull, which can be adjusted. I did this by installing some shims to help take up the slack. All told, the initial shooting session was a positive experience. At 12 yards, I had no doubt that with proper points Watson's crossbow would do the job.

When chronographed with the practice points, this crossbow generated a velocity of 162 fps and only 14 foot-pounds of energy at 10 yards, a relatively slow speed caused in part by the energy lost in accelerating the heavy steel prod and string. This performance is keeping with period

Wood shafts made by David Watson for replica medieval crossbows are combined with Fred Bear's field points for hunting. Ventilated broadheads with cutting surfaces parallel to the deck and the fletching help ensure accuracy.

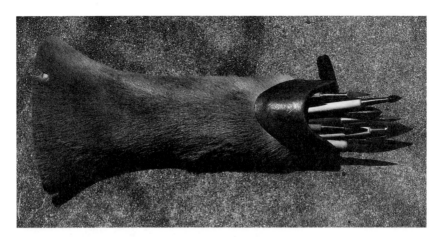

A replica of a traditional crossbow quiver, where the points were carried up for quick selection. When using today's razor-sharp points, it is safer to carry them point down and color the nicks to differentiate among different style points.

illustrations that show crossbow arrows sticking out of the game, rather than passing through the animal as usually happens with modern crossbows. I would have to experiment with points and arrow weights to achieve optimum penetration.

With some two-bladed Fred Bear chisel points, the wooden arrows used on my primitive Watson started out striking 9 inches high at 5 yards and reached a midrange trajectory of 25-plus inches at 20 yards. At 35 yards, the arrow started to descend but still shot 15 inches high. At 25 yards, the shaft penetrated 6.5 inches of block Styrofoam, but at 35 yards, its penetration had dropped to 6 inches. Such results indicated that the arrow from this crossbow could penetrate into the chest cavity of a deer at 25 yards but likely would not exit. If I could master the needed hold-under, I was confident that I could take a close-range deer with this primitive instrument.

FINE-ART CROSSBOWS

Crossbows have a habit of turning up at some unexpected places. Consider that at the 2005 Blade Show held in Atlanta, Georgia, a one-hand crossbow with an under-slung spring-release bayonet made by Jack Levin of New York won first place in the International Blade Show's fantasy category. The crossbow has an all-steel body with steel limbs, and the grip and end cap are made of carved ivory with high-relief carvings of medieval crossbowmen cocking their crossbows. The remainder of the crossbow is decorated with engravings and sculptured metal panels.

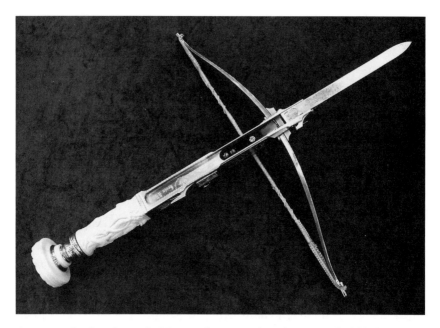

A true work of art in steel, this crossbow pistol with an attached blade won Jack Levin of New York a first-place award at the 2005 International Blade Show. The pistol uses a screw-type cocking mechanism in which a round ivory knob at the back of the pistol is turned to cock the crossbow.

Levin has a personal interest in making high-art crossbows, which would equal or surpass any seen in today's museums. However, the crossbow at the Blade Show was fully functional with an ingenuous threaded screw-cocking mechanism, which could span the crossbow by turning a knob at the rear of the crossbow after the string was fixed in the lock. If anyone wants to commission a functional crossbow that looks like a piece of art worthy of hanging in any museum in the world, contact Levin at jacklevin@yahoo.com.

3

Understanding the Crossbow

A crossbow propels an arrow by holding energy in a bent member or members (bow, prods, or staves) fixed in a stock and transmitting it to a string, which is typically released by a trigger or tickler. In the past, crossbows were used to throw a variety of projectiles, including short bolts and darts, stones, shot, and arrows designed to tumble in flight. Darts were employed mainly for target use, and the stones, shots, and tumbling arrows were used for hunting small game and waterfowl.

Crossbows were developed on the Eurasian continent, and practically every culture from Southeast Asia, through the Middle East and Africa, and into Europe had knowledge of the crossbow. During the Vietnam War, a crossbow was even credited with downing a U.S. helicopter. In the Middle East, crossbows were considered hunting implements, and their use continued long after firearms became commonplace. Because modern scholarship and writing about the crossbow have almost completely focused on European versions, the sometimes overlapping and confusing technological vocabulary used in modern literature is derived from various European languages.

HOW A CROSSBOW WORKS
In the "at rest" position, crossbows are commonly displayed with the prod (horizontal bow) bent and under slight tension from the string. The stock is longer than the prod, and its general appearance is not unlike a fluked Admiralty anchor with a long shank and hooked ends. To cock the crossbow, the string is pulled rearward to the point where it is caught by a hook, which is then put under tension. A sear fits into a notch on the bottom of the restraining hook. Once cocked, an arrow is placed into the crossbow in contact with the string. Now the crossbow

Dan Miller with an Excalibur Vixen crossbow and a Canadian bear. Miller prefers this easy-to-cock 150-pound pull weight recurve crossbow and has taken a number of deer and bear with it.

is ready to be aimed and fired. When the trigger is pulled, the string flys forward and the arrow or other projectile is released.

A crossbow may be cocked manually or by using a rope cocker or various mechanical devices to augment the leverage exerted by the arm. Such devices can reduce the force required to cock a crossbow by fifty to ninety percent, and this reduction in cocking pressure makes the crossbow an ideal instrument for anyone who, because of age, disability, or injury, doesn't have the strength to hand-cock a crossbow.

DEFINITIONS SURROUNDING THE CROSSBOW

air deck–A crossbow bed in which the arrow is not in contact with the deck of the crossbow and not contained in a groove. Instead, the arrow is supported by the string and a rest at the end of the arrow. Because of the lack of bed friction and the minimal contact with the crossbow, this type of rest is used on many target crossbows.

The crossbow looks like a fluked Admiralty anchor, and it sometimes feels like one when you are trying to maneuver it through thick brush.

arbalest (arbalist)–A crossbow maker, of Latin origin.

armbrust–Crossbow in German.

arrow–The projectile, typically fletched with plastic veins or feathers and with a metallic point, used by both crossbows and bows. Bowfishing shafts are commonly made of solid fiberglass and are often fletchless.

back–The side of the crossbow's prod that is under increased amounts of tension when the crossbow is cocked.

Traditional-style crossbow points. The unmounted point is designed to penetrate plate armor. The others are replicas of original designs for use against lightly armored or unarmored individuals.

ballista–An outsize crossbow developed by the Romans to propel extremely heavy arrows against ships, fortifications, and massed troops.

bastard string (bracing string)–An auxiliary string used to cock a crossbow so that a string can be installed or removed.

barrel–A groove made traditionally of a slick, natural material such as bone or ivory but now more commonly made of machined aluminum, which supports the crossbow arrow. Also, the hollow tube of a bullet-throwing crossbow.

barrel (rail) lube–A moderately thick grease or wax used to lubricate the rail of a crossbow. This lubricant reduces friction and increases arrow speed.

belly–The portion of the prod that is facing the shooter and is under compression when the crossbow prod is under tension.

belt hook–A hook on a belt commonly used as a cocking aid on light-to-medium draw weight crossbows.

bending lever–A whippe-type cocking device in which a long lever is used in conjunction with a hook and a hinged section with a fork to catch the string. This device, which is nearly as long as the crossbow, enables heavy crossbows to be cocked with much less force than would be required if cocked by pulling the string with the hands.

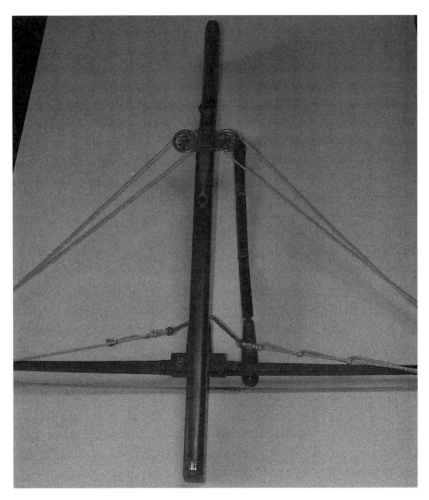

A nineteenth-century bullet crossbow with a split barrel and wheel-controlled string. This crossbow could have come from anywhere in Europe, but its stocking appears more English than continental. It was probably used to eliminate garden pests. A modernized version would be fine for controlling the population of squirrels and pigeons in city parks.

binding–Leather and/or cordage used in early crossbows to bind the prod to the stock.

bolt–A short projectile, usually from 4 to 6 inches long, fired from a crossbow and used in target competition. In modern use, the term bolt refers to the arrow shot by a crossbow.

bow–A vertical bow, which may be a self bow, made from a single stave of wood, laminated wood, fiberglass, composite materials, horn, or much less commonly steel. The bow may have straight limbs when unbent and be recurved or employ metallic wheels to change the bow's draw characteristics. Sometimes, and confusingly, bow is used as a synonym for prod.

bowhunter–An individual who hunts with a bow.

bow irons–Parts made of forged iron or cast bronze that are bolted to the front of the crossbow and used to retain the prod.

bowstave–The prod, or horizontal bow, of a crossbow.

bowsteel–The steel prod of a crossbow.

bowyer–Bow maker.

brace height–The distance in inches of the crossbow string at rest from the center of the prod.

bridle binding–A leather or rope binding used to fasten the prod to the wooden stock of the crossbow. The binding, which was also sometimes made of sinew cord, was passed through a hole in the stock and tied to the limbs of the crossbow.

bullet-shooting crossbow–A crossbow that shoots a lead, stone, or clay bullet and was commonly used in the 1800s for small-game and target shooting. Sometimes a circular barrel would be used, but earlier it was common for bullet or stone-throwing crossbows to employ two strings with a connecting pouch.

Detail of round pulley on the compound limbs of the Horton Safari Express. Pulley technologies have changed so that the high-let-off cams used on compound bows now reduce the pressure on the string-retaining catches and the trigger pull weights.

butt–Rearmost portion of the crossbow stock. The modern crossbow employs a butt style obviously derived from firearms, but early crossbow butts ranged from little more than squared-off planks to stocks elaborately carved and fitted with cheek pieces.

cases–Crossbow cases, which can be hard or soft, are designed to contain an assembled crossbow and are sometimes required for legally transporting a crossbow, whether cocked or not, to and from the hunting area. Frequently when transporting a crossbow on an airplane, the limbs may be removed so that the crossbow can be carried in an ordinary suitcase.

catch (latch)–The fingers, nut, or pin that restrains the crossbow string.

center-shot crossbow–A style of crossbow in which the arrow passes through a hole in the middle of the prod or limbs of the crossbow. This style was often used in split-limbed crossbows.

clip–A spring, most often made of metal but sometimes of horn, used to retain the rear of the arrow in the barrel of the crossbow.

clout (similar to flight shooting)–Long-range shooting with archery equipment. In Europe, this target is 15 meters in diameter.

cock–To draw a crossbow string from its at-rest position to where it is caught and latched by the fingers or hooks of the firing mechanism.

cocking effort–The force required to cock a crossbow, usually categorized as "extremely difficult, difficult, and moderate."

cocking peg–A pin, sometimes made of wood, horn, ivory, or metal, used to set the crossbow trigger prior to firing.

cocking ring–A ring on the front of the crossbow used in conjunction with some cocking aids.

commando–A military-issued crossbow employed by Green Beret and Ranger units during the Vietnam War. Although the crossbow was quieter to use than a gun, a person hit with an arrow still could raise the alarm before he expired. The military commando crossbow, which used a combination tubular stock-cocking rod to cock the crossbow, was a quiet shooter but not necessarily a quiet killer.

compound limbs–Single or multiple limbs with wheels on the ends designed to produce higher velocities in a shorter-limbed crossbow and alter the pull characteristics of the crossbow.

cord and pulley–A cocking device in which a pulley is hung on the crossbowman's belt. One end of a cord is fixed on a peg or ring on the body of the crossbow, and the free end is run through a pulley hanging on the crossbowman's belt, then passed through the eye of a metal hook (or a combination pulley-hook) connected to the bowstring. A foot is placed in the stirrup to fix the crossbow in place, and an upwards pull on the running end of the cord enables the crossbow to be cocked with only half the force needed if the crossbow were cocked by pulling directly on the string.

crannequin–A device, employing a crank, gears, and a notched steel rod with string hooks, used to cock a crossbow. The crank is turned to operate a gear that engages the teeth of a notched rod with hooks on the end. The hooks grab the string and move it to where it could be caught by a notch connected to a sear and trigger. The crannequin differs from wind-up cockers, which employ no strings or pulleys. Sometimes crannequins are built onto the crossbow.

crossbow–A device most frequently used to launch an arrow. The propelling energy is held in a bent stave fixed in a stock and transmitted to a string, which is typically released by a trigger or tickler.

crossbowman–A person in a military unit who is armed with crossbows or, in more modern usage, anyone who shoots a crossbow.

deck–The top of the crossbow stock on which the arrow rests in a groove or barrel or on a bone or metal arrow support.

double string–Two strings with a leather pouch between them used to hold lead, ceramic, or stone projectiles that are launched from a bow or crossbow.

draw length–The length, in inches measured from the front of the crossbow, in which the crossbow arrow is drawn back.

draw weight–The force, most often reported in pounds in English-language publications, needed to draw a crossbow from rest to full cock.

dry fire–Shooting a crossbow without an arrow or projectile. Dry firing can result in broken crossbow strings and damage to the limbs and other components of a crossbow. The greater the pull weight of the crossbow, the higher the likelihood of doing significant damage when the string is inadvertently released.

end caps–The flat rear end of a crossbow arrow, frequently containing hollow, threaded centers to accommodate arrow pullers or fletching aids. Excalibur, TenPoint, and most recently Bear recommend that only flat-backed arrows be shot from their crossbows.

endless loop (English) string–A type of string commonly used on today's crossbows that consists of fiber strands initially looped around two mandrels set on a board. The end loops are served and then wrapped together with additional serving, leaving open eyes at the ends of the string. The center of the crossbow string now is served and ready for use. Compared to the Flemish string, the endless loop string forms a loop using just half of the fiber bundle and is not twisted when strung on a bow.

Flemish string–A type of string often employed on crossbows and regular bows, which uses a complicated pegboard in its construction yet is fast to produce. Lighter weight, stronger, and more efficient than the endless loop string, the Flemish string must be twisted to retain its fibers and readjusted from time to time to make sure it is has retained its proper brace height. In the absence of any definitive information on the number of twists needed for crossbow strings, turn the string thirteen times and adjust from there until the proper brace height and pull weight are achieved.

fletching–Feather or plastic fletch used on today's crossbow arrows. Feather fletching is lighter in weight, is more forgiving to shoot, and won't stiffen in cold weather. Plastic veins are not affected by water, whereas feather fletching becomes nearly useless if wetted by a severe rain.

flight shooting–Shooting to determine the maximum cast or throw of a projectile from a bow or crossbow.

gaffle–See *goat's foot.*

gastraphetes–An ancient Greek weapon that is an ancestor of the modern crossbow. A powerful short crossbow shot from the stomach, hence the "gastra" prefix, this early derivation of the crossbow was most effective against close-range targets, especially armor penetration in close combat, since the weapon did not require room to pull and shoot it.

goat's (dog's) foot–A crossbow-cocking device with a long arm and two thin arms. The two split arms of the goat's foot are run behind the string and in front of the cocking pin in the middle (and usually thickest) part of the stock. When the lever is pulled toward the shooter, the string is pulled back until caught by the latch. This cocking device sometimes employed a short, pivoting section with hooks to catch the string, or when used on low-powered bows, it might have no moving parts.

grip safety–A safety button or bar on the stock of the crossbow that must be depressed to allow the crossbow to fire. This device is principally used to discourage shooters from placing their fingers in the way of the string, and causing a severe injury.

groove–The open-topped barrel of the crossbow.

horizontal bowhunter–An individual who hunts with a crossbow.

Italian Federation of Crossbowmen–A group organized around crossbow competitions held in five cities in central Italy—Massa Marittima, San Sepulco, San Marino, Gubbio, and Lucca—in which exacting replicas of medieval tickler-triggered crossbows are used. Contestants must attempt to hit a dime-size bull's eye at about 40 feet. With the competition as much pageant as contest, contestants dress in period garb and may invest thousands of dollars in their crossbows and costumes. The shoots have evolved into tourist attractions.

This thumb safety on a TenPoint crossbow helps prevent fingers from being clipped by the string as it is forcefully propelled forward. It also provides a second, silent safety for the crossbow.

inch-pounds of power–A means of measuring the power of a crossbow, in which the pounds it takes to draw a bow are multiplied by the number of inches that is drawn. Thus, a bow with 150 pounds of draw weight that can be drawn 14 inches has 2,100 inch-pounds of power.

latch (catch, release mechanism)–The lock of a crossbow that is used to catch and hold the string.

lath (prod)–The horizontal bow used in a crossbow. Although the term lath implies a stave with a uniform composition, crossbows have historically used laths made of steel, wood, bone, or horn composites. Ancient crossbows were frequently wrapped in ox sinew to provide added force and elasticity.

limb (prod)–The energy-storing components of a crossbow. Limbs may consist of a single piece of steel, fiberglass, or composition materials, be split into right and left halves, and contain single or multiple staves.

lugs–Pins, usually made of metal but sometimes bone, used as leverage points for a mechanical cocking mechanism, such as a goat's foot.

manuballista–Literally "hand ballista," this form of Roman crossbow could be carried by one man and fired using only his hands. Like its Greek predecessor, it may have been pointed from the waist, rather than aimed and fired.

nock (end cap)–The flat end cap or half-moon nock, depending on the maker of the crossbow, of a modern crossbow arrow. As pull weights increase, it is important to use only the manufacturer's recommended nocks and arrow weights.

Notre Dame des Victories–A late Gothic church in Brussels, Belgium, that was financed by crossbowmen and built between 1338 and 1400, the time at which the crossbow reigned supreme as the most powerful military weapon in Europe.

nut–The roller release, typically made of horn or ivory, used on traditional crossbows.

Ok Meydan–Literally "place of the arrow," a location in Constantinople where notables of the Ottoman Empire exercised their bows and where, in the late 1700s, the Emperor Sultan Selim shot an arrow 835 yards with a composite horn bow followed by a second shot that traveled nearly the same distance. A stone marker was erected on the grounds in his honor. In his book *The Crossbow*, Sir Ralph Payne-Gallwey reported that the notables shot with very short flight arrows, using a primitive overdraw technique involving a piece of horn on the archer's left wrist, which allowed a light cane-shafted arrow to be propelled remarkable distances.

package–A crossbow sold with a variety of accessories, often including a quiver, arrows, and a scope or other sight.

pavise–A large shield used to protect crossbowmen while they were recocking their cumbersome instruments. A pavise could be cut out at the top to provide a front rest for a crossbow. In military use where crossbows performed a function similar to artillery, crossbowmen were subject to counterfire from their opponents.

popinjay–A crossbow target often carved in the shape of a bird and used at least since the fourteenth century.

power stroke–The length, in inches, an arrow travels before it leaves the crossbow.

prod (bow, lath, limb)–A stave that supports the crossbow string and provides the power to propel projectiles thrown by a crossbow. Traditionally made of wood, laminated wood, whalebone, horn, and composites of these and held together by sinew and/or glue, crossbow prods are made of aluminum, steel, and fiberglass in modern times. Fiberglass limbs may or may not contain laminates of other materials.

quarrel–A crossbow arrow with an armor-piercing head, often with four sides sharpened to a cone or pyramid. Although they could penetrate armor, these arrows caused less dangerous wounds than the willow-leaf-shaped arrows used against lightly armored individuals.

quiver–A container used to hold arrows for a bow. Quivers for crossbows are usually shorter than those employed by conventional archers. Modern crossbows often use a detachable quiver, although it is always possible to carry crossbow arrows in a belt quiver, which is more convenient for target shooting.

red-dot sight–A no-magnification battery-powered scopelike sight with one or more illuminated red dots. Adjustments for windage and elevation may be made so that these dots correspond to the point of aim at various yardages. Red-dot sights work well under low-light conditions but tend to wash out in bright light and must be reduced in power near dark to prevent "flaring" and obscuring the target with unwanted light.

repeating crossbow–Light draw weight repeating crossbow with a vertical magazine over the crossbow deck designed to shoot poisoned arrows at an approaching enemy. In more recent times, a pump-action repeater with a 28-pound draw was built in the 1970s and used by the female shooting team, the Crossbowetts.

A red-dot sight mounted on a Fred Bear crossbow. Red-dot sights are fine for dim light but become unusable in very bright or very dark conditions.

riser–A component typically made of metal that joins the stock of the crossbow to the limbs. In most modern crossbows, these components are held together with one or more bolts.

Saint George Arbaletriers de Bruxelles–A crossbow society founded in Brussels in 1381 that continues to hold regular competitions.

safeties–A device located on the rear of the crossbow, above the trigger assembly or on the trigger, and intended to prevent misfirings. Safeties can be automatic or manual, depending on the maker of the crossbow. Excalibur uses a manual safety, but most other makers employ an automatic safety.

scope–A device providing modest degrees of magnification, up to four-power, to allow better target definition under low-light conditions and sometimes equipped with convenient sighting bars that enable the hunter to quickly compensate for arrow drop at various ranges.

self-cocking crossbow–A crossbow containing a mechanism that allows the bow to be cocked without using an external device such as a windless.

serving–A thin, hard cord wrapped around the bowstring to prevent string abrasion caused by the deck of the crossbow and "picking" of the string when it comes in contact with the arrow nocks.

set triggers–Two triggers, one behind the other, used to provide a low-pressure release on a crossbow's trigger. Designed to overcome the

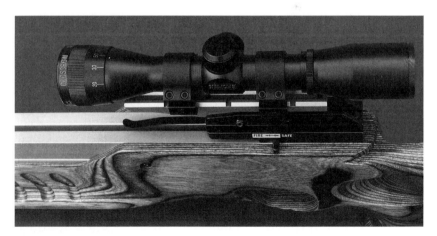

Cabela's Simmons crossbow scope mounted on a wood-stock Outfitter crossbow. Scopes make excellent sights for most crossbows. The hunter appreciates the scope's ability to slightly magnify the target and pick out unobstructed shooting lanes and its added light-gathering capabilities that help the hunter see at dawn and dusk.

hard trigger pulls typical of early crossbows, set triggers allowed the crossbows to be shot with a greater degree of accuracy.

sights–A device enabling a crossbow user to accurately aim a crossbow at a target. The earliest crossbows did not have sights, and later models often had adjustable sights that enabled the shooter to hit more distant targets. In between having no sights at all and the later metallic sights, a 6-to-8-inch grooved strip of wood was screwed to the top of the crossbow and used as a sight.

sled–A device, made of metal, bone, or ivory, used in conjunction with a rope or wind-up cocker to catch the crossbow string and pull it to the full-cock position.

slurbow (barreled crossbow)–A type of crossbow that uses a barrel to guide a featherless arrow. The barrel is split to allow for the passage of the string.

sound suppression–Padding located between the limbs of the crossbow and the riser and/or between the riser and the stock of the crossbow to reduce vibration and noise.

spanner–Any mechanical devise used to cock a crossbow, such as a goat's foot or wind-up cocker.

span (spanning)–To cock a crossbow.

stonebow–A bullet- or shot-throwing bow or crossbow used for shooting wild game and waterfowl. The decks of these crossbows, which often employed a large rectangular front sight, were frequently bent into a vertical C-shape to allow the unimpeded travel of the stone.

stirrup–The piece on a crossbow in which a foot or feet are placed to stabilize the crossbow while it's being cocked. In some cases, the shooter bends his legs, puts two feet in the stirrup, and uses the strength of both legs to cock a strong crossbow.

stock-mounted cocking lever–A cocking lever inlet into the comb of the stock that is used to cock the crossbow.

string–The part of a crossbow that is drawn back to release an arrow or other projectile. Now commonly made of synthetic fibers such as Fast Flight, crossbow strings were originally composed of a variety of elastic fibers and were much thicker than their modern equivalents. A lighter string achieves a higher velocity and increases the speed of the arrow. Two types of strings in common use today are Flemish strings with twisted fibers and endless-loop (English) strings with parallel fibers.

stringer–A cord, somewhat resembling a bowstring, used to help string a recurve-prod crossbow. When the stringer is held in the full-cock position, the pretwisted crossbow string can be easily slipped over the limbs of the crossbow.

string loop–A loop placed in the center of the string to engage the latch, generally used on low-powered target crossbows. This loop not only reduces wear on the string, but it reduces the potential strength of the crossbow because it shortens the total draw length in proportion to the length of the loop.

string twisting–The method in which Flemish-style crossbow strings are made of whatever fiber and adjusted to length by twisting the strings. The more twists, the more tension put on the crossbow limbs and the higher the obtained velocity. In the absence of other instructions, try thirteen twists to provide pretension to a new string before installing it on a crossbow.

table–The top of the crossbow containing either a groove or barrel to steady the arrow or a V-shaped arrow support, which supports the front of the arrow.

tassel–A rag hung on the belt and used for wiping crossbow arrows.

teeth–What a crossbow is said to have if its violent recoil propels the stock against the shooter's face with enough force to hurt. More commonly today, it would be said to "bite."

thumb piece–A cut, frequently made of horn or ivory inlay, dished out to receive the user's thumb at the rear of the crossbow so that the thumb and hand are consistently positioned from shot to shot. It serves the same function as a spot-weld used by modern riflemen to hold a weapon in the same relative position in respect to the sights.

tiller–The stock of a traditional crossbow that resembles the tiller on a small boat.

tickler–A long curved wooden or metal member extending below the stock on medieval and Renaissance crossbows. Modern crossbows most often employ a trigger to activate the string-release mechanism.

tommy bar–A threaded rod used instead of wedges to tighten the prod-containing bow iron.

toxophilites–Archers, particularly those belonging to longbow shooting clubs in England during the nineteenth century.

wax–A stiff product applied to the crossbow string to reduce internal friction of the fibers and prolong string life. Some crossbow makers use the same wax to lubricate the barrel of the crossbow, while others use stiff grease.

whippe (bending lever)–A cocking device with a long arm that is hooked onto a ring at the front of the crossbow and hinged to a sliding block. Hooks in the moving block catch the string and move it to the full-cock position as the lever is pulled toward the shooter.

windlass (wind-up cocker)–A device with one or two cranks most frequently used to draw water from a well but has been adapted for use in cocking a crossbow.

wind-up cocker–A system containing gears and cables (or strings) and attached to one or two cranks used in conjunction with hooks to catch the string and pull it to the full-cock position. A cocker allows a crossbow to be cocked with little force compared with manually pulling the string back to the full-cock position. Some modern versions may be operated by a battery-powered screwdriver.

4

LEGAL AND CULTURAL ISSUES

To say that hunting with a crossbow has caused some controversy in North America is a considerable understatement. Maine, for example, had a period when even possessing a crossbow was a crime. More recently, Maine's laws have been modified, and crossbows may now be used by hunters who are physically impaired, but this bias against crossbows continues to exist across the country.

In 2005, Pope and Young, the organization that recognizes and registers trophy-game animals taken by hunters using self bows, recurve bows, and compound bows, removed any question as to its position on the crossbow. The organization's policy reads: "Consequently, the Pope and Young Club does not consider the crossbow to be a hunting bow and will not accept any trophies collected by crossbow hunters. Further, the Pope and Young Club considers the use of the crossbow during bowhunting seasons to be a serious threat to the future of bowhunting. The Pope and Young Club therefore recommends the crossbow should not be considered for use in any bowhunting season. Also, the club strongly recommends that crossbow hunting be abolished from all existing bowhunting-only seasons and the use of the crossbow for hunting be restricted to firearms seasons."

In the modern media, archers such as Errol Flynn in *Robin Hood* are viewed as heroic figures, whereas the crossbow is used by the evil forces of darkness as in the case of the Earl of Nottingham's minions in Kevin Costner's movie of the same work. In literature, the only truly heroic crossbowman that I can bring to mind is the Swiss William Tell, who was forced to shoot an apple from his son's head with a crossbow and later led a successful rebellion.

Arguments raised against the use of the crossbow have often been based on incorrect information about the physical capabilities of the crossbow, the level of training and proficiency of crossbow users compared to archers, the intentions of a new influx of hunters going into the woods during crossbow season, and the removal of excessive numbers of game animals. Opponents also argue that the bow is more "culturally appropriate" than the "evil" crossbow for the hunting of big-game animals.

Sheila and Bob Foulkrod with Sheila's first crossbow bear. Bob filmed this hunt, thus preserving the image of his wife taking a bear.

These not-well-founded arguments and prejudices lead many bow-hunters to believe that crossbow hunting should not be allowed during "their" archery seasons. Some, however, now that they are older and have physical problems, either have changed their minds or want to keep this option open in the eventuality that age, injury, or accident prevents them from using their bows.

One well-known bowhunter who first opposed and later supported crossbow use was Bob Foulkrod. He explained that, at first, he went along with the prevalent opinion among bowhunters that crossbows should not be allowed in Pennsylvania. He once wrote, "I will do all in my power to oppose the crossbow, but if it is legally allowed, I will accept it." His opinion has changed since the use of a crossbow allowed him to hunt three additional years with his 84-year-old father. He also appreciated that his wife, Sheila, who cannot draw a hunting-weight bow, could easily use a crossbow. She demonstrated this on a 2005 bear hunt when she took a 260-pound Canadian black bear with a single shot, just one of a number of filmed big-game hunts with a crossbow that her husband has released on a commercial video and DVD.

THE REALISTIC CAPABILITIES OF THE MODERN CROSSBOW

Any user of traditional or modern bows has a considerable advantage over a crossbow user: His bows are lighter weight, easier to maneuver in the woods, and, most importantly, are more efficiently reloaded for follow-up shots. If an archer initially overshoots his animal and the deer runs away from the noise caused by the arrow's impact, it commonly moves closer to the hunter. When this happens the archer can quietly put another arrow in his bow and, this time, kill the animal. I have killed deer this way, as has almost every bowhunter who has hunted for more than a few years.

A crossbow user, on the other hand, does not often have the opportunity to make a rapid follow-up shot because of the movement and noise caused by recocking his crossbow. If a person wanted to poach game with archery equipment, a modern compound bow, with its inherent ability to provide a rapid second shot, would be a much more effective (and more readily available) hunting implement.

Crossbows, like compound bows, are best employed at short ranges. Like most bowhunters, crossbow hunters like to shoot their game at 30 yards or closer. In theory, the longer, heavier arrow thrown by a bow should be a more effective killer than the lighter projectile thrown by the crossbow. However, such a property is difficult to demonstrate, and historically bows and crossbows have vied with each other as the most effective archery implement. The Genoese crossbowmen at Agincourt were surprised when the English longbowmen made pincushions out of them at what they thought was a safe distance. Should either tool be used in an attempt to take game at 100 yards? No. Both are short-range hunting implements and are at their best when used within 40 yards.

One thing the crossbow allows the hunter to do is to wait for the perfect shot and precisely place that shot. Although modern high-let-off compound bows have eased this problem, bow shooters have the problem of having to hold back the bow for perhaps considerable periods of time before the deer moves into a good shooting position. When hunting with recurves and longbows, the hunter feels considerable strain on his arm and this may lead to a hastily released arrow and poor hit. Given equal abilities and the fact that both hunters "kept their cool" in the presence of game, crossbow users can reasonably expect good hits and quicker one-shot kills than their bowhunter counterpart.

Better shot placement with the crossbow results in faster kills more often than any increased energy carried by crossbow arrows at 20 or 30 yards. In the final analysis, the ability to make hits in the vital areas of big-game animals is what kills them, whether the projectile is a bullet, arrow, or spear. With a poor hit, the animal will run and may not be recovered. With a good hit, the hunter will shortly have work for his skinning knife.

ARGUMENTS AND REFUTATIONS

David P. Robb of TenPoint Crossbows systematically categorized the anti-crossbow arguments in an article published in the first issue of *Horizontal Bowhunter*, the official publication of the American Crossbow Federation. In later issues, he refuted these arguments one by one. I can imagine some readers thinking at this moment, "Hold up. What would you expect him to say? After all he owns part of the business. Can we trust his statements?"

In brief, yes. His comments can be trusted because his arguments stand up to examination, which is different from listening to two groups of protestors standing on opposite sides of the street with one side shouting, "I'm right," and the other side shouting, "No. You're not." Once you consider the facts and real-life experiences of crossbow use in a number of states where they are permitted during archery seasons, these loudly voiced protests evaporate into nothingness.

I have borrowed Robb's list of anti-crossbow arguments and wrote my own refutations. I am a hunter and bowfisherman. I hunt with black-powder guns, crossbows, recurve bows, compound bows, and knives. I am not and have never been employed by a crossbow-manufacturing company or any company that retails sporting goods. As a technical writer of books about subjects as diverse as geology, architecture, and even AIDS, I bring a trained objectivity to this subject material.

Faced with rising populations of deer and a declining number of hunters, game management departments in many states are looking for ways to get more hunters in the woods to remove the excessive number of deer. Authorizing crossbow use may help motivate hunters to be more active during deer seasons and, incidentally, may result in a reduced number of urbanized deer.

Ohio, Arkansas, Georgia, Ohio, Tennessee, Virginia, and Wyoming have legally recognized the crossbow as archery equipment and permitted its use during their archery seasons as of mid-2005. The trend is that one or two more states each year are allowing their residents to use crossbows during bow season. In my home state of Georgia, retailers reported a large increase in crossbow sales (about 14,000) during the first year following the crossbow's legalization. Such purchases were made by those who had never hunted during the archery season and former bowhunters who could no longer operate their bows effectively and wished to hunt. After the first two years, crossbow sales fell dramatically, but sales of archery equipment remained strong as archers upgraded their equipment and a new generation of bowhunters bought their first bows.

Nothing in these states' laws mandates that bowhunters give up their bows and switch to crossbows. Outside of the two-year spikes in crossbow sales, the number of bowhunters in these states remained relatively stable. If numbers have declined, it is because age is taking its toll on our generally middle-aged and older population of hunters, and new hunters are not being recruited fast enough to replace the losses. If you want to grow the population of archers, take a youngster hunting. If it is easier for him to use a crossbow, let him. As he grows physically stronger, get him started with a compound bow that has enough pull weight to be effective.

Addressing Specific Anti-crossbow Arguments

The crossbow is the preferred weapon of poachers. Although I imagine that some poachers have used crossbows, the majority of illegally shot game has been taken by gun hunters. Poachers who want to work silently find that compound bows are more effective and allow for rapid second shots, something that cannot often be done with the crossbow because of the movement and noise necessary to recock the crossbow.

Michael J. Budzik, former director of the Ohio Division of Wildlife, wrote in 1999, "From a law-enforcement standpoint, violation statistics are just about equal between crossbows and vertical bows, and the total of both is an extremely small portion of the overall enforcement effort."

The crossbow is not a bow. First of all, crossbows are defined as archery equipment under the Pitman-Robertson Act, the legislation that enabled taxes on sales of sporting equipment to be collected for the benefit of wildlife. Second, the crossbow propels, under string pressure, an arrow that is a shortened version of the same shafts used by longbows, recurve bows, and compound bows. The crossbow also generates the same low energies, less than 100 foot-pounds, generated by a bow.

The crossbow is a long-range weapon. Most crossbow users, like most bowhunters, want to take their deer at 20 yards and preferably no farther than 35 yards. The more distant the game is from the crossbowman, the more likely game such as deer will "jump the string," and a missed shot will be the result.

The crossbow has the knockdown power of a firearm. Rarely do deer come down immediately when shot by an arrow fired from either a bow or crossbow. The animal may have received a fatal hit, but its usual reaction is to run. Arrows shot from either a bow or a crossbow usually register between 70 and 90 foot-pounds of muzzle energy, a far cry from even the relatively puny 500 foot-pounds of energy still retained by the .44 Remington Magnum pistol cartridge at 100 yards, much less the 2,800 foot-pounds of energy generated by a 150-grain .30'06 bullet at the muzzle.

Crossbows shoot as flat as a black-powder rifle. Once beyond 20 yards, which is spear-throwing range, an arrow from a crossbow starts to drop rapidly. At 40 yards, the typical crossbow arrow had dropped around 20 inches, while the round ball from a 50-caliber muzzleloader is still shooting to the point of aim. At 100 yards, the typical round-ball load from a muzzleloader hits 6 inches low, compared to 100 inches low for the crossbow arrow.

Crossbows are unsafe. Crossbows manufactured by recognized makers are well-made instruments that perform safely when used according to the directions in the instruction manual. Of course, a crossbow hunter may injure himself when using a crossbow, just as archers or gun hunters may also be injured by their hunting implements. However, the crossbows themselves are safe and reliable tools. Will parts break? Yes, just as parts of conventional bows and guns. All mechanical objects will someday fail, but the modern crossbow is no more intrinsically unsafe, or safe, than modern bows or guns. The most common type of accident associated with crossbows is a hunter jabbing himself with an arrow, which incidentally is also the most commonly reported accident involving bowhunters.

Crossbows shoot farther and faster than compound bows. Crossbow arrows do get off to a faster start than the typical full-length arrow shot from a modern compound bow, but they decelerate rapidly. Maximum effective ranges will differ, depending on the characteristics of the individual crossbows and bows, but in reality, no real difference exists between the effectivenesses of crossbows and bows at reasonable hunting ranges.

The crossbow is too easy to use. It is a lazy man's weapon. If you really want an archery challenge, cut your own stave, make your own bow and string, fashion your own arrows, and point them with an obsidian arrowhead. A small group of primitive archers actually do this, but most of us use off-the-shelf equipment. Crossbow hunters do have a faster learning curve than conventional bow hunters and less physical conditioning is required. Does this somehow negate the crossbow to a lesser status? The challenge in hunting is not so much the instrument being used, but the getting close enough to the game to make a killing shot. If I take a homemade bow and shoot a deer at 20 yards, the hit is not going to be as precise as it would be with either my compound bow or my crossbow. I greatly improve my chances of making a shot that will quickly kill a deer when I use more modern equipment. I want my percentage of fast kills to be as high as possible, out of respect for the game, and to do this, I prefer to use a precision-shooting instrument, such as the modern crossbow.

Permitting crossbows in archery season will decimate the deer population. Crossbow legalization does put more hunters in the field during the archery season, and it might reasonably be expected that some of these additional hunters will kill deer. Will they "shoot them all out?" Not likely. If deer are overharvested in a particular area, state authorities are quick to readjust the season. In northern states, winter kill has a much more devastating effect on the deer herd than total hunting pressure. The added crossbow take is not really significant. Most hunting in the eastern half of the nation is on private land, where landowners can control the deer harvest and restrict it if the harvest is thought to become excessive.

Allowing crossbows will threaten the existence of, or at least the length of, archery-only seasons. Weather and land-use factors have a much greater effect on the health and numbers of deer available to hunters than archery kills from bows or crossbows. If any adjustments to the length of hunting seasons are made by state authorities, it will be in response to the total population of deer, taking into account winter kill, disease, and, increasingly, vehicle-deer collisions. More bow and crossbow hunting is allowed in urban areas to help control deer populations.

Yes, a number of factors may cause the alteration of some bow seasons, but archery opportunities are increasing, rather than decreasing, nationwide. Bowhunters, like any other hunters, must be flexible and take advantage of new hunts offered in nontraditional areas.

Crossbow hunters are less ethical, dedicated, and proficient than vertical bowhunters. Just as there are ethical and unethical lawyers, doctors, clergy, and police officers, ethical and unethical conventional bowhunters and crossbow hunters can be found. Assertions about the personal values and ethics of any class of people cannot be proven or disproved. Perhaps new crossbowmen in the woods are less proficient during the first couple of seasons, and some will try to overreach the capabilities of their equipment. Some may take the crossbow out of the box and put it together incorrectly, and others may not shoot well with their unfamiliar hunting tools, but these conditions work themselves out in time. After a disappointing trip or two, some hunters may abandon their crossbows and go back to gun hunting, but far more will learn from their experiences and become increasingly more proficient.

Crossbow hunters will overcrowd the woods, decreasing the chances of success for the vertical bowhunter. This statement, more than any other, reveals the real reason that many bowhunters don't want crossbowmen in the woods: They don't want anyone "killing their deer." If this is so, then they should lease or purchase enough private land so that they can hunt when they like, as they like, without competition. For hunting as we know it today to survive in North America, we need numbers. Bowhunting, crossbow hunting, and black-powder gun hunting are not allowed in much of Europe, and the anti-hunting fraternity would like nothing better than to close down hunting one step at a time in our country. First, these opponents would seek to outlaw trapping, then dog hunting for big game, followed by dog hunting for all game. After that, bow and crossbow hunting and eventually black-powder hunting would come under attack, until finally a ban on all hunting would occur. To prevent this, we should seek more hunters in all aspects of the hunting sports, not a decrease in numbers for our own temporary advantage.

Ohio has allowed crossbows to be used alongside vertical bows since 1976. The result? The archery season has not been shortened, and crossbows have done nothing to diminish conventional archers' chances of success. Instead, the deer population has increased, the season has been lengthened, more areas have been opened for hunting, more hunters have participated, and hunter success percentages have dramatically improved. A rapidly increasing deer population more than absorbed the increased numbers of hunters, about half of whom now use crossbows.

Vertical bowhunters fought too long and hard for their season, and crossbow hunters have not earned the right to be in the woods. To all who promoted and ultimately were successful in getting state legislatures to pass laws permitting a separate archery season, we owe considerable thanks. Many of these same individuals are now reaching an age, or various conditions of infirmity, where they can no longer use their vertical bows. Are bowhunters as a class willing to cast away those who did so much for the sport because they can no longer physically use a bow? Crossbows can both get a youngster into the woods at least five years before he can draw a legal-weight bow and extend the bowhunting life of an older person by decades. Are these opportunities to be denied? Most states have provisions for allowing crossbows to be used by hunters who are physically disabled, but what formerly robust guy wants to go to a doctor and admit, "I am not as good as I once was"? Better shots on deer and greater competence will result if a hunter becomes accustomed to a crossbow before becoming seriously disabled or before hunting at age 80 or 90.

Because of their dedication to their craft and their respect for nature and the tradition of bowhunting, bowhunters have a mystical bond with the animals they pursue, a bond that a crossbow hunter could never understand or ever hope to achieve. Hunters may feel attachment to their grandfather's gun or the first bow they used to kill a deer, but to feel any mystical bond between the deer and deer hunter is something more imaginary than real. One can and should respect the game animals that are taken. This respect for nature, sometimes lost in modern societies, was often highly developed in what are now considered primitive cultures, such as the Native Americans. Game vital for a group's survival was considered a gift, not a statistic. Sure, such cultures had waste and even some responsibility for the probable extinction of species, but they also had a respect for the game that today has often been replaced by trying to fill bag limits or hanging the largest set of horns on a wall. In my opinion, the highest and best use of game is its consumptive use. After all, shouldn't the taking of the life of one species to give life to another be the essence of hunting?

GEORGIA, A CASE IN POINT

Nick Nicholson, a senior wildlife biologist who has been monitoring Georgia's wildlife harvest for more than a decade, was interested in learning what effect the state's inclusion of the crossbow has had on the archery season. Georgia has among the longest deer seasons and one of the most liberal bag limits in the nation. During the season, which typically runs from late September through the first part of January, each licensed hunter can take by any means up to ten does and two bucks, and deer harvested during managed hunts on wildlife management areas do not count against a hunter's tags.

Occasionally, individuals will take their dozen deer, but I personally don't know any. Only on a hunt lease, which has a serious goal of adjusting the doe-buck ratio, would a hunter be apt to shoot anything close to this number of deer.

With the announcement of a crossbow season, the first notable effect was a marked increase in the sale of crossbows. Some 14,000 crossbows were sold in the state in preparation for that first season. The majority of those buying crossbows were former gun hunters who wanted a chance to take a deer during archery season, but some were older bowhunters who wanted to continue archery hunting but for various reasons had not previously qualified or applied for a special permit for the disabled. Still others were hunters who had taken deer with guns, muzzleloaders, and conventional bows and wanted to see for themselves what the new crossbows could do.

Nicholson sent a summary of his first two years of data to *Horizontal Bowhunter*, which published the summary in its Fall 2004 issue. It is reproduced here with the permission of the publisher.

I have just completed looking at Georgia's 2003–2004 hunter survey results. Because of the interest in crossbow hunting, we decided to take a closer look at crossbow harvest. I have included excerpts from the annual report below.

The 2003–2004 hunting season marked the second year that crossbows were legal for the majority of hunters in Georgia. Previously, only those hunters with certified disabilities were permitted to use crossbows.

The number of crossbow hunters and their harvest during 2003–2004 increased by 55.3 percent and 168 percent respectively over 2002–2003.

To put these numbers more in perspective, crossbow hunters comprised 24.8 percent of archery hunters and 9.1 percent of all hunters for 2003–2004. Crossbow harvest comprised 21.8 percent of archery harvest but only 2.6 percent of the 2003–2004 total Georgia deer harvest.

Thirteen point five percent (13.5%) of crossbow hunters indicated they previously had used a crossbow under the handicap permit system.

Thirty one point one percent (31.1%) of crossbow hunters (6,884) indicated they had not hunted with archery equipment prior to using a crossbow.

To estimate the real impact crossbow hunters have on total harvest, we must make several assumptions. The first is that new crossbow hunters who already participated in archery hunting did not increase their harvest by changing from compound/recurve to crossbow. The success rate for crossbows (.49 deer/hunter) is comparable to that of compound bows (.51 deer/hunter).

Our survey indicates that 78.5 percent of archers use compounds and it is less likely that a traditional archer would switch to a crossbow.

There was a significant increase in the number of archery hunters for 2003–2004. The raw estimates give us about 9,300 additional archers. A large part of this increase can be attributed to the 31.1 percent of crossbow hunters (6,884) who indicated they were new to archery hunting.

Additionally, age structure indicates an influx of older hunters into the crossbow hunter ranks. A portion of these individuals are likely retired archery hunters who were attracted back into archery hunting by the legalization of crossbows.

If we assume all additional archers hunted with crossbows and the .49 deer per hunter harvest rate for crossbows is additive for both of these groups, then 4,557 additional deer would be attributed to additional archery (crossbow) hunters. The 95 percent confidence interval for total harvest is plus or minus 7,818 deer. These data and assumptions suggest that any additional harvest attributed to the legalization of crossbows is not significant at a statewide level.

During 2002–2003 there was a small tendency for crossbow hunters to be older than the general hunter population. That trend continues for 2003–2004, particularly in age classes over 50 years old.

Thirty four point six percent (34.6%) of the general hunter population is over 50 years old. Older age groups show greater crossbow use for both seasons crossbows have been legal; however, there also was an increase in crossbow selectivity this year by the 25–29 year age group. The average age for the general hunting population is 43.8 years. The average age for crossbow hunters is 45.3 years.

The results of this study showed that more hunters, particularly older hunters, were able to take advantage of the archery season because of the crossbow, but the increased harvest did not significantly affect the overall harvest of deer in the state. Information on geographic locations of deer kills was not included. I suspect that a significant portion of the crossbow kills were deer taken from archery-only areas around metropolitan areas and urban deer taken from the outskirts of the state's numerous small towns.

STATE LAWS

I had reservations about including a section on state laws since conditions change so rapidly that information quickly could become obsolete. For the most recent information on crossbow legality and seasons, consult your state's fish and game regulations. Another good source is the magazine *Horizontal Bowhunter,* which does an annual update of crossbow regulations throughout the nation. TenPoint Crossbows's website, www.tenpointcrossbows.com, also keeps an updated list of legislative activity related to crossbow hunting.

The information below is simply a time capsule reflecting conditions as they existed in mid-2005. To date, crossbow use has never been rescinded, once it has passed through the state legislatures. In fact, the national trend has been to steadily expand, rather than restrict, crossbow use.

As of mid-2005, four states have made the crossbow, for all practical purposes, illegal: Oregon, Nevada, New York, and West Virginia. There has been a long-term movement in New York to liberalize crossbow use, at least for someone less than profoundly disabled, but to date it has not been successful.

A much brighter picture emerges in Alabama, Arkansas, Georgia, Ohio, Tennessee, Virginia, and Wyoming, where crossbows may be used during designated archery seasons and in most cases during muzzle-loading and gun seasons.

Eighteen states permit crossbow use during archery season only by certified disabled hunters: Connecticut, Hawaii, Idaho, Illinois, Iowa, Kansas, Maine, Minnesota, New Jersey, North Carolina, North Dakota, New Mexico, Okalahoma, Rhode Island, South Dakota, Utah, Vermont, and Washington.

Twelve states permit qualifying disabled individuals to use crossbows during archery season and anyone to use them during some or all of gun or firearms seasons: Alaska, Arizona, California, Colorado, Delaware, Pennsylvania, South Carolina, Kentucky, Texas, Michigan, Missouri, and Nebraska.

Three states permit the use of crossbows by permit-holding disabled hunters of any age and all hunters over the age of 65: Louisiana, Mississippi, and Wisconsin.

Montana permits the crossbow to be used by anyone during some or all of firearms season but has no provision for handicapped hunters.

Five states have legislation allowing crossbows during particular seasons or parts of seasons: Florida, Indiana, Maryland, New Hampshire, and Pennsylvania. Pennsylvania also has recognized the particular aptitude of crossbows for taking urban deer and, although restricting crossbow use for deer to disabled individuals, permits anyone to take deer in designated urbanized areas during any established deer season.

Crossbow use has been increasing nationwide. Will the use of crossbows increase to such a degree to make up 50 percent of all archery hunting as it has in Ohio? That is a more difficult call to make. Whatever the increase in crossbow use, much of it can be attributed to older hunters who are staying in the woods longer and frequently taking their grandchildren, nieces, and nephews with them. Watching an 8-year-old take his first deer with a crossbow that granddad cocked is often more of a thrill for granddad than if he shot the deer himself.

5

SELECTING AND SHOOTING THE MODERN CROSSBOW

Crossbows are available in a variety of configurations, weights, styles, and even modes of operation. They range from historic medieval reproductions to comparatively simple low-cost instruments to crossbows with sufficient shooting aids to satisfy even the most gadget-happy among us. Choosing the most appropriate crossbow should depend first on its likely use and whether it is powerful enough to do its intended job. Next, consider whether it is appropriately sized and accessorized for you. And, finally, can you afford it?

Shot placement is more important than raw power. A crossbow with a 150-pound pull weight will send a shaft through the chest of any North American whitetail at a range of 30 yards, assuming a leg bone is not hit. Upping the poundage to 175 speeds up the arrow, flattens the trajectory, and provides something extra to kill bear and the larger members of the deer family. Although the 200- and 225-pound crossbows may be used on smaller game animals, these powerful crossbows are best employed with exceptionally heavy arrows and twin-bladed cutting points on the world's largest beasties, such as buffalo and elephant.

One way of producing more power out of a crossbow is to increase the barrel, or deck, length of the crossbow. However, the longer the crossbow, the more difficult it becomes for shorter-armed individuals to cock the bow using either their hands or a rope cocker. I am 5 feet 10 inches tall and do not have particularly strong arms, yet I have never seen a 150-pound pull crossbow that I cannot hand cock with reasonable ease. With a rope cocker, I can easily cock 175- to 200-pound draw pull crossbows with the same barrel lengths. Increasing the barrel length 2 inches causes me to have to pull the last little bit with my arms at nearly shoulder level, which is a bit of a strain. The lesson here is if you are 6 feet or taller you can comfortably shoot the heavier draw weight, longer-barreled

The risk of buying a used crossbow is that the instrument might have been previously damaged. Carefully examine the prod and compound wheels (if any) before purchasing a used bow. If the only thing wrong is a worn string, that can easily be replaced. Keep in mind that such makers as Horton, Parker, Excalibur, and Fred Bear can completely refurbish crossbows made in the last decade.

Shooting a replica of a medieval crossbow made by Texan crossbow maker David Watson. Although this crossbow had no sights, the user can shoot over the arrow shaft, like the rib of a shotgun, to ensure sufficient accuracy to make hits on a deer-size target out to 40 yards. However, the comparatively small delivered energy of the bow restricts shots on game to within 20 yards.

crossbows, but if you are a more slightly built individual, the lighter draw weight crossbows will be more comfortable to shoot, and most importantly, you are more likely to practice with them.

Cocking aids are the most important accessory for anyone with weak arms or physical impairments. They are discussed in chapter 6. As for crossbow sights, some users will need magnifying scope sights, and some prefer red-dot sights. Still other users find the old reliable peep-and-pin system works best. Crossbow sights are covered in detail in chapter 7. TenPoint crossbows now have an extendable monopod, which is particularly designed for disabled shooters but is also a useful accessory to use in ground blinds. The key here is don't be in a hurry to purchase a crossbow. Do your homework and buy one appropriately sized for you that has the accessories that you'll need.

Unfortunately, price is the most important discriminating factor for many would-be crossbow purchasers. Crossbows that will kill deer are available for less than $150, indeed some even less than $100, but these crossbows are not as well designed or supported with accessories, spare parts, or information as the higher-priced versions. If taking one of these on a hunt in a distant location, carry two of them. In fact, it is not a bad practice on any hunt to take two crossbows of different configurations, say one with iron sights for rainy days and one with a scope or

Kath Throubridge shooting an Excalibur crossbow from a blind. Blinds help to conceal the hunter and control his scent. Hunting from blinds near waterholes or food plots is the surest way to make close-range kills on turkeys and big-game animals.

red-dot sight, but if you are using bargain-basement crossbows, taking along more than one is a necessity. Cheaper crossbows will work, but they cannot be expected to be as easy to shoot or as durable as more expensive crossbows. If you want to hunt with your crossbow year after year, choose one in the $300 to $400 range.

THE CROSSBOW'S MOST IMPORTANT COMPONENT

To paraphrase a comment Chuck Buck of Buck Knives says about his knife blades, "The prod is the thing," and this holds true for crossbows. Without the prod, the remainder of the crossbow is an assemblage of nonfunctional components. One might be able to scavenge the sights or perhaps even the trigger and use them on something else, but without the prod the crossbow has no utility. Historically, crossbow prods have been made of wood, bamboo, horn, laminated woods, steel, aluminum, and fiberglass. Nowadays, prods usually are made of synthetic composites, often with graphite or other space-age fibers, that may carry multiple laminates designed to have optimum compressive or tensional strengths, depending on their positions in the limb.

The greatest stress on a crossbow comes not when it is at rest, cocked, or even fired. Instead, the greatest stress is imparted when the string under high velocity is suddenly arrested at the end of its travel after it has discharged the arrow. The string first moves forward of its "at rest" position, is stopped, and under tension from the opposite direction rebounds rearward of its rest position. Then it is forced forward again and rebounds back. With a springy prod, this cycle would repeat several times. With a stiff prod, the vibration-rebound cycle is shortened. In any event, arresting the motion of the string asserts the greatest stress on the prod, the string, and all the connective hardware of the crossbow.

An important thing to remember here is that this shock tends to loosen bolts. Before going on a hunt, and from time to time if you are shooting at targets, check to make sure the screws retaining the prod are tight.

Prods must restrain this cocked-fired-and-rebounding stress without literally flying apart. Most medieval crossbows before the fourteenth century used composite horn bows, which also contained wooden or bone components wrapped in sinew and fastened together with fish glue. These prods were thick, rounded, and bulky but could generate sufficient force to be useful. The Assyrians developed the technology of making horn bows, and their powerful, short recurve bows along with chariots propelled their war machine. This technology, which was passed onto and improved by the Huns and Arabs, was ultimately adopted by European crossbow builders, who recognized that short horn prods could store

Here, the glass fibers in fiberglass are drawn before being placed in a mold with resin to be cured into crossbow limbs for an Excalibur crossbow.

A modern Excalibur recurve limb is formed by placing the parallel fiberglass fibers in the limb mold with resin and curing the resin with heat.

more energy than wooden prods. Arguably, the most sophisticated horn crossbow prods were produced during the golden years of the Ottoman Empire.

After the fourteenth century, steel manufacture became sufficiently advanced that crossbow prods were increasingly made of steel, although woods, such as yew, remained the preferred material for European longbows. Steel bows were tested in England and elsewhere in the 1500s but were never adopted in large numbers. Steel longbows even had a brief resurgence in the United States during the 1950s but quickly lost the competitive battle when Fred Bear and others introduced fiberglass-laminated wooden recurve bows.

Whatever the composition of the prods, crossbows, from the earliest surviving examples to the 1950s models, used some variant of the recurve design. Commercial crossbows manufactured in Europe and the United States almost universally used steel prods on hunting bows, although fiberglass prods increasingly appeared on advanced designed and low-end crossbows starting in the mid-1950s.

Modern compression-molded fiberglass limbs have brought crossbows a long way since the bows mentioned above. Pressure molding has allowed fiberglass-resin limbs to be made stronger and much lighter

Heat and compression are used to form the fiberglass limbs for a Fred Bear crossbow.

than those cut from flat sheets. In molding technology, the fiberglass fibers are not cut, which gives them full strength and makes it much less likely that the limbs will split apart.

Improving the strength of the crossbow's prods has brought some inherent problems. The more tension placed on the trigger mechanism, the harder the trigger is to pull. Also, to give the arrow the smoothest acceleration and to lessen the chance of the string jumping over the top of the arrow, the limbs of the recurve prod tended to be long. Short, thicker limbs could store the same energy, but accuracy was sacrificed, and as this energy was expended more rapidly, the recoil forces on the crossbow were harsher.

SELECTING YOUR CROSSBOW

If the modern crossbow designer was to "have his cake and eat it too," his ideal prod would be short, exert less pressure on the trigger's components for a lighter trigger pull, and build up pressure on the arrow as it traveled down the rail instead of applying a maximum amount of stress on the arrow at the outset. That "cake" turned out to be the technology applied to the dual-round-wheel compound bow and later high-let-off cams. Interestingly, Fred Bear Crossbows solved the trigger-pull problem another way when the company employed "no let-off cams" to achieve maximum velocity from its crossbows.

It took some years after the first compound bows were introduced before crossbow makers such as Barnett and Horton, who had long histories of making recurve-prod crossbows, added compound crossbows to their lines. Although Barnett still offers recurve prods on its lower-priced crossbows and Horton still has one recurve, the SteelForce, in its line, most of the crossbows made and sold by these companies today are compound crossbows.

Horton's first compound crossbows were the Safari Express with a polypropylene thumbhole stock and the LS Express, which featured a wooden stock. Both used compound wheels held in brackets suspended from the crossbows' prods. Introduced in 1975 as 150-pound draw weight crossbows, both were sold alongside Horton's recurve-prod Safari Magnum. For a time, the public was ambivalent about compound crossbows, and Horton continued to market both types. Today, the SteelForce remains Horton's last recurve-prod crossbow.

Many of the newer companies in the crossbow field, such as Parker and TenPoint, have never made anything but compound crossbows. When Fred Bear, the successor to the famous Bear Archery Co., decided to offer its first crossbow, it was a compound crossbow designed by Tom Jennings. PSE's first crossbow was also a compound design. In North

America, Excalibur is the only company that produces high-end hunting crossbows with recurve limbs. A reasonable question is, "Why?"

Bill Throubridge, Excalibur's founder, president, designer, and spokesman, explained, "We kept the recurve design because it has fewer components that might potentially fail. In addition, a recurve crossbow is a lighter, simpler design." Anyone who has ever replaced strings on both types of crossbows can attest that it is easier to restring a recurve than a compound crossbow.

When comparing power and speed between recurve and compound crossbows, no practical difference between the two types can be found. Power depends on the pull weight of the bow and the travel length of the string, which gives thrust to the arrow. Velocity figures are not directly comparable unless the crossbows are shooting the same arrows.

On the downside, the Excalibur's recurve limbs, which are longer than those of compound crossbows of comparable power, are more awkward to use in tree stands and blinds. The trigger pulls on Excalibur bows are excellent, and the tension of the string against the bed of the crossbow and the flat back of the arrow prevents the string from jumping over the shaft. Excalibur's recurve crossbows have a proven track record on game and have taken all North American species of big game and most African game.

Bear Archery created an interesting mating of Excalibur's crossbow design with compound limb technology with its Buckmaster MaxPoint. To make this crossbow, Bear placed its newly manufactured riser and compression-formed quad limbs on Excalibur's frame, stock, and trigger mechanism. Both 150- and 175-pound versions were produced, and the MaxPoint crossbows remain one of the best hunting crossbows to

The Buckmaster MaxPoint by Fred Bear combines an Excalibur body with split-limb prods to make an excellent crossbow, albeit one that is no longer made.

date. Fred Bear now makes 175-pound draw weight laminated-wood-stock versions of its F-340 crossbow for Cabela's called the Outfitter Series XB-340.

Recurve crossbows are preferred over compounds when the bows are rigged for bowfishing. Recurves have fewer metallic components on the front end of the bow to be corroded by saltwater and/or gummed up with fish slime, mud, or scales. If one is going to bowfish with a crossbow, a recurve crossbow would tend to have fewer problems.

Whichever style of crossbow you choose, it should suit you and your pocketbook. Any recurve or compound crossbow of 150-pound pull from a recognized maker can be expected to give good results on deer-size game as long as you take the time to choose compatible arrows and points, sight in the crossbow, determine its trajectory out to 40 yards, and maintain your equipment. A crossbow is not a tool you simply take out of the box and go shoot something with it. If you take the time to learn your equipment, you will be better prepared technically, physically, and psychologically when you finally have a shot at a nice head of game.

UNPACKING AND ASSEMBLING YOUR CROSSBOW

A natural response to receiving any new shooting implement is to throw it together, take it out, and start punching holes in something. Restrain yourself. Instead, look at the accompanying video, read your instruction manual, find the assembly instructions and tools, and then start assembling your crossbow. Because compound crossbows come with the limbs already attached to the riser and the strings and cables preadjusted, the limbs should fit into the stock-deck assembly smoothly. Now you will need to secure the limbs with several screws. When installing the screws, keep in mind that you are putting a steel screw into aluminum or fiberglass. Snug up the screws, but do not overtighten or you will strip the threads in the softer host materials. The cables connecting the crossbow's limbs typically have a small plastic cable guide that fits into a raceway slot under the crossbow's deck. You may have to twist the strings slightly to properly orient the guide.

On recurve-prod crossbows, the prods are not strung. Make sure you read the directions carefully on how to install the string. If the crossbow is shipped with a Flemish string, you will have to give it a set number of twists to put the needed amount of tension on the prod. If the crossbow has an English, or continuous-loop string, twisting will not be necessary. On most recurve crossbows, a slave string will be provided to cock the crossbow and allow the crossbow string to be easily attached.

Otherwise enlist your best buddy to pull the prod's ends together so you can slip the string onto the other prod.

SHOOTING YOUR CROSSBOW

Before shooting your crossbow, apply a coating of string wax to the string and cables and a small amount of deck grease to the barrel of the crossbow. Do not put any grease on the serving. The string should be rewaxed after each shooting session, and after every twenty shots, apply additional lubricant to the crossbow's deck.

Select the arrows you wish to try and install a field point. Crossbow arrows have excellent penetration and, when used in practice, require a stout foam or cloth-filled bag for a backstop. Arrows shot into grass are hard to recover as they will typically bury themselves well beyond the fletching. Place your target and backstop 10 yards from the shooting bench.

Before cocking the crossbow, take a white marker and stripe the crossbow string on both sides of the barrel. This will help ensure that the string is properly positioned in the sear when the crossbow is fully cocked. If the string is pulled off center, the arrow will be cast to the left or right of the point of aim. Carefully take aim and shoot an arrow at the center of the target. Walk forward, pull the arrow, and take another shot. This shot should be in practically the same hole. Adjust the sights to hit about

The high velocity of crossbow arrows requires a stout target to catch the shafts. Sometimes it is necessary to drape a piece of carpet material over the target to prevent the arrow from passing completely through the target.

Shooting from a bench allows for maximum accuracy when initially sighting in a crossbow. Shoot only one arrow at a time to prevent damaging the shafts and fletching. Begin at 10 yards and shoot at 20, 30, and 40 yards, recording drop information as you go. Like all arrows, those shot from crossbows are subject to wind deflection, so your best targeting will occur on windless days.

2 inches above the point of aim. Then move to 20 yards and shoot again, using one arrow at the time to keep from damaging your arrows from repeated impacts. Now adjust the sights at 20 yards to hit the point of aim.

Once you are confident that you can hit the bull consistently—all of the arrows from a crossbow fired at a rest should be within 1 inch—then move the target to 30 and 40 yards. Do not adjust the sights anymore. Practice holding over the target until you are satisfied that you can drop the arrow into the center of the bull with every shot. Record the amount of hold-over for each range, and paste this on the inside of a limb on your crossbow so that you have it for easy reference.

CHRONOGRAPHING: WHAT IT MEANS

Assuming two crossbows have the same efficiency, which is often not a good assumption, crossbows with the same rated pull strength should launch an arrow of same size and weight at about the same velocity. In reality, playing around with lightweight shafts and points can provide a large range in velocities and easily increase the velocity to the seemingly magic 300-fps threshold that appears to define a modern crossbow. Readers want high velocities, and even the Brand X makers can produce it if they use very light arrows. Some advertisers of inexpensive crossbows also bend the truth a bit about the supposed draw strength of their prods.

Chronographing involves shooting the arrows through both detectors without hitting them. Shooting the same arrows from different crossbows will help to separate fact from advertising fiction and enable the amount of energy actually delivered to the target to be calculated.

Any user who cocks a few so-called 150-pound draw crossbows will find that some cock with much less strain than others.

The following series of chronograph tests were made with various crossbows. The results, although not representative of all crossbows, demonstrate considerable variations with the same advertised pull weights. Because it is not practical to shoot arrows with the same length and weight in all crossbows for safety reasons, the length and type of shafts are recorded in the table. All of the points used were 100-grain field tips.

CHRONOGRAPHING CROSSBOWS

Type	Arrow Characteristics	Velocity fps
Watson replica 150-pound draw	³⁄₈-inch wood shaft field point feather fletching 13⁵⁄₈ inches 288 grains	162
Brand X folding-limb crossbow	Horton Lightning Strike 7 shaft 18-inch aluminum 341 grains	161
Brand X	2018 aluminum 14 inches 304 grains	175/250**
Barnett Ranger 150-pound draw	Horton Lightning Strike 7 shaft 18-inch aluminum 341 grains	205/225**
Horton SteelForce 150-pound draw	Horton Lightning Strike 7 shaft 18-inch aluminum 341 grains	213/240**
Horton Hawk SL 150-pound draw	Horton Lightning Strike 7 shaft 18-inch aluminum 341 grains	245/260**
Fred Bear F-300 150-pound draw	Carbon Express 20-inch carbon arrow 376 grains	247/300**
TenPoint XQ4 185-pound draw	Beeman Thunderbolt 20-inch carbon arrow 421 grains	281/313**

** advertised velocities

During the shooting tests, the Competitive Edge Dynamics Chronograph was consistent with velocities between repeat shots only varying between 1 and 2 fps. The Brand X crossbow was shot first and at the end of the shooting session and reported an identical 161 fps velocity both times. Empirical data indicated that the reported trends were correct: The crossbows that reported higher velocities were harder to cock, and the arrows penetrated deeper into the Styrofoam target.

What do these figures tell us about today's crossbows? So-called 150-pound draw weight crossbows may develop anywhere from 175 to 245 fps, with the more expensive crossbows coming closer to actually producing advertised velocities. The Brand X crossbow, even with the smaller diameter lightweight shaft, was 75 fps shy of its advertised velocity of 250 feet per second. The simpler and lighter Barnett Ranger was only about 20 fps short of obtaining its full advertised velocity with an 18-inch shafted aluminum arrow.

With all this information, what did it take to reliably kill deer? I knew from experience that the Barnett Ranger, even at around 200 fps, would produce 32 foot-pounds of muzzle energy, enough to shoot an arrow through the ribcage of an 80-pound deer. What about arrows traveling at only 162 fps and producing 16.78 foot-pounds from the Watson crossbow? Would these poke through an animal with deadly results? Was I willing to take the relatively lightweight but low-velocity Brand X crossbow on a black-tailed deer hunt on Kodiak Island? These were decisions that I would have to make, and the chronograph figures gave me a solid basis from which to draw an informed conclusion.

DETERMINING YOUR CROSSBOW'S TRAJECTORY

Velocity figures showed me that the Barnett Ranger might be the better choice to take to Kodiak Island on a black-tailed deer hunt than the Brand X crossbow, which produced 44 fps less velocity. My next task was to enhance the Ranger's capabilities and discover how it performed at longer ranges. I had to answer some critical questions:

1. Could I shoot this lightweight crossbow effectively from off-hand positions since I would probably have to stand to see a deer over the top of Kodiak Island's alders and tall grasses?
2. Would I be able to see my target well enough to hit it?
3. What was the trajectory of the arrow at ranges of 30, 40, and 50 yards?
4. What would be the longest range that I would have a reasonable chance of making a killing shot at a deer?

During my first shooting sessions with the Ranger, I found that holding my supporting left arm close to my chest with my left hand cupping the bottom of the pistol grip provided the most stable off-hand shooting position. This pose, identical to one used by off-hand rifle shooters, works just fine for crossbows. The most serious detracting components for off-hand shooting were movement of the crossbow on the target and a long, mushy trigger pull. I typically needed to take two breaths to get off a good shot. Off-hand shooting could be done, but only if considerable care was taken.

Excalibur sent me a scope sight, which has dial adjustments for different velocity crossbows and redicle points below the main crosshairs to allow for compensation at longer ranges. The lowest adjustment on

BARNETT RANGER TRAJECTORY

Range	Velocity fps	Energy foot-pounds	Drop or Rise in inches
Crosshairs			
10 yards	205	32	+3
20 yards			+1
25 yards			0
30 yards			−3
First marker			
30 yards			+3
35 yards			0
40 yards			−4
Second marker			
37 yards			0
45 yards			−3
50 yards			−6
Third marker			
50 yards			+4
52 yards			0
55 yards			−4

The author installed an Excalibur scope on this Barnett Ranger to see if the lightweight crossbow would be useful for an Alaskan hunt.

the scope for velocity—225 fps—was close enough to zero in the scope for the Ranger's achieved 205 fps. An unexpected result was that I could see the target and the crosshairs on the scope most clearly when I was not wearing my glasses, and this would allow me an increased possibility of making a good shot.

Using the intermediate markers in the scope certainly helped when I was judging the amount of hold-over/under necessary to hit the target at various ranges. Although the eye can fairly easily judge a hold-over of 2 to 6 inches, determining the exact hold-over between 16 and 21 inches becomes more of a problem, particularly if you also have to hold off the target to compensate for the wind.

While shooting at the longer ranges, I noticed that if the crossbow arrow was pushed all the way back to the string, it was elevated slightly off the deck of the crossbow, and the arrow would fly high at all ranges, up to a foot or more at 50 yards. The little Ranger was very touchy, and I discovered that everything had to be exactly right for it to perform well. The arrow had to be laid in flat on the barrel, the crossbow had to be held still as the shot was discharged, and I had to hold my breath to keep from wobbling off the target. The crossbow could hit the target, but only if all of the above conditions were met.

Are all crossbows this hard to shoot? Certainly not. The better quality crossbows from any maker, including Barnett, will be easier to shoot and will perform better. In choosing the Ranger, I had decided to save weight while sacrificing ballistic performance and operational characteristics. Besides lightweight, the Ranger also was quieter to shoot than any of the crossbows that I owned. In the relatively noisy conditions found on Kodiak Island, it might be possible to get a second shot if the first arrow did not spook the deer.

Kinetic energy is calculated by using the formula

$$\frac{velocity^2 \times arrow\ weight\ (in\ grains)}{450,340} = kinetic\ energy\ in\ foot\text{-}pounds$$

Even at 10 yards, the 32 foot-pounds generated by the Ranger was far short of the 50 foot-pounds recommended by Chuck Adams for animals weighing between 300 and 700 pounds. Sitka blacktails top out at about 200 pounds, and the white-tailed deer that I had taken with the little crossbow weighed about 80 pounds. The crossbow had shot completely through the smaller deer at 20 yards, but did it have enough "stuff" to handle a deer twice as large? Recalculating the needed energy for a 200-pound animal (50:300 as X:200), the recommended energy figure came

With a deer in sight, now is not the time to worry if a crossbow arrow has enough retained energy to cleanly kill the animal. Ideally, you should have chronographed the crossbow with an appropriate arrow and point to establish its maximum kill range. If no chronograph is available, crossbows from reputable makers come closer to developing their advertised velocities (and energies) than unknown brands.

out to be 33 foot-pounds, which told me that the arrow from the Ranger could not be depended upon to pass through a 200-pound deer's ribcage at 20 yards.

A likely result of using the Ranger on Kodiak's deer would be that the animal would receive a hit, but the arrow would not exit the deer, reducing the amount of blood released by the animal and making it more difficult to recover in the island's tall grass and brush. And if it ran some distance, I might find that I was not the only creature following the blood trail as Kodiak bear like to eat deer, too. If I were to put an arrow into a Sitka blacktail, I had to bring it down as quickly as possible. Whatever the desirable characteristics of the Ranger might be, this was not the crossbow to take on my Alaskan hunt. I could use it confidently on whitetails at home where I had dogs to help recover my deer, but not in far-off Alaska.

It was time to look at other options. Horton's SteelForce generated 34 foot-pounds at 10 yards with the same weight arrow, but the crossbow would not give me much flexibility in regards to range. At 245 fps, the 7-pound Hawk generated 45 foot-pounds and was capable of successfully completing a pass-through at a slightly longer range. During my selection process, I discovered the 150-pound pull Fred Bear F-300 crossbow was a $1/2$ pound lighter than the Hawk due to its split limbs and hollow buttstock. The crossbow also came with Carbon Express arrows. Clearly, I needed to investigate this option before making a final decision.

TRADE-OFFS: IDENTIFYING THE MOST IMPORTANT FEATURES

So far, for my Alaskan trip, I had eliminated two crossbows, both of which were light in weight and promised to be easy to carry, because they did not appear to develop sufficient energy to produce reliable pass-through shots on 200-pound deer. They also were "touchy" to shoot. Both had long—two-breath—trigger pulls, which would pose no particular problem at a stationary target, but what if I was offered a single optimum shot for only a split-second, as frequently happens in real-world hunting? The deer could be there and gone while I was still pulling the trigger on either the Brand X or Barnett Ranger.

I wanted a crossbow that was lightweight and small, but I knew that making a rapid, deadly shot that would dump the deer in a hurry was more important. The unavoidable conclusion was that I needed to use a more powerful crossbow, even if it was larger and heavier. The smaller, weaker crossbows would be fine choices for smaller deer closer to home, where if the arrow went into the deer's chest cavity and did not exit, my dogs would find the animal, or if something broke, I could walk back to the house and get another crossbow. Neither of these options would be available in Alaska.

Fred Bear's F-300 crossbow has a light, clam-shell stock design with efficient pressure-formed split limbs and a good trigger, and it would readily accept a scope, red-dot, or ring-and-peep sights. Of all the 150-pound pull-rated crossbows, the F-300 took the most force to cock, and I suspected that it would report a higher velocity when I had the opportunity to chronograph it with its 20-inch Carbon Express 376-grain arrows.

As I suspected, the Fred Bear crossbow did develop higher velocities and energies than the other 150-pound pull-rated crossbows that I tested. The difference was not spectacular—only 2 foot-pounds greater than the Horton Hawk—but the arrow the F-300 shot, which was 2 inches longer and 35 grains heavier, promised to have better flight and killing characteristics.

FRED BEAR F-300 VELOCITIES, ENERGIES, AND TRAJECTORY FROM 10 TO 40 YARDS

Range	Velocity fps	Energy foot-pounds	Drop or Rise in Inches
Ring and pin			
Setting no. 1			
5 yards			0
10 yards	247	50.9	0
20 yards	243	49.3	0
25 yards	241	48.5	−3
30 yards	235	46.1	−4
35 yards	234	45.7	−6.5
40 yards	233	45.3	−12
45 yards			−20
Setting no. 2	Zeroed at 25 yards		
Setting no. 3	Zeroed at 27 yards		
Setting no. 4	Zeroed at 29 yards		
Setting no. 5	Zeroed at 32 yards—straight down		
Setting no. 6	Zeroed at 34 yards		
Setting no. 7	Zeroed at 37 yards		
Setting no. 8	Zeroed at 40 yards		

The more I shot the Fred Bear F-300 crossbow, the faster the advantages mounted up. The stock felt good, and the crossbow balanced well. The trigger pull was a little mushy at the start, but it broke nicely. A 1/2-pound weight advantage over the SteelForce also enhanced the Bear crossbow's portability. I liked the simplicity of the ring-and-pin sights, which would eliminate problems with fogging optics. All these physical characteristics combined strongly indicated that the F-300 would be the appropriate crossbow to take to Alaska.

With the Carbon Express arrows, the Fred Bear crossbow basically shot flat out to 20 yards and was only 4 inches low at 30 yards, providing a 30-yard kill zone without having to bother with sight adjustments or hold-over. This put-the-pin-on-the-deer-and-shoot capability was vital for

This Fred Bear crossbow, shown propped against an enormous mushroom anchor, was used to hunt black-tailed deer on Alaska's Kodiak Island.

the close-range, but fleeting, opportunities that I might have. The arrow's 45.3 foot-pounds of retained energy at 40 yards increased the possibility that I would be able to make a pass-through shot even at what most consider to be the longest acceptable shot with a crossbow. With the animal in sight, I could dial up the sight to the no. 8 position, aim directly where the arrow needed to go, and make the shot to kill the deer.

Few crossbow shooters go through such an elaborate shooting determination to know how their crossbows will perform at various ranges. Usually, they will take the crossbow out of the box, fit it out with whatever points are furnished, target it in at 20 yards, shoot a few shots at 30 and 40 yards, and then take it hunting. Some hunters erroneously assume that the crossbow is "sighted in" out of the box. TenPoint does a rough sighting in, but even so, this does not tell the crossbow buyer what its long-range trajectory may be or what the various dots and crosshairs on his sighting equipment really represent. To determine this vital information, the user must shoot the crossbow at various ranges with hunting-weight arrows and points. Crossbow hunting has no place for the "Hail

Mary" approach where the shooter launches an arrow that does not have a ghost of a chance of hitting a vital area of the target.

The only way I know of determining a crossbow's trajectory is to shoot it with the arrows that are going to be used at various ranges and plot the results. I usually recommend shooting from a bench as this helps eliminate errors, but I wanted to see how the crossbow actually shot from an off-hand position. I chose a nearly windless day to try this approach, and the results I achieved are shown in the preceeding table.

MAINTENANCE OF YOUR CROSSBOW

Today's crossbows may be made of a variety of synthetic and nonferrous components, but they still require regular cleaning and lubrication. The steel bolts, screws, and components of the cam system must be protected from rust. Even rust-free aluminum cams rotate on steel axles. The trigger assembly is the most delicate part of most crossbows. Most of the time it is imbedded deep in the stock and may not be removed, but a drop of oil a few times a year is usually sufficient to clean and lubricate the mechanism, provided that the crossbow has not been exposed to a driving rain, salt water, or dropped into a pond.

Most damage occurs to hunting crossbows when they are dropped from tree stands, fall over, or are backed over by a vehicle. To protect your crossbow when it's not in use, hang it by its foot piece. If that's not possible, lay it flat resting on its stock and empty quiver. You also could prop it up on the end of one limb and stock and lean the other limb against the wall, although this is not recommended for compound crossbows with exposed cams that would rest against the ground or floor.

To avoid dry firing, which is probably the second most frequent cause of crossbow damage, make sure that you are not distracted when you shoot and that you actually have an arrow in the crossbow before you fire. TenPoint has an anti-dry firing mechanism on some models of its crossbows, but the best preventative is a little attention.

When walking through the woods with a crossbow, you will notice that leaves and twigs sometimes get caught by the strings and dragged up into the cams where they may lodge quite solidly. Carry a pocketknife with a pick or awl to help clean these cams, and take care to remove the leaves and twigs without bending the thin walls of the aluminum cams.

As crossbow technology becomes more complex, the shooter plays less of a role in changing parts or repairing any significant damage to the crossbow. All North American manufacturers have maintenance centers for their crossbows, usually located somewhere other than the factory, although TenPoint still offers factory cleaning and maintenance. If purchasing a recurve crossbow, be sure to acquire a spare string and some replacement limb tips, if replaceable tips are used.

CROSSBOW STORAGE

Never store your crossbow cocked or in extremely hot conditions. By investing in a crossbow case, you will keep your crossbow clean and in proper shooting condition for decades. Like firearms, crossbows should not be stored in foam or cloth cases as the moisture held by these cases will tend to rust any ferrous components and oxidize aluminum, particularly if any residues are present from exposure to salt or brackish water.

6

COCKING TECHNIQUES

Before obtaining accuracy with a crossbow, a new shooter has to grasp how to properly cock the hunting implement. If not, a crossbow string pulled to one side or the other will result in arrows scattered left and right. This lateral dispersion can be difficult for the first-time crossbow shooter to understand, especially if the shooter is used to slamming a cartridge into a rifle's chamber and pulling the trigger.

The best way to prevent string misalignment is to mark the string on both sides of the barrel with white paint or to sew a piece of colored string onto the string so that its correct alignment may be checked at a glance.

The tension on either side of the crossbow's limbs (two, four, or eight) will determine the horizontal direction of the arrow's flight. Before a compound crossbow leaves the factory, the tension on the limbs is carefully adjusted by twisting the auxiliary strings or cables to apply the same pressure on the limbs so that they exert symmetrical forces on the string. If this is either not done or done incorrectly, the crossbow will shoot a tight group of arrows to one side of the central axis of the crossbow. Some crossbow makers carefully measure and match the bending modules of each limb so that balanced sets are used to build each crossbow.

Flemish-style crossbow strings must be twisted when they are put on a crossbow, or the crossbow will not develop full power. The number of twists helps to determine the strength of the crossbow: The more the prod is tensioned at the "rest position" prior to cocking, the stronger the crossbow's pull weight. For starters, twist a Flemish crossbow string thirteen times and try it. Leave the string on the bow and shoot a couple of arrows. Then check the brace height. If it is not braced where it formerly was, twist or untwist the string until the correct distance is

Manually cocking a crossbow is quicker than using a cocking aid, but the hunter also has a greater chance of pulling the string to one side and seriously deflecting an arrow.

achieved. Because Flemish strings will slowly stretch, it is a good idea to check the brace height and tighten the string if necessary after the first few shooting episodes.

Endless loop, or English, strings have parallel fibers and are not twisted when used. String length may be shortened by twisting an endless loop string, but crossbow strings of this pattern are usually designed to be installed without twists. These strings are less trouble to use and install and now appear on many crossbows, but they are heavier than Flemish strings, are not as strong (only half of the number of strands are used to form the end loops), and take more time to make. Because they are easier to use and take less skill to install and maintain, endless loop strings are growing in popularity.

Assuming the tensioning cables on a compound crossbow are correctly stressed and the bowstring has been positioned at the proper brace height, symmetrical cocking of the crossbow may be done by a variety of manual or mechanical means.

COCKING METHODS, HISTORICAL AND MODERN
Manual Methods

Historically, only crossbows with the lightest pull weights are cocked by bending over and pulling up the string with the arms. Most reasonably robust individuals can hand cock a 150-pound crossbow using their arm and shoulder muscles. The foot stirrup is used to restrain the end of the crossbow, and the person reaches down, grabs the string between the fingers of both hands and pulls upward. Anyone sound of limb and nimble of body can get away with this on a relatively weak crossbow.

Hand cocking stronger bows requires bigger muscles, and just as it is better to lift a load with your legs rather than bending your back, cocking one of these bows works best if you use your strong leg muscles instead of the relatively puny muscles of your arms and back. When cocking the crossbow with a leg, place a foot into the stirrup, bend the knees, grab the string, and then straighten the legs. Not only will this method reduce pressure on the back and arms, but it allows you to hand cock a 165-pound or heavier bow.

In medieval times, crossbows were often described as "one-foot crossbows" or "two-foot crossbows." To employ a one-foot crossbow which was relatively easy to cock and light to medium in weight, one foot was placed on a limb of the crossbow (later in a stirrup), and the leg muscles were used to cock the crossbow. On the more powerful two-foot crossbow, the stirrup was large enough to accommodate two feet, and both sets of leg muscles were employed. Depending on the crossbow and the individual, this cocking method could be used while standing, sitting, or lying on one's back. To use this method, the crossbowman did not have to carry any mechanical devices.

On a derivation of this technique, a hook (or sometimes double hooks) was run through the crossbowman's waist belt and used to catch the string. A standing crossbowman bent his leg at the knee, put his foot in the stirrup, and pushed down with his foot until the hook or hooks on his belt pulled the string up into the cocked position. This method only worked when the draw of the crossbow was comparatively short, 8 to 10 inches, which was typical of early crossbows.

Another method replaced the belt hook with a pulley. One end of the pull rope was attached to the crossbow, and the rope was run through the pulley on the crossbowman's belt and then through an eye (or second pulley) on a hook (or hooks) that caught the string. A foot placed in the stirrup held the crossbow in place. When the free end of the rope was pulled upward, the string would be pulled back to the latched position.

The pulley system allowed the crossbow to be cocked with half the force required to cock the crossbow in a conventional manner.

When using a crossbow with foot stirrups, the shooter must exercise care because if a crossbow should slip off the foot while it is being drawn, it could spring back and strike the user in the groin, chest, or face with sufficient energy to do serious damage. When cocking crossbows by hand, always wear stiff-soled shoes and retain the foot stirrup just forward of your heel. Most accidents involving this type of crossbow are caused because shooters wear soft-soled athletic shoes or the crossbow slips off a wet, slick shoe sole. Don't wear oversize rubber boots and winter overshoes, because they are too large to fit into a crossbow's stirrup. A wet or snow-covered rubber boot can slip off the crossbow. An expedient way to cock a crossbow is to cut down a small tree or branch, hook the stirrup on the branch, and use it, rather than the foot, to hold the crossbow while you pull back on the string.

String cockers provide an effective and lightweight means of cocking a crossbow. Most adult hunters who can stand and have use of both arms can use string cockers to cock crossbows with pull weights of up to 175 pounds. Stronger individuals can cock crossbows with pulls of 200 to 225 pounds.

Rope, nylon, or leather cocking stirrups have been used on various crossbows, such as this Horton Safari Magnum. These fiber stirrups are lightweight but must be positioned an equal distance on the prod, as on the Horton SteelForce, and periodically examined for wear. Care must also be taken that no part of the stirrups extends above the shooting deck and interferes with the flight of the arrow.

A bent steel cocking stirrup on a crossbow of reputed Vietnamese origin. This lightweight stirrup was designed for a low-powered crossbow.

Although a strong individual can place a lightweight, modern-stocked crossbow on his chest and cock the crossbow by pulling the string back toward him, this method is not recommended. The chance of the crossbow slipping off the sternum and flying back to strike the user are too great to offset any speed gained in cocking the crossbow from the chest. Furthermore, anyone who has had heart surgery or sustained injuries where the sternum has been split and repaired should avoid this cocking method.

Rope Cockers

Rope cocking aids equipped with either a sled or hooks and pulleys are the lightest and fastest of all mechanical cocking aids and can reduce the amount of force needed to cock a crossbow by fifty percent. In medieval times, a pulley was attached to the crossbowman's belt, but in the modern adaptation, the rope is passed around a groove or through a hole in the rear of the stock with the hooks hanging on both sides of the

Two versions of the author's homemade rope cockers. The more sophisticated version was made for something less than $5 from a nylon fish stringer purchased at WalMart and two carabiners. The tricks to getting this simple system to work successfully are to adjust the rope to proper length and to tie the end loops with nonslip knots.

crossbow's barrel. The crossbow string is pulled up slightly to engage the hooks, and the user puts his hands through the loops on the string and pulls uniformly on the string until it is firmly latched by the crossbow.

TenPoint Crossbows incorporates its string cockers into a box held in the crossbow's stock. Other makers, such as Horton, Fred Bear, and Excalibur, use separate string cockers, which may be slipped into a pocket when not in use. Excalibur employs hooks on its string cockers, whereas Horton has a rope cocker with a sled that slides along the top of the aluminum barrel of the crossbow. This sled, which is a metal component with hooks that engage the string, must be used right-side-up, and it takes a bit longer to untangle and deploy than the twin hooks used on rope cockers.

You can make a simple rope cocker with a length of nylon rope and two carabiners. I do this on Horton's SteelForce crossbow, which has a hole in the rear of its stock that allows the cocking rope to pass through and become what is, in effect, a pulley. The rope is threaded through the hole, and the carabiners, which are slid onto the rope just forward of the knots on the hand loops, are snapped onto the string in symmetrical positions and pulled up with equal force to make sure that the string stays properly aligned with the crossbow's barrel.

Even when using a rope cocker, you may misalign the string, so the index marks on the string must be checked each time the crossbow is cocked to ensure that the string is in proper position for accurate arrow flight.

Goat's Foot and Whippe-type Cocking Levers

These devices employed a detached lever with a pivot and two arms to push the string back into the fully cocked position. Typically a large iron pivot pin was placed through the thickest part of the stock. Two arms of the goat's foot were placed back of the pin, and hooks on the pivot were used to grasp the string. A pull on the lever transported the string back to where it was caught by the sear. Although lighter in weight, smaller, and faster to deploy than a whippe-type cocker or a crannequin, the goat's foot was another accessory that had to be carried in the field. In addition, because it did not develop sufficient leverage, it could not cock the strongest crossbows.

A longer lever and better mechanical advantage were achieved by the whippe-type cockers, which employed a hook to catch on a ring on the front of the crossbow and a hinged lever with pivoting arm that engaged the string. The long operating arm was almost as long as the crossbow itself and almost as cumbersome to carry. It was probably most often used

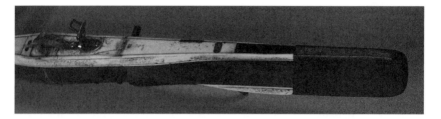

The strong steel pin in the middle of the stock of this medieval German crossbow was used as a pivot for a cocking device.

with target shooting or when the crossbow user was firing from behind a fixed position.

A variation of the whippe-type cocker was sometimes built into the butt stocks of nineteenth-century crossbows. Inlet into the comb of the stock, it could be operated by raising a knob that allowed a metal catch to move forward to engage the bowstring.

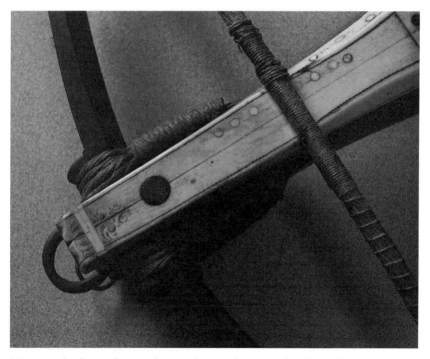

Rings on the front of a crossbow, when not being used to hang the instrument, provide a front attachment for a cocking mechanism.

Crannequin

A crannequin used a lever to turn a gear and engage a toothed rod, which pulled the crossbow string to its cocked position. This device was sometimes permanently attached to the crossbow, but was most often carried as a separate accessory. The turning crank frequently was placed on the top of the deck of the crossbow and operated horizontally, although some were placed on the side of the crossbow and turned on a vertical axis.

Crannequins, which were expensive to make compared to other medieval cocking mechanisms, accompanied only the highest-grade crossbows used by the nobility and by elite knights fighting on horseback. The common crossbowman had to rely either on muscle power or the much less expensive wind-up cocker.

Windlass or Wind-up Cockers

In contrast with mechanical cocking aids that attached to the front or middle of the crossbow, wind-up cockers were attached to the rear and operated by a crank, or very often two cranks. When these cranks were turned, cords were wound on an axel to pull the bowstring back. Unfortunately, the crossbow windlass, which was a simple adaptation of the windlass used to draw water from deep wells and pull up ores from ancient mines, took too much time to straighten out the cords, install the device on the crossbow, and wind the crossbow string to its full-cock position.

Wind-up cockers offered by most crossbow manufacturers today are descendants of these early winders. Today's models sometimes slip over the buttstock or, in the case of TenPoint, are contained within it as an optional extra. These devices can operate with 5 to 7 pounds of pressure, so even disabled individuals are able to cock their own crossbows. Usually the cranks are detachable, and some may be operated by a battery-powered screwdriver.

Screw-type Cocker

A historical method of cocking a crossbow used a long threaded screw that ran the length of the crossbow's stock. Rotating the screw downward moved a sliding grasp, which hooked the string. When the opposite motion was applied, the string was drawn up to the desired distance. On some crossbows, the firing mechanism was built into the grasp, but in others a more conventional rotating nut was employed. Jack Levin used this type of mechanism on his recently built high-art crossbow pistol with an attached bayonet, which won the fantasy knife category at the 2005 Blade Show.

Horton winder with a newly designed metal gear to replace a reinforced-polymer component that sometimes failed. Once while on a hunt, the author saw a hunter with a 175-pound crossbow experience gear failure with his winder when the crossbow was being cocked. This effectively destroyed the winder and ended his hunt. Because mechanical instruments do fail, it is wise to carry a second crossbow when going on a hunt.

Horton's Electric Cocker

In the 1970s, Horton offered an electric cocking mechanism that could be affixed to the front of the crossbow. It had a forked arm that slid down the crossbow barrel, caught the string, and under battery power pushed the string back to the full-cocked position. This cocker, which was about a foot long and 4 inches high, was cumbersome and heavy, and when it did not receive much user interest, its production was discontinued.

If you are seeking maximum accuracy out of a crossbow, particularly one with a pull weight of more than 150 pounds, a mechanical cocker will provide more precision in cocking and string alignment than

Horton's Activator electric cocking mechanism installed on a Horton Express. Although mechanically successful, the cocking mechanism received insufficient demand to justify its continued development. The device, which employed D-cell batteries, was bulky and heavy.

can typically be managed with hand cocking. The heavier the cocking poundage, the more a person has to struggle to correctly cock the crossbow, and the higher the likelihood of making a poor shot on a game animal.

7

SIGHTING SYSTEMS

S ights were commonly used on crossbows in the fifteenth century, but not until the twentieth century were they applied in similar numbers to conventional bows. For five hundred years, the crossbow was supreme in its ability to place an arrow on game or on a target at exactly the point it needed to be. Its precision was so applauded that target-shooting events and hunting with crossbows continued into the twenty-first century, long after firearms became commonplace.

Compared to early matchlock guns, which were typically about .75 caliber, heavy, and smoothbored, the crossbow was reliable, quiet, accurate, and less expensive. Both were slow to reload, but the crossbow had a technological edge in this department. The crossbow also had no components that were likely to blow up its user. Musketeers carried lit matches (nitrated ropes that were lit at both ends) and loaded their

Adjustable brass sight on an antique German crossbow. The sight has been bent, but it was clearly designed to be adjustable for elevation.

guns from wooden bottles of black powder strapped across their chests, and unintended explosions regularly occurred.

Early crossbow sights varied greatly according to the era and skill of the fabricator. Many crossbows used no sights whatsoever. Their users shot bare crossbow in the same manner that archers shoot with a sight-less bow: They lined up the centerline of the arrow, elevated to whatever degree appeared appropriate, and fired. With handmade prods of different draw weights and strings having different characteristics, little uniformity was found from crossbow to crossbow. Nonetheless, just as instinctive archers can shoot with remarkable accuracy, crossbow shooters, once they were well practiced with their instruments, could hit their targets with regularity. For long-distance shooting, they would drop the rear of the crossbow down to their chest so that the crossbow could still be inclined at a high angle and the target could be seen over the point of the arrow. In modern terms, this technique would be similar to inclining the barrel of a potato gun to strike a target 80 yards away with the low-velocity spud.

The thumb wrapped over the top of the crossbow may have provided the earliest type of sight, as some have asserted, but this would only work with crossbows that had short ticklers, or triggers, and long stocks. When the crossbow was mounted and the thumb wrapped over the top of the stock, the thumb could have acted as a rear aiming point while the tip of the arrow provided a front sight. This "self sight" would have been an individualistic approach to crossbow sighting. (I am personally not sure about this. I have looked at period prints that show the shooter using his thumb to help hold down the rear of the arrow, but I think using the thumb as a sight would be more of a bother than an aid because the thumb would obscure the target.)

Sighting along the thick arrow shafts provides a convenient and reasonably accurate way to sight a crossbow that is employed against either men or big game. For close-range shooting, nothing else is needed.

Thumb pieces located near the rear of the crossbow were used like a modern shooter's "spot weld" to make sure that the crossbow was consistently positioned from shot to shot. In period prints of people using medieval crossbows, the thumb is nearly always shown at the very rear of the stocks positioned well below the eye, indicating that the thumb was obviously intended to be a spot weld, rather than a sight.

A single vertical pin in the center rear of the crossbow is likely to have been the next development in the evolution of sights. One bow of reputed Vietnamese origin used a rear pin capped with a round piece of brass that was lined up between two pins on the front of the crossbow on either side of the arrow.

Front sight pin on early Horton crossbow. This simple sight is most effective for shooting at ranges of up to 40 yards. At longer ranges, the pin obscures too much of the target for precise hits to occur.

V-notched rear sights are now so regularly used on firearms of Western origin that it is difficult to imagine that other types of rear sights were in common use elsewhere, but they were. In Japan, for example, rectangular and square block sights were used as front and rear sights on matchlock guns. Lining up the edges of the blocks sighted the gun and enabled precise hits to be made at 50 yards. Practically every culture had its idea of what crossbow sights ought to look like, and no doubt an extensive collection of crossbows from around the world would show many variations in sighting systems.

A precise sighting system was developed to compensate for arrow drop. Several screw eyes were installed on the side of the crossbow, and a colored target was painted on the prod facing the crossbowman. The shooter would focus his eye through a "peep" at the rear of the crossbow, and by aligning the "peep" with a central ring and a round "target" on the back of the prod, he could target his crossbow in at a given distance. Different "peeps," rings, and targets on the side of the crossbow would be used for various distances. Although this method precisely compensated for the arrow's drop, the hunter could not simultaneously

Japanese matchlocks used rectangular and square block sights with hollow centers that allowed small sticks with glowing coals to be set in them. In this manner, the gun could be aligned at a target at night.

focus on the game, so this sighting system was fine for shooting at ranks of advancing troops but not at individual game animals.

MODERN CROSSBOW SIGHTS
Iron Sights
V- and square-notched rear sights coupled with a pin front sight are used on many inexpensive crossbows made by Barnett and Brand X makers of unknown parentage. The rear sight is supported by a spring and elevated by turning a knurled knob, whereas the front sight is typically supported on a slotted bracket and adjusted for elevation by tightening and loosing screws on the sides of the bracket. Adjustments for windage are provided by another knob that moves the rear sight left or right to adjust the strike of the arrow on the target.

By moving the rear sight in the direction that you want to move the strike of the arrow on the target, the sight position changes. The front sight is adjusted in the opposite direction: The higher the front sight is elevated, the lower the crossbow arrow will strike on the target.

An "iron" sight is inexpensive to make and is effective once adjusted for a given range. The difficulty with this type of sight arises when shots occur at random ranges. The hunter who uses an iron sight will have to wait until the animal happens to walk by at the range that exactly matches the sighted-in range of the crossbow or hold-under or -over for shorter or longer ranges.

Ring-and-Post Sights
Often thought of as the most "modern" type of adjustable sights, the ring rear sight with either a front bead or post was commonly used through-

Ring-and-pin sights on a Fred Bear-built Buckmaster MaxPoint. These rugged sights are most useful in wet weather when sights with optical components may become fogged. When hunting away from home, you may want to carry a crossbow equipped with this simple sight system along with a crossbow with a scope or red-dot sight.

out the 1800s on muzzleloading and cartridge firearms. Yet ring-and-post sight systems were found on crossbows, particularly for target use, for hundreds of years before they appeared on guns. This sighting system is quick—the eye automatically aligns the pin in the center of the sight—and it may be employed in comparatively low-light conditions when used with fiber-optic pins.

An interesting multiple-reticle ring sight was developed by Hank Robertson of Longmont, Colorado, when he designed a unique metal-framed crossbow with a 6-inch sight bar containing a variety of reticles set in a glass slide. The user could either choose a particular reticle or use different parts of the reticles at different ranges.

Most crossbow makers offer the ring-and-post sights as standard on their lower-cost crossbows. Resist the temptation to immediately take it off and install a scope or red-dot sight, since the ring-and-post sight is particularly useful in rain or snow and under other conditions that might render sights with optical elements impossible to use. Instead, when going on a crossbow hunt, I suggest always having a crossbow with a ring-and-post sight so that if the weather turns bad, you will have a hunting system that is useable under these conditions. The ring-and-post sights are also preferred in the rough and tumble world of bowfishing.

Horton crossbows have a Dial-A-Range sighting system that can elevate the rear sight for various ranges. With this sighting system, and with

Sights on the Robertson crossbow are effective enough for short-range hits to be made on game.

a similar one offered by Fred Bear, the numbers on a dial correspond to a given amount of elevation adjustment. However, the number "2," for example, does not indicate 20 yards or any other particular distance. The

Reticles on a Robertson crossbow sight not only allow a great amount of choice of hunting distances, but are adjustable for elevation to compensate for various distances.

crossbow with such an arrow-point combination must be shot at various ranges and the dial settings used to zero the point of impact at those ranges. Rather than trying to remember, for example, that the number "3" represents 25 yards, write the zero settings for various ranges on a piece of masking tape and attach it to the inside of a crossbow limb where you can readily see it.

Red-dot and Holographic Sights

Red-dot sights range from simple models that cost just a few dollars to sophisticated versions with multiple dots and a wider range of illumination adjustments. In such sights, a red dot is generated by a tiny glowing diode and projected in the center of the scope, but unlike laser sights, this dot does not project onto the target. Red-dot sights are most effective under cloudy conditions when it may be difficult to see conventional iron sights.

Sighting systems offered by Horton include two scopes (top) and two varieties of red-dot sights at prices that fit all pocketbooks.

Under either very bright or dark conditions, red-dot sights do not work well. The dots wash out in bright light and become very faint, even when the power settings are turned up to their maximum settings, and when it is dark, the red dot appears to flair and will completely obscure the target.

Holographic sights project a dot, crosshairs, or other sight patterns in front of the shooter. These sights are lightweight and just as easy to mount or zero than a scope or red-dot sight, and although they may look strange to some shooters when mounted on a crossbow, they do work.

Red-dot and holographic sights require batteries, which have been known to physically fall out of some inexpensive sights and will eventually run out of power. I always carry a couple of replacement batteries with me when I hunt with a crossbow using red-dot sights. I also save on battery power by only turning on the sight just before I shoot. Doing this means I must remember one extra thing when it's time to shoot but it's better than the alternative—draining my battery power while waiting for game only to look through a tube devoid of any aiming point when the largest beast I have ever seen is standing only a few yards away.

Some inexpensive red-dot sights are so unreliable that they are not worth the little money charged for them. I discovered this with a BEC Miradot sight packaged with a Brand X crossbow. Not only was the sight's battery use excessive, but the left adjustment arrow was pointed in the wrong direction. I have run into this problem previously with inexpensive optics designed and assembled in countries where English was not a native language. I thought the BEC sight looked good, but it cost little and was worth less.

With the use of multiple dots on a red-dot sight, such as those available from Horton, TenPoint, and others, you can instantly select various yardages for different aiming points. At a given yardage, say 20 yards, the top dot is zeroed to strike at the point of aim. When the crossbow is shot at longer distances, the ranges at which the lower dots shoot to the point of aim are recorded. For example, the second dot may provide bull's-eye for your particular arrow and point at 18 yards, rather than 20 as you would have thought. The lowermost dot may be right on at 33 or 45 yards, rather than 40. Always confirm the zero ranges for your dots before taking the crossbow on a hunt and after you arrive at a distant hunting camp.

Laser Sights

Laser sights also use red-sighting elements, but this time the red dot is projected on the target. A laser sight is an excellent teaching tool because a student can see exactly where he is aiming on the target when the trigger is released. It is also a great confidence builder for the novice shooter or hunter since the dot will show him exactly where his point of impact will occur on the target. Because the red dot is projected instead of actually visible on the interior optics, laser sights allow shots to be made under low-light conditions that would not be feasible for a red-dot sight.

Scope Sights

Scopes have become the "standard" sighting system in firearms, and many shooters have never fired a gun that was not equipped with a scope. Whether used with a gun or a crossbow, a scope provides good target definition and increases light-gathering capabilities. Unlike most riflescopes, which are designed for long-distance shooting, scopes made for crossbows are parallax-adjusted to allow a clear view of the target at very close range. Only scopes designed specifically for pistols, shotguns, and crossbows are really suitable for mounting on crossbows. Although rifle scopes will physically fit in the mounts, close-range targets will be blurred.

The more sophisticated crossbow scopes have multiple crosshairs to provide shots at various ranges. Although these scopes are set up to allow for arrow drop at approximately 10-yard intervals, you should confirm these ranges by actually shooting your hunting arrow-point

Scope sight with multiple statia lines on a Horton crossbow. These lines allow the crossbow to be quickly elevated to allow for arrow drop at various ranges. To establish the exact amount of drop represented by the lines in the scope, you must shoot the crossbow with a hunting arrow at various ranges.

combination at various distances. You cannot simply sight in at 20 yards and assume the lower crosshairs are for 30 and 40 yards. If you don't confirm these settings, you may well miss the animal.

Excalibur now sells a crossbow scope with a dial that allows ranges to be adjusted for arrow speeds of between 250 and 350 fps. This adjustment feature permits the scope to be used on a wide range of crossbows and arrow weights.

Because scopes have a low-magnification power of only about 1.0 to 4, they allow sight-impaired shooters to better see their targets once iron sights no longer help. I like to use scopes on crossbows when I am hunting bear and hogs, animals that are often shot in dim light.

Are sights a one-size-fits-all crossbow option? I don't think so. Rather than changing sights on a crossbow to suit different hunt conditions and then having to rezero the crossbow with each setting, I prefer to take two crossbows sighted for the same arrow-point configuration. This way, I can use iron sights for poor weather and a scope or red-dot sight for ordinary hunting conditions. As an alternative for when you can't take along another crossbow, carrying a spare set of iron sights, which do not weigh much, may save a hunt should your red-dot or scope sight decide to quit working.

8

Choosing Arrows and Points

B efore the modern era, crossbow arrows had undergone a long and complex evolution. Many styles with different points and fletchings had been developed for a variety of hunting and military purposes. Early shafts, which were wood and typically feather fletched, were often fairly short because the handheld crossbows of the day had relatively little draw length, often less than 10 inches and frequently about 8 inches. Today, we think of arrows as straight shafted, but the projectiles thrown by these crossbows often purposefully swelled in the middle of the shaft and tapered more strongly toward the fletching than the point. Some more nearly resembled long darts than conventional straight-shafted arrows.

On the end of some shafts were baskets designed to hold stones or shot used for waterfowling. Other shafts, which were rear weighted and heavy, were designed purposefully to tumble in flight so to break the wings and necks of geese. Yet others used a wide Y point or had multiple prongs to increase the hit area on small game. Other varieties were fitted with blunt, or bag, tips for use on small game or targets.

Short fletchless bolts were also employed for target use, and all-metal bolts, where the fletching is sharpened steel designed to cut on impact, thus, practically eliminating the shaft, have been around since the early Greeks.

If these various arrow types are technologically possible, why don't we see some of these forms on the market today? Government policies have effectively eliminated some potential crossbow hunting tools. For example, waterfowling with a bow and arrow is permitted under a treaty among the United States, Canada, and Mexico, but the use of a crossbow is not specifically allowed. Also, various states demand that crossbows employ arrows of a certain length or that points used on big game have a minimum cutting area.

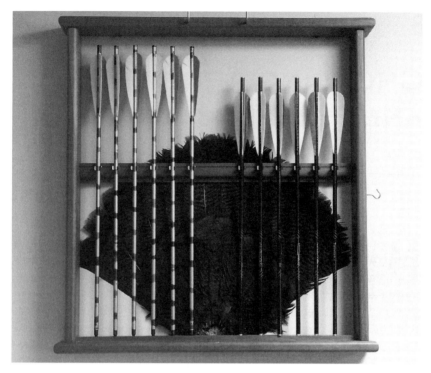

The fan of an eastern wild turkey, with conventional-length arrows on the left and crossbow arrows on the right.

While we're on the subject, crossbow waterfowling would be an excellent way to reduce the population of urban geese. During the Renaissance, crossbows were used alongside stone-throwing bows and muskets to shoot ducks, geese, and swan in Europe. If permitted, crossbows could still perform that task today and open another opportunity for hunters to take surplus game animals that have become real pests.

Since the twentieth century, like their counterparts for conventional bows, crossbow arrows have been made with wooden shafts, hollow-spun fiberglass, fiberglass-wrapped wood, solid fiberglass, folded aluminum, extruded aluminum, wrapped graphite, and extruded graphite. In contrast to the wooden shafts used in the 1950s, modern shafts are straighter, stiffer, and stronger, fly better, and are more trouble free.

CHOOSING ARROWS

If you purchase a crossbow from a Brand X supplier or pick up one from a pawn shop, you most likely will find little or no information supplied about the arrows or points that the crossbow was designed to shoot.

A variety of points, such as these offered by Fred Bear, are designed for field, target use, and big game. Not all points, even if they have the same weight, will shoot to the same point of aim.

Without question, the easiest way to get information about your most recent crossbow purchase is to place a call to the manufacturer to request an instruction booklet for the crossbow or to ask the help desk for specific information. Some companies will be able to respond better than others. More recent entries into the crossbow market, such as Ten-Point and Excalibur, will have readily available information about all of their crossbows. Older makers, such as Horton and Barnett, may have to scratch around to provide information about any of their crossbows not made within the past ten years.

Over the years, Bear and PSE have experimented with some radically different crossbow designs. Bear's Devastator and Lightning crossbows and PSE's Foxfire used arrows with conventional archery nocks and fletchings in their trackless crossbows, a natural for companies with strong archery perspectives. Just as with their compound bows, the arrows for their new crossbows were supported by being knocked by the string and by arrow rests.

But when the power of these crossbows was increased from 125 to 150 pounds of pull, problems arose. The nocks were too weak and the arrows too light. Although the same diameter and wall thickness, the shorter 22-inch shafts on the crossbow arrows were stiffer than the 29- to 30-inch shafts used by most full-draw compound bows. These shafts worked for a time, but as had been discovered in medieval times, more powerful crossbows required heavier, stiffer arrows.

By 1989, Bear, now Jennings-Bear, had designed a heavy-duty cross-bow nock for its crossbow arrows and had recommended that 22½-inch 2219 anodized aluminum arrows be used for its Devastator crossbow. Two years later when the Bear QuadPoint (the last crossbow made with a Dev-astator stock) was introduced with its split limbs, the recommended arrows were to have a minimum spine of 2117 and be used with heads weighing at least 100 grains.

Although aluminum shafts are still available and are still used on crossbows, carbon arrows are increasingly popular and appear likely to be the dominant shaft type used on crossbows in the future. Usually, each crossbow maker has its own shafts that it markets with its crossbows. Horton, for example, has an extruded carbon shaft called the Carbon Strike, which is a 20-inch arrow recommended for all of its crossbows except for the SteelForce, which uses a 17-inch arrow. The company also markets aluminum Lightning Strike 2 (430 grains with a 100-grain point) and Lightning Strike 2 (Lite) (395 grains with a 100-grain point) arrows. The even lighter LS7 (Lite) (341 grains with a 100-grain point) is specifi-cally designed for the recurve SteelForce crossbow.

A general rule is that as draw weight and power increase, the weight and stiffness of the arrow and point also must increase to absorb more of the energy of the crossbow. If in doubt, it is better to go with a heavier rather than lighter arrow. For large game, such as buffalo, arrow-point combinations weighing up to 700 grains are used. An extreme in heavy-weight arrows are solid fiberglass and stainless steel versions used for bowfishing. Crafting these arrows is covered in chapter 15.

NOCKS

Four types of nocks have been used on modern crossbows: two arrow-style, half-moon, and flat. The two arrow-style nocks (discussed in the previous section) are necessary for the Jennings-Bear Devastator and the PSE FoxFire crossbows, which support the rear of the crossbow arrow on the string. Barnett and Horton employ half-moon nocks, which fit against the string and help index the fletching in the correct position in the barrel of the crossbow. Excalibur and Fred Bear crossbows use a flat nock that is threaded at the end for an arrow extractor, which allows the arrow to be pulled straight out of a foam target without bending the shaft.

Use only the recommended styles of nocks with a given crossbow. Half-moon nocks may be filed flat and used with modified arrows in a

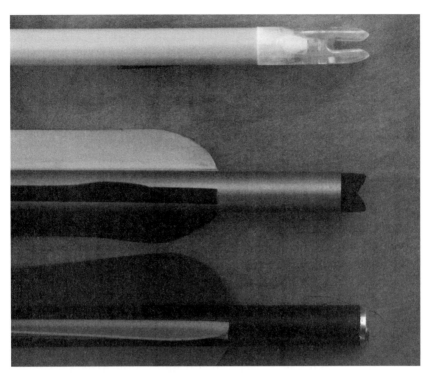

Different nocks have been employed on crossbow arrows. On top, a conventional nock used on arrows shot from conventional bows, a half-moon nock center, and at the bottom a flat nock. Horton crossbows use half-moon nocks, and Excalibur crossbows employ flat nocks. To prevent the string from "jumping" the arrow and dry firing the crossbow with potentially dangerous results, use the appropriately styled nocks designed for your crossbows.

crossbow that requires square-backed nocks. If you use half-moon nocks, inspect them regularly as they may become either brittle and shatter or too soft and deform and have rough edges. Not only could this affect accuracy, but a broken half-moon nock is a safety hazard as the string easily could jump over the arrow and, in effect, cause the crossbow to dry fire.

POINTS

With so many excellent big-game points available today from a variety of sources, it is difficult to imagine a time in the 1970s and '80s when few points were offered on the market and none were specifically designed for crossbows. Hunters such as Dan Miller, Bill Throubridge, and George Wagner recall spending hours filing their welded Zwickey broadheads in an effort to get them to fly well from their crossbows.

Ventilated three-bladed and mechanical points have helped to overcome crossbow arrow-flight problems by cutting wind resistance and preventing the point from steering the arrow off target. Even two-bladed arrows needed for the deepest penetration on dangerous game will fly better with ventilated rather than solid points.

Technology and experience were combined to come up with two solutions to the arrow-flight problem. Ventilated 100-grain broadheads with three replaceable cutting surfaces, such as those popularized by Muzzy, provided the necessary good flight characteristics and cutting surfaces needed to make killing shots, and mechanical points were created with blades that only expand on impact. These two developments not only helped to solve arrow-flight problems, but they considerably improved the crossbow's performance on thin-skinned animals such as deer.

For maximum penetration of heavy animals, a two-bladed cutting point performs better than three-bladed designs. Throubridge prefers a two-bladed point made by Sam Magnus for maximum penetration on water buffalo and similar animals.

Any crossbow arrow-point combination must be spun to ensure that it is wobble free and will fly correctly. To do this, put the point on a surface and spin the arrow with the thumb and forefinger just as you would spin a top. If you see a wobble, either the shaft is crooked (less common with today's high-quality shafts) or the point is slightly crooked in its alignment with the shaft. Trying different points on different shafts will occasionally work, but sometimes shafts will have to be discarded or used for only close-range shots.

When target shooting, be careful to shoot only one arrow at a time and to pull the arrows straight out of the target. Do not allow a friend, however well meaning, to pull your shafts for you. If your shaft is bent during test firing, then all the other work you have done is meaningless.

Once the "spin tests" are completed, align the point's cutting veins with the fletching and shoot the arrows at a target. You may have to install a small O-ring between the point and the shaft to achieve proper alignment of some points.

Just because crossbows typically deliver higher initial velocities doesn't mean you shouldn't have razor-sharp cutting edges on your arrows. If you don't know how to sharpen broadheads, then install new blades before you hunt. The best way to learn how to sharpen blades is to do it. You'll need a set of vise grips with very small jaws to firmly hold the blades, a fine metal whet or Arkansas stone (and sharpening oil if you use a stone), and cardboard or leather as a strop.

With the vise grips, securely grasp the blade as far back from the edge as you can. Use a shallow-cutting angle to move the blade with a rotating motion on the edge of the flat of the stone or whet. After eight to ten circular strokes, reverse the process and sharpen the other side. Check the blade edge from time to time. When satisfied that you have a good edge, reposition the vise grips and strop the edge once on each side on a leather strop or piece of cardboard to polish the edge and remove any tiny slivers of metal hanging onto the blade. Then lightly oil your blades and penetrating points before storing them away in your broadhead box or quiver.

Take the manufacturer's suggestions for arrow-point combinations seriously. Not just any arrow-point combination will work reliably, and the worst of them fly terribly. An ill-matched arrow-point combination can easily miss deer at 15 yards. But if you hit a deer with a sharp arrow point, the animal sometimes will not even realize that it has been struck

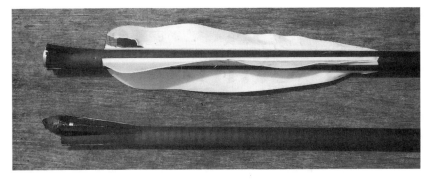

When target shooting, be careful to shoot only one arrow at a time to prevent damaging shafts, as was done here.

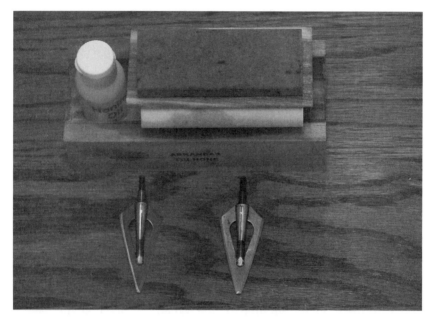

You need sharp broadheads to kill, and this three-stone sharpening set will sharpen a broadhead to a razor edge. Points stored in a quiver dull as they abrade against each other and therefore periodically must be retouched as must any arrow that touches the ground. If you don't know how to resharpen an arrow, use only new points when shooting at game animals.

and will resume feeding. Sharp arrows reduce pain, penetrate better, and kill quicker. To be ethical hunters, we should never use anything less.

Always recover your arrows after a hunt or shoot. Not just because you want them to be a part of your trophy or because the points and arrows are expensive, but because an arrow left behind may injure another hunter. Every year or two, I recover someone else's arrow from the woods. Even if you only hunt on your own property, protect yourself. You don't want to walk into one of your own arrows either. Remember, if you shoot an arrow in the woods, you are ethically bound to retrieve it.

QUIVERS

Crossbows with detachable quivers are so common that it is difficult for many modern users to think of having a crossbow without one. Detachable quivers certainly are convenient for making sure you always have your shafts with you, but when you're in a tree stand, they can get in the way; also, when you're taking an already unwieldy crossbow through brushy country, they can catch a lot of twigs and briers.

When sitting in a tree for hours with a crossbow, I often remove the quiver. Not only does the crossbow become more comfortable to hold, but a detached quiver eliminates the possibility of catching the arrows on the stand when the crossbow is raised and thus making enough noise to alert game. For these reasons, I prefer crossbows with easily detachable quivers. Some makers use quiver-attachment screws, but these are a bother to remove and reinstall when 30 feet off the ground. If you are shooting from a roomy box blind where you'll have enough space to hang a cross-bow when it is not in use, it makes little difference if the quiver is on the crossbow or not. But most hunters make do with less commodious quar-ters where it is convenient to reduce the crossbow's bulk.

If your crossbow does not have an attached quiver, then use a sim-ple target quiver that hangs on the belt. Because shorter crossbow shafts are often completely contained within the belt quiver and the arrows may rattle with every step, stick a glove between the shafts to keep them sep-arated. Hip quivers are quieter, but they will catch as much brush as the crossbow. Conventional back quivers are so deep that the crossbow arrows must be fished out after the quiver is unslung from the shoulders.

How did crossbowmen from centuries ago solve the quiver dilemma? They discovered a better way to carry their arrows. The crossbow quiver they carried was suspended on a belt and designed with a wide foot to sit upright on the ground. Because a great variety of different point styles were available to them, the arrow points were carried up to offer instant

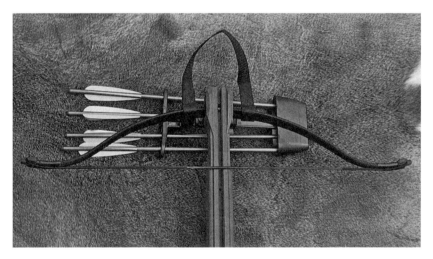

Attached quivers such as this one displayed on a Horton SteelForce are a quiet, convenient, and efficient way of carrying arrows.

point selection. However, when retrieving an arrow from among the points-up shafts, these early crossbowmen had to take great care, something akin to removing a single quill from a porcupine.

If you want a convenient belt quiver today, the best alternative is to take a tanned hide and build your own. You can make the quiver as stiff, which the old ones were, or as soft as you like. I recommend using a wood base covered by a piece of foam to keep the shafts from poking through the bottom. Since the modern hunter usually uses just one style of point, I would also recommend that the arrows be carried points down and fletching up to prevent unnecessary cuts. You can identify different point types by marking the nocks with different colored paints.

9

HUNTING TECHNIQUES

The thrill that comes from taking game at close range makes hunts with short-range hunting implements particularly memorable. I enjoy having game at rock-throwing distance whether I am armed with spear, crossbow, bow, or muzzleloader. The paramount objective of this "Don't shoot until you can see the whites of their eyes" experience is to have the game so close to you that your shot almost certainly will have a deadly result. Even so, there are no guarantees in hunting.

Once, I nearly set the woods afire with a flintlock pistol when I shot from a two-handed, sitting position at a 200-pound hog 5 yards away and missed it. I had practiced with a .58-caliber pistol, and even without a rear sight, I could reliably shoot a saboted .45-caliber bullet out of it with sufficient accuracy to land eight out of eight shots in a 3-inch circle at 15 yards. Unbeknownst to me, however, the .45-caliber bullet had dropped from the sabot the day before, but even when I checked the barrel, the ramrod hit the sabot, leading me to believe that the gun was fully loaded.

When I shot, the black-powder charge did not develop sufficient pressure to completely combust the powder, and the pistol acted more like a flamethrower than a firearm. Instead of a bullet, the hog was hit with the tumbling lightweight plastic sabot, and although a bit singed, the surprised animal was none the worse for the encounter.

Think the equivalent can't happen with a crossbow? Think again. I missed a standing deer with a crossbow at a range of 8 yards. When I returned home, I shot the X from the center of a 20-yard target using the same crossbow and arrow. How could I have missed during the hunt? The crossbow shot, the arrow shot, and I thought that I was calm. Nonetheless, the arrow hit the dirt under the deer. I have never completely explained this miss, but most likely it was caused by human error, rather than the fault of the crossbow or the arrow. I suppose I lifted my head at the shot and allowed the crossbow to drop so that the arrow passed beneath the deer.

The three "secrets" of successful crossbow hunting are to get close, know the range, and keep the crossbow rock-steady while the arrow leaves the bow. Do these three things, and your ratio of shots-to-kills will be extremely close to 1-to-1.

STALKING

Stalking big game is so ingrained in the hunting mystique that the mere mention of "hunting" brings to mind the image of a hunter stealthfully making his way through the woods while approaching a big-game animal. This is an exciting type of hunting for a person armed with a crossbow. The unhandy shape of the crossbow, the need for the bow's limbs to clear any surrounding vegetation, the time required for an arrow to be put in the crossbow once game is spotted, the noise from the shot, and the inability to rapidly reload all argue against success for stalking big game.

To cite a recent example, I employed stalking while on an African hunt, armed with a .45-caliber in-line muzzleloader and chasing zebra. My guide and I attempted to stalk three different herds in scattered acacia thickets separated by smaller areas of grass, and only on the third herd did we approach close enough to take an 80-yard shot at the stallion.

Stalking with a crossbow sometimes pays off, but not very often. The hunter will obtain more success in a blind or stand where the game can approach the hunter.

Stalking worked because we saw lots of animals, and if one stalk was unsuccessful, we could easily locate another group. Even so, the closest we could approach the herd with its 15 pairs of eyes was 80 yards, much too far for a crossbow shot.

During the five-day hunt, we did close to 40 yards on one group of wildebeest that were distracted because the bulls were sparring among themselves. Although we were often able to approach closer while in the safari car, this was the only close-range encounter that we had with African game on foot. Admittedly, the three of us—myself, a professional hunter, and a tracker—may not have been as careful as a lone hunter dressed in camo who paid close attention to the wind would have been.

No matter what type of game you are stalking, the best time to do it is following rain or snow when a hunter can slip through the woods without alerting everything for a half-mile that he is coming.

WATERHOLE SHOOTING

Because almost all species of game require water to live, staking out a waterhole is one of the most productive methods of hunting with a crossbow. Even so, it is not a sure thing. The animals may be watering at night, or, if it has rained recently, water may be so abundant that they don't need to travel to permanent water sources. Some species don't need water every day; others may water at different locations. One of the most effective methods of waterhole hunting is to use blinds made of natural materials gathered from the area or cut out of standing vegetation. The American pronghorn does not seem to be bothered by temporary tent blinds, but blinds in deer country work best if they have been installed for some time prior to deer season.

If hunting from a waterhole blind, allow for shoots in several different directions, as the beasties will invariably come from your "off" side. If you have a rifle or handgun, you merely have to swing the gun to the other side, but crossbows require enough nonobstructive space for the limbs to function.

BAITING

Shooting animals over bait is a feasible option when an abundance of game requires large numbers of animals to be killed to reduce their population to sustainable levels. Bait may include a mechanically operated feeder turned on at a given time, grain scattered along a road or sendero (a cleared dozer track), or feed dispensed regularly in troughs or pans. Often the bait stations will have a block of salt nearby.

I view hunting over bait as more of a culling operation than hunting, but baiting does give the crossbow hunter, hidden in a blind, the

Baiting is used to entice bruins within sure-kill crossbow range. Although frequently used in Canada, bear baiting is less common, and often illegal, in much of the United States. Alternatives include spotting and stalking bears or hunting them with dogs.

opportunity to get close-range shots at undisturbed animals. If it is legal to hunt over standing cornfields specifically planted to attract game, it seems something of a fine point to make it illegal to scatter corn in exactly the same spot after the crop has been harvested. For the health of the animals, bait stations should be moved periodically so that the grain does not accumulate and become moldy (which may be deadly to deer) and disease does not spread among the animals.

Deer, hogs, and bear are commonly shot over bait, and I have described the typical Canadian bear hunt over bait in chapter 12. Stalking, although possible in much of Canada, is much more time-consuming and less productive than hunting over bait. Even so, hunting over bait for any animal provides no guarantees. During a week's hunt, for example, no trophy animals may present themselves, hot weather may keep them from moving, or the animals may come to the bait every night but never during daylight. The African bushpig, for example, frequently feeds at night, but a light turned on to illuminate a bait can offer the crossbow hunter a shot at this animal.

This tree dripping with ripe, yellow plums provides prime bear feed and is a natural bait station. Although in many states hunters could not legally pour out a half-bushel of plums to attract bear, they could legally hunt in an orchard where the trees are dropping fruit.

CALLING

Calling big-game animals such as elk and moose is a thrilling way to hunt. By making some seductive cow calls, the hunter may find himself staring down a bull that has literally come on the run looking for that cow. Typically, the person doing the calling is located somewhere behind the hunter who is positioned along the path of a responding animal's likely approach. Since you'll be shooting at less than 10 yards, it helps to have some brushy cover to help conceal you.

Sometimes, however, hunting after calling an amorous bull may be so unnerving to the archer that he cannot shoot. One western outfitter described what happened after a guide attracted a bull's attention with some cow and bull calls for a young archer. "It was a huge bull elk with antlers extending over half its back. It had just wallowed and came in covered with mud, blowing snot out of its nostrils, and ready for a fight. The young hunter took one look at the red-eyed bull charging in, threw down his bow, and ran. His parting words were, 'You shoot him. I'm outta here.'"

Calling, usually thought of in connection with turkey hunting, also works on occasion with deer, moose, elk, bear, and alligators.

Obviously, hunting under such conditions is going to be exciting, if not nerve-wracking, but a hunter must still get the job done. If hunting did not have an element of excitement, it would not be worth doing. Keep cool, aim at the right spot, and get a smooth arrow release. Elk are big, moose are bigger, and it may seem impossible to miss one at 8 or 10 yards, but believe me it can, and does, happen. A single crossbow arrow delivered in the right spot will take these animals cleanly; an entire quiver-full shot at random will not.

Calls, including mouth calls and rattling horns, will sometimes work on rutting deer. Staging a mock fight will also work from time to time on deer, moose, and turkeys. Many companies now market calls for small game, big game, and predators. Most hunters may not think of using calls on bear, but a fawn-in-distress call or a predator call can entice a bear to come to the hunter for a close shot.

BLINDS

Blinds both offer protection from the sun, rain, and cold and shield the hunter from game. A built-up blind on a well-established hunting ranch may have all sorts of amenities, whereas a pop-up blind thrown up on a field edge will be quite spartan in comparison. Both can work, particularly if they are prepositioned prior to the hunt. Blinds also help control the hunter's scent, although often at the expense of preventing ventilation. Behind a blind, a hunter can engage in a small amount of low-volume conversation, hide his movement of taking down and mounting a crossbow, and muffle the noise of loading a shaft or clicking-off a safety.

I have used commercial blinds, stick-build blinds on pilings, homemade blinds made out of painted canvas and PVC pipe, and blinds made of cut palmetto fronds, and I have found it particularly effective to hunt wild turkeys from blinds. In all cases, you'll want sufficient room to operate the crossbow and a shooting rail to provide support for your bow. TenPoint now has a swing-down monopod, which provides a great deal of stability when used in conjunction with a ground blind.

Shooting from a blind not only supplies the hunter with cover, but it provides scent control and protection from the elements. Such confined quarters become even tighter when a guide and cameraman accompany the hunter inside the blind.

Excellent locations for blinds are within shooting range of topographic bottlenecks, at waterholes, along the edges of food plots, near agricultural fields, and on trail intersections. Territorial markers such as rubs and scrapes, breeding areas such as strut zones and leks, and favored defecation locations (especially for members of the horse family and some antelopes) may also be productive.

It requires patience to sit in a blind for hours, and perhaps days, waiting for game. What may have been an expressed desire to hold out for a huge animal at the start of the hunt changes by the end of a five-day hunt when any legal animal looks promising. As consolation, keep in mind that younger animals, of whatever species, are always better for eating. In addition, if you take a small animal this year, you'll find it comparatively easy to take a better specimen on the next trip.

Younger hunters who are strong of limb and stout of heart but short on patience may have trouble spending hours sitting in a blind. My best recommendation is to take along a book. As a teenager, I thought I was physically ready and psychologically capable of running down the deer, grabbing it by the throat, and killing it with my teeth. This never happened. In fact, although I jumped deer from time to time while rabbit hunting, I never killed one until I was almost in my 20s and able to hunt with a degree of deliberation. Even this was an accidental encounter.

One day while seeking woodcock among the viney islands and brushy banks of the Kitrell Creek, I heard the sounds of a dog chase taking place in the uplands some distance away. I exchanged the bird shot in my 16-gauge L.C. Smith double with two loads of number-1 buck, and, stepping in the creek to listen, spotted a buck easing along a deer trail on the side of the creek. Because he did not expect danger from the creek, he did not look in my direction. His attention, like mine had been, was focused on the sounds of the dog pack. I raised the shotgun, aimed behind his shoulder, and shot both barrels in quick succession. After considerable tracking, I found the deer and finished it off with a duck load in its neck.

It had taken three or four years of looking for deer as incidental game before I was ever able to shoot one. Once I had matured enough to be able to sit for long periods in a blind or deer stand, I started taking several deer a year. If you want to be a consistently productive hunter, you are going to have to learn to sit.

There is a truism that says, "The mind can absorb only what the butt can endure," and this saying certainly applies to deer hunting. The most reliable aid to killing deer is not deer attractant, scents, rattling horns, or mystic portents offered at midnight by the light of the hunter's moon. All of these may work from time to time, but what works every time is a comfortable cushion that allows the hunter to sit still long enough to actually see deer. Sitting on a stand for four to six hours, or even all day, may be tough, but it's necessary to consistently kill game.

TREE STANDS

I like to hunt from tree stands, especially lightweight climbing stands that I can take with me and set up in little time. Whatever type of tree stand you use, remember two rules: Practice with it before going into the woods, and always use a safety harness. On the property adjacent to my house, I seldom hunt from the same tree two days in a row. I may leave a stand on a favored tree and use it when the mood strikes me or if the

Portable, lightweight climbing stands may be used anywhere that you find straight-trunked trees. When hunting near home, I seldom hunt a stand more than a single day. Constantly changing stand locations keeps the deer from patterning the hunter and makes the view more interesting for the hunter. A comfortable cushion is the best accessory for a stand.

wind is particularly favorable. Whatever tree stand I use, I am sure to stay in it from daylight until at least 11 A.M., no matter what happens.

This rule was severely tested one year when at about 8:30 A.M., I heard the "crunch, crunch, crunch" of a four-footed animal approaching my stand. I turned and saw Persephone, my black Lab, playing her favorite game of "finding Hovey in his tree." She looked up at me in my stand, gave a satisfied look, and curled up and went to sleep at the base of my tree.

It was too early to go in, and the woods were too noisy for me to move so I sat there and fumed while "Hound Dog" slept blissfully in the leaves. After about an hour, I heard another "crunch, crunch, crunch" of an animal approaching. Only this time it was a doe. I raised my muzzleloader and took aim when the deer became curious about the black blob curled up in the leaves. She started to go away, but then returned, and when she offered an open shot, I nailed her through the spine. The deer went down within 10 yards of where the dog was sleeping, and, Persephone, who became unglued by the unexpected noise of the shot and nearby thrashing of the dying deer, went over, grabbed the deer by the throat, and finished it.

On the drag back to the house, my proud Labrador led the way, confident that she had attracted the deer and killed it, as she indeed had. Since then, Labrador retrievers as deer decoys have not been incorporated as part of my standard deer-hunting strategy, but this incident does illustrate the importance of forming a good hunt plan and sticking with it, despite seemingly adverse events.

The farther one travels from the Midwest to West, the fewer good climbing trees will be found. In those locations, bolt on or chain or strap-on tree stands are more useful than climbing stands. Whichever type of stand is used, the crossbow hunting techniques remain the same. Cock your crossbow on the ground. Then, after making sure the safety is on, hoist it by rope up to the stand. I can't overemphasize the importance of putting on the safety before hoisting the weapon. If the crossbow trigger would catch a twig or vine, the crossbow could fire, the string and/or limbs could be damaged, and the hunt could be ruined. Once you have it on the stand, detach the quiver and put an arrow in the crossbow. Then you are ready to hunt.

At the end of the sit, remove the arrow and lower the crossbow to the ground. If a crossbow falls, most likely it will fall limb-end down and cause the end of one of the limbs to strike the ground. Such a fall could seriously damage a compound crossbow, since the wheels, which are, by far, the most delicate part of the entire bow, could become bent out of

Strap-on tree stands, such as this one used on Rio Bonito Ranch in Texas, allow a hunter to rise high enough above the brushy cover to get a good shot. The closer you hunt to arid parts of the midcontinental region of North America, the more difficult it is to find small straight-limbed trees to support climbing stands. In these environments, strap-on stands are popular and almost the only option for hunting from a tree.

line or the string could no longer work freely through the pulleys. If this happens, the hunt effectively would be over, a disappointing end if you are hundreds of miles away from home. Because of such hazards, always take a spare crossbow if traveling a distance for a crossbow hunt. It does not have to be the most expensive crossbow, just something that you can shoot, along with a matched set of arrows and points, in the event your primary crossbow becomes damaged.

The limbs of a recurve crossbow, whether strung or not, respond better when dropped from a tree stand. The spring of the limbs may bounce the crossbow some feet away, but as long as the trigger retains the string, the crossbow may come through the event without any damage. A piece of string weighs almost nothing, and it is far better to lower the crossbow to the ground than to attempt to climb down or up with it in your hand or on your back.

Recocking the crossbow in a tree stand may be done using a variety of techniques, depending on the crossbow and the configuration of the stand. If you are in a large box blind with a floor in it, cock the crossbow in the traditional fashion using a stirrup—just like at home. If the crossbow has a light draw weight (150 pounds or less), place a foot through the stirrup to push the crossbow away from you while holding the string with the hands. A rope cocker may be used in the same manner, but its use requires considerably more fumbling. Individuals with strong arms and stout breast bones (not anyone who has had heart surgery) can place the stock of the crossbow against the sternum and, by pulling back with both hands, cock the crossbow. Wind-up cocking devices may also be used to easily recock the bow. Unless you have a particular reason to recock the crossbow in the stand, such as a struggling animal beneath it, it is always best, and safest, to return to the ground to recock the crossbow.

Because any of the above techniques require considerable movement in the stand, the hunter and his crossbow and assorted arrows run the risk of falling from the stand. Before you ever climb a tree, practice recocking a crossbow on the ground to find out which method works best for you. The greater the crossbow's pull weight, the more difficult it is to cock in confined spaces. Always wear a safety harness when hunting from a tree stand, and no matter how tempted you are to do otherwise, keep the safety belt snapped on while attempting to recock a crossbow.

DOG HUNTING

Hunting deer, bear, hogs, and mountain lion with the aid of a pack of dogs has a long tradition in Europe and the United States. Although dogs have a legitimate place in the hunting world, they are not universally applicable for all purposes. Coursing game with dogs requires some room, typically several thousand acres. Typically, in a dog hunt, the dogs are released to drive game to hunters positioned on strategically located stands. When they hear the dogs approach, the hunters get ready and shoot once the game appears in range. Often the animals will be at a dead run, but sometimes they will sneak along and offer a reasonable shot for a person with a crossbow. Many times, hunters using this method are not very selective, and on many European hunts, any game that moves may be taken.

Deer respond differently to different types of dogs. Beagles with their short legs are not considered much of a threat to a deer, which at a walk can outdistance a beagle. However, because the deer will more often walk, rather than run, beagles are often used in the Southeast to chase deer.

Larger hounds are used to chase hogs, which will run until they back themselves into some cover and then stand to fight the dogs. The hunters pursue at a dead run until, nearly breathless, the crossbowman has a good shot at the hog. Care must be taken not to pass an arrow through a dog or get chomped by the hog. Treed mountain lions may

The author with a pistol and deer alongside Demeter, part of the author's deer-recovery team. Although not allowed in every state or on many public hunts, dogs are extremely useful for recovering game.

also be killed by crossbow, but if the cat climbs a thickly branched western oak instead of a comparatively clean-limbed ponderosa pine, the hunter must wait for a clear shot.

Catch dogs, usually bulldogs, are typically used to hold a hog until the hunter can catch it by hand or kill it with a knife or spear. If a hunter is close enough to stab a hog with a knife, he is close enough to take it with a crossbow, although the bow is considerably more cumbersome at close quarters. A knife or spear, causes more tissue damage and thus kills faster than crossbow arrows.

Hunting with dogs requires rapid movement through brush, swamp, and briers and a higher degree of mobility than I now possess, but it is an exciting way for young hunters in good physical condition to hunt. Horses can be of considerable aid to a hunter who is a skilled rider. However, horses are a hazard to the inexperienced. More hunters are injured each year in accidents involving horses than in encounters with big-game animals.

In my part of Georgia, it is legal to run deer with dogs, and I use dogs to hunt every year, but not in the manner described earlier. I find that dogs are unexcelled at recovering wounded animals when, despite our best efforts, game is hit but not quickly killed.

I once used my dogs for tracking a buck that my brother-in-law wounded. After he and his partner had looked for the deer for several hours without success, I put my canine deer-finding team, Saladin, Ursus, and Demeter, to work. They started following a deer trail, but that deer was not the one we were after. Returning to the area, I found fresh blood and put them on it. Quickly picking up the scent, they discovered that the deer had backtracked and was moving up the creek bed through a series of beaver ponds. Soon I heard barking as they bayed the deer. Approaching closer, I could see my white Lab, Ursus, standing in water and barking at the deer concealed by the root ball of a downed tree. Saladin was on the other side. I climbed up the roots and saw the deer, which was lying in a pool of water and looking at Demeter who was immediately in front of it. I could not use my buckshot-loaded muzzleloading shotgun for fear that the pellets would strike one of the dogs, so I drew my single-shot .50-caliber muzzleloading pistol and shouted for Demeter to move. Once she was out of the line of fire, I placed a bullet in the deer's spine to end its struggle. Thanks to the dogs, this deer would not be left to the coyotes and buzzards. Demeter, who was then the matriarch of the pack, claimed "her" deer and would not let the other dogs approach it.

Outside of good shot placement, the use of trailing dogs will result in more deer being recovered than any other factor. However, in many states the use of dogs for deer hunting, in any fashion, is illegal. Instead of this short-sighted approach, a better law would be to allow leashed dogs to be used for deer recovery and hunters to carry one firearm to kill the deer if necessary. A crossbow used under such circumstances would be a safer tool than wrestling with a deer and breaking its neck, something I have done but do not recommend.

SCENTS AND SCENTING

We humans are woefully deficient in our sense of smell, a fact brought home to me forcefully a few nights ago when Demeter was tracking a crossbow-shot deer. My hunting buddy Paul Presley had made a bad hit on a doe from 15 yards; he thought he may have become excited, jerked at the hard trigger on his Horton SteelForce crossbow, and pulled the shot. Although the arrow had no blood on it, a small amount of red blood was found on the ground. On this hunt, he had shot at three deer: He missed one, grazed another, and more seriously injured this one. We had no choice but to put a dog on the deer's trail. Because it was already dark and the weather was hot, we feared the deer would spoil if we left it overnight.

We had some early hope of success as Paul thought he had heard the deer "crash." Demeter was certainly eager to work, but we had to keep her on a leash because we couldn't move through the cutover area with its fallen tops, briers, and rank stump sprouts as fast as she could. Using a Q-beam and two flashlights, we trailed in the dark for more than two hours, as Demeter followed the blood scent. Occasionally, we would find a small amount of blood, but mostly it was drop by drop.

While watching Demeter trailing, I had a visual realization of how the universe of scents must appear to her. Rather than invisible organic molecules wafting in the air, I imagined the scents in full color and in three dimensions. Each drop of blood was the apex of a bright red plume of scent that dissipated downwind in the air and formed spherical and pear-shaped clouds, which became progressively orange and yellow as the scent dispersed. In my vision, the drops almost formed a connect-the-dots line along the doe's travel path, which if seen from above, would have traced a very irregular J shape for almost two miles as we tracked the animal. Her path took us toward a pond, back up on the benchlands, and into a swamp, where we lost the scent.

Coming out of the swamp, Demeter started to trail a second deer, and with only one weakly burning flashlight between us, we discontinued the search. Demeter had done well. As long as the blood trail was on land, she followed it without a misstep. She only lost it when the deer went to water among the streams and beaver ponds. I went back with her the next morning, but we could not pick up any fresh sign of the deer.

To complete the visual analogy, I imagine the world of scents would be a psychedelic experience to a dog. Intersecting the red-hot blood trail would be pink trails of other deer, orange hot-spots where a buck had been pawing, circular and oval yellow trails of squirrels, pink scents from vegetation, and green tracks from a day or two ago that still retained some scent. Mix these up, take them in different directions, and you begin to have an appreciation of what a dog experiences. Scent is a complex world that humans can't begin to experience. We just don't have the equipment for it. Technology, although it offers optical enhancements, has not improved our ability to smell anything except perhaps what canines must consider the rankest of odors.

10

Deer Hunting with a Crossbow

Religion and crossbows crossed paths in 1139 when Pope Innocent II called the crossbow "deadly and hateful to God and unfit to be used against Christians." In my case, the biblical admonition "If you have done it to the least of these you have done it to me" influenced the selection of my first crossbow. Because of a writer's perpetual state of poverty, I decided to try to take a deer with the least expensive crossbow that I could buy. If I did, I figured there may be something to this crossbow stuff.

Sportsman's Guide, the discount catalogue company, featured an ad for a Barnett Ranger at $130, which included a red-dot sight, quiver, and four arrows. It was a price that I could afford, but would the Ranger kill deer? The crossbow was advertised with a 150-pound pull, which would give the crossbow adequate power to take deer-size game. With its skeletal stock, it had a total weight of slightly less than 5 pounds, an important feature since I planned to take it on a hunt to the Cumberland Island National Seashore, a wilderness area that required me to pack in all of my stuff and drag out any game I shot.

When the crossbow arrived, I found it to be a simple instrument with a fiberglass rod for a prod and an inexpensive Chinese red-dot sight with two different brightness levels. I tried it out and found it shot adequately with Barnett's 412-grain Stalker arrows and Muzzy's 125-grain skeletal broadheads, a heavier point than is usually used on crossbows but since I owned them I thought I would use them. (This was not a bad selection for my purposes because many first-time crossbow buyers install the same points on their crossbow arrows that they previously used with their conventional bows.)

I was impressed with how the little crossbow shot. It may not have been a tack driver, but I had no problems keeping broadheads in less than 2-inch groups at 20 yards. I also shot the crossbow at 30 and 40 yards and taped the amount of drop for each range below the shooting rail for easy reference.

I decided to try out the crossbow on 13 acres of undeveloped urban wetlands in my hometown. I often bowhunted there, and although it was a small parcel, I invariably saw deer. My game plan was to sit inside the woods within sight of a small grain patch that I had planted. With any luck, the deer would walk to the edge of the woods, and I would have a shot. The first afternoon, I discovered I was too far back in the woods, and the buck stayed just out of range until dark. The following afternoon, I moved my stand closer to the food plot and resumed my hunt.

This time, a doe came out of the woods opposite me and walked toward my stand. When she was about 20 yards away, she turned broadside. I had already switched on the red-dot sight and taken the safety off the crossbow as she approached. When the red-dot sight landed behind the shoulder, I pulled the trigger. The deer bounded away, ran 30 yards, and went down. The crossbow arrow penetrated the deer, and I saw it sticking into the ground. Because the deer was slowly walking, the arrow hit the rear of the lungs. I should have aimed a bit forward on the shoulder to compensate for the deer's movement. Even so, the deer was decisively killed by the little crossbow.

Looking back, what could I have done better? I should have used a lighter weight mechanical point for a faster arrow and better hit. The heavy broadhead I used was reasonably accurate and killed the deer, but a mechanical point would have been more accurate and killed equally well. In addition, the faster arrow would have hit the deer before it had moved quite so far. Nonetheless, my first crossbow hunt with less than optimum equipment was a success.

FIRST-TIME CROSSBOW HUNTER

In many ways, my sometimes-hunting companion Paul Presley is typical of many first-time crossbow hunters. In his mid-30s, he is married and has four children, and the end of the month does not leave him with much excess money to spend on hunting equipment. When I asked him if he was interested in using a crossbow instead of his bow during archery season, he assented, and I equipped him with a Horton SteelForce. Since he did not have much time to work with the crossbow, I thought that this relatively simple crossbow would enable him to get hunting in a hurry. To enhance the crossbow's capabilities, I mounted an Excalibur scope on it and adjusted the power setting to reflect the relatively low 265-fps velocity generated by the SteelForce's arrow and 75-grain Muzzy points. After a brief orientation, I set him off to find game.

Paul Presley with his first crossbow deer taken with a TenPoint crossbow. Presley missed one animal and grazed another with a Horton SteelForce with a hard trigger pull before he succeeded with the much easier-to-use TenPoint crossbow.

Things did not go well. Although the SteelForce functioned reasonably well for a low-cost crossbow and its light weight was a favorable characteristic, its hard trigger pull was so difficult for Paul to overcome that he could not use the crossbow effectively. On his first hunt, he missed a deer. On his second, he made a grazing shot. The third evening, he hit a doe in a nonfatal area and he spent several hours tracking the animal at night. When we returned to the range, I found that he still shot the crossbow adequately. We reshot the crossbow and checked his arrows and points after each episode, and they were fine.

I thought about his experiences on his hunts. His second shot at 40 yards was a grazing hit, which I chalked up to his being somewhat over-confident of his abilities with the crossbow. The shot where he wounded the deer was at 15 yards, certainly within range. After talking it over, we both concluded that he had jerked the hard trigger and pulled the crossbow off the point of aim, not an unusual occurrence in real-world hunting situations.

A change was needed. Nothing could be done to improve the trigger pull except for putting a drop of oil on it, and fiddling around with the arrows and points would do no good. I did have another crossbow that he could try. This 185-pound pull TenPoint was a top-of-the-line crossbow with an Acudraw cocking mechanism, grip safety, and three-position red-dot sight. I zeroed it in with 100-grain Wasp Boss points and got it ready for our next morning's hunt.

Paul arrived before dawn. I set up a target on the back porch and had him fire one shot at 12 yards. He hit it dead center on the bull. After reviewing the more complex procedure of using the winding mechanism and the three-step process needed to fire the crossbow (operate two safeties and pull the trigger), we started out.

He had been on the stand for an hour when the sound of the crossbow and the thud of the arrow hitting the ground indicated that something had happened. From 300 yards away on the other end of the field, I could see a deer run toward the center of the food plot. Was this the deer Paul shot? I had no way of knowing, and it was still too early for me to climb down. Twenty minutes later, I had a doe approach me from behind. Even though she was only 3 yards away, I could not turn to shoot before she smelled me and was gone.

With the sun hitting my tree and illuminating me like an orange Christmas ball, I decided that it was time to come down. We either had to retrieve a deer or have Paul practice some more with the crossbow.

When I arrived at his location, he was standing over his deer. He had made a good behind-the-shoulder hit and fallen in love with the Ten-Point crossbow. "It was heavy enough to be stable when I put it on the deer," he said. "The trigger pull was no problem, and it was so fast that the arrow passed through the deer the instant I pulled the trigger. I know this crossbow cost much more than the other one, but it is worth it!" The price differential between the two crossbows is significant: The SteelForce with scope costs about $200, whereas the TenPoint would retail for about $1,200. Paul was disappointed about the size of his deer and wanted to continue hunting until he collected a "more worthy" animal.

After returning to the house, he shot the TenPoint crossbow at 5, 10, 20, 30, and 40 yards. Up to 30 yards, the hits were solid and predictable, but at 40 yards, the group shot from a sitting position opened up to about 6 inches. He found that between 5 and 20 yards he could use the uppermost of the three dots on the scope and at 30 yards he could aim 6 inches low to hit the point of aim with the second dot. Unless shooting from an absolutely rock-solid rest, he would have to limit his shots to about 30 yards with this red-dot sight-crossbow combination.

The next week, again with the crossbow, he hunted urban deer with me on my in-town property. Paul had two shots. On the first, at 38 yards, his arrow penetrated to the fletching on a buck. On his second shot, this one at a three-point buck at 15 yards, the arrow passed through the deer's spine and exited the belly. The blades on the Wasp Boss point were considerably banged up from its passage through the deer, but they remained intact. That deer fell where it was hit. We tracked the first deer both manually and with dogs, but it apparently made it to a brush-choked pond and escaped. If the arrow had penetrated the deer, we could have followed a better blood trail, and the deer might have expired sooner. The 185-pound pull crossbow shot and functioned well. If there was a fault, it was Paul's for pushing the 40-yard maximum range of the crossbow.

OPTIMUM EQUIPMENT, OPTIMUM RESULTS

Bill and Kath Throubridge are not only president and vice president of Excalibur crossbows, but they are an effective husband-wife hunting team that often goes after whitetails. Both are experienced crossbow shooters who compete in target-shooting events. With an entire company's line of crossbow products at their fingertips, what do they use and why do they use it?

An old hunting adage renders, "Beware of the man who only owns one gun. He can probably shoot it." The Throubridges feel pressure to use each year's new products so that they have firsthand experience on how their crossbows and components perform. However, once a crossbow is selected, they will use this crossbow on as many hunts as possible during the year so that they get the "feel" of the crossbow and know, without question, how it performs. By using one crossbow during an entire hunting season, they can quickly detect any problem, such as loose bolts, that needs to be adjusted.

Almost every game animal that I have taken has been shot with a different crossbow, sight, arrow, and point. I've done this because I wanted to gain field knowledge of as many crossbows as possible in the shortest possible time. Is this approach recommended for the average hunter? Certainly not. Buy the best crossbow that you can afford and use it as your primary crossbow. You should also purchase a less expensive crossbow for a backup in case the guide backs the truck over your primary crossbow, the mule kicks it, or it falls from the tree stand.

The last time I had the opportunity to hunt with the Throubridges, Bill was using his new ExoMag, which has a 225-pound pull weight, and Kath had an Exocet 200. They used these crossbows on everything they

Bill Throubridge with a 150-class Mexican deer taken on one of his annual hunts with his Excalibur crossbows.

shot that year, including whitetails. Before the introduction of the Exocet 200, both most often used the Exocet 175-pound pull bows, which are overly powerful for white-tailed deer but will certainly get the job done. Dan Miller, a long-time Excalibur user, uses a 150-pound pull weight Vixen, with which he has taken a large number of deer.

For arrows on deer-moose (and sometimes even larger game such as the Australian scrub bulls), the Throubridges typically use the Gold Tip carbon shaft and 100-grain, triple-bladed Wasp Boss point, which have a total weight of about 450 grains. These arrows fly well from 150- to 200-pound pull-weight crossbows and can shoot through deer and moose with broadside shots. This pull weight and arrow selection are excellent choices for this class of game, and the Throubridges' videos certainly show this.

While hunting whitetails from Canada to Mexico, the pair has hunted from ground blinds and elevated shooting platforms, over bait, overlooking sinderos, and at field edges. They have both done a small amount of stalking and taken deer during accidental encounters.

One of Bill Throubridge's most memorable deer was a mostly white speciman that he had seen around his Ontario farm for some years. Although he had permission to hunt his neighbors' properties, it was under the expressed condition that the "white deer" not be shot. "I was

Bill Throubridge with an unusual white-pigmented deer that was taken on his property in Canada. This deer proved to be the most expensive animal he had ever taken, as he first remodeled his house, and later his office, to properly display the full-mounted deer.

hunting my own property, and there was the deer at 12 yards," he recalled. "That deer was at least eight years old, and it was time for it to die. One arrow and it was mine."

In a classic case of "beware what you wish for, because you may get it," the deer turned out to be the most expensive one that Throubridge ever killed. Because of the unique character of the animal, it had to be mounted whole, a costly undertaking. Then an addition had to be built onto the house so that the mount would fit in the living room. Ultimately, it was moved into the factory display area, which also required enlargement and renovation. By the time all was done, the price tag of that deer had risen to between $30,000 and $50,000, depending on how you count the required renovations.

MULE DEER

Taking a trophy mule deer has always been an historic part of the hunt package in the western United States. In the old days, fellows such as Teddy Roosevelt would go west for buffalo (already uncommon in Roosevelt's time), moose, elk, mule deer, and antelope. The mule deer, the most elusive of the five, was often the more difficult to hunt, even with firearms. Although herds would be seen, approaching the crafty animals was difficult, and few hunters with black-powder rifles were rewarded with a nice set of mule deer horns for above the fireplace.

The best place to hunt for mules was in broken country where the hunter sometimes could spot a deer and pull off a successful stalk. This spot-and-stalk method prompted the development of optics powerful enough to locate potential trophies and sharp enough to judge the quality of the animals' horns from a distance.

Mule deer like to lie just under the rim of a canyon so that they can see approaching danger. When disturbed, they quickly rise, jump over the crest, and flee into the next canyon, leaving the hunter with only a fleeting glimpse of the elusive animal. At one time, mule deer were said to be in the habit of stopping, turning, and looking back, apparently to see what had disturbed them, but since all of the stupid deer have been shot, this one-time trait cannot be counted upon anymore.

Hunting trophy deer with a crossbow adds another degree of difficulty. Not only must the crossbow hunter do the usual spotting, trophy judging, and stalking, but he must get within 40 yards of the animal for a reasonable shot. Then, once he gets that close, he runs the risk of having his arrow deflected from a piece of tough sagebrush.

Often the best opportunity to bag a trophy mule deer is to hunt on a private ranch with a local guide. Such hunts benefit the ranch owner by keeping the deer population under control and providing extra income. The guide, for his part, is given an area to hunt where his clients will see little competition from other hunters, and the paying hunter has a chance to shoot deer that have had the opportunity to grow to trophy size. Everybody wins.

Although most hunters think antelope and vast plains when considering Wyoming, the state hosts mule deer in the broken foothills and lower parts of the mountain ranges. Paul Vaicunas, under the guidance of Ron Mobley of Miller Outfitting in Gillette, Wyoming, hunted mule deer on a ranch below what is appropriately named the Big Horn Mountains.

After two days of scouting and glassing, without any success stalking a muley, Vaicunas and Mobley were taken by ranch owner Doug Miller to a more distant part of the ranch where Miller had seen a big buck. It was a pounding trip over rutted, muddy roads in a four-wheel-drive jeep to get to this area, which was on higher, even more broken country.

Settling down on a high point, they resumed their now-accustomed glassing. When the trio spotted a small herd of mule deer below them, Miller acknowledged that the largest buck was the "big one" that he had seen. Vaicunas used an optical doubler to convert his 10X binoculars to a 20X spotting scope and confirmed that this deer's head gear was intact with no broken-off tines. They had spotted the deer at first light, and by 8:30 A.M. the deer had bedded down.

As Vaicunas describes it, "The challenge would be not to lose sight of the buck once I began the stalk. . . . I had to plan a route and stay on course until the moment came to pop over the top and take my shot."

After an hour of negotiating the intervening washes and ridges, he was able to use the broken country and favorable winds to his advantage and close within 100 yards of the bedded deer. He knew where the deer was, but he did not know if his approach might spook some unseen deer and bust the stalk.

By crawling on his belly and pushing the crossbow ahead of him inch by inch, he snuck up to within sure-killing range. After another hour, at 60 yards away, Vaicunas spotted the tips of the horns sticking over the rim of the wash. The crosswind carried his scent away from the animal, and maybe, just maybe, he would have a shot if the wind held true and some small noise did not alert the deer. At 50 yards, he was tantalizingly close but not close enough. He had to crawl another 15 yards and find a shooting lane through the knee-high sagebrush. Loading an arrow in the crossbow, he began his final push toward the deer.

The bedded deer was lying down and still looking down the draw when Vaicunas had his first close-range look at it. The deer looked even better than when he first saw it. He used his rangefinder to confirm that the distance was less than 25 yards and fired. At the shot, the deer exploded in a cloud of dust and sage. The 175-pound draw weight Horton Hunter and its 100-grain, three-bladed broadhead had done its job. The deer gross scored $172^4/_8$ inches and is a pending new world record in Safari Club International's crossbow category.

ALASKA BLACK-TAILED DEER

The U.S. Army located its Arctic Test Center at Fort Greeley, Alaska, because this state's harsh climate will quickly show any faults in the design and materials of its new fighting gear. Using the same logic, I took a Fred Bear 300 crossbow on a hunt for black-tailed deer on Kodiak Island. My friend Roger Kicklighter, his business associates W. C. Copeland, Victor Gregory, and Ed Foster, and Victor's brother-in-law Jim Hopf had planned the hunt of three years, but when another potential member canceled, I had the opportunity to fill his slot.

Alaska Coastal Marine, the hunting outfitter, used a boat, the *Spirit*, to transport us to different locations in the area of Alitak, Deadman,

Akhiok, Alaska, under fresh snow cover. Snow forces the black-tailed deer to come down from the mountains and feed closer to the coast. In this extreme setting, hunters must not only fight the usual alders and steep slopes, but travel through snow that often drifts up to 4 feet thick and across partly frozen creeks and ponds covered with a thin layer of ice and snow.

Portage, and Moser Bays on the southwestern end of Kodiak Island. We enjoyed hot meals and dry bunks on the boat but were taken each day to shore on a Zodiac. Since this was not a guided hunt, once on shore we hunters were on our own.

Blacktails, the smallest of mule deer, are distinguishable by their relatively small eight- to twelve-point racks, a dark black patch on the crown of their heads, and two white throat patches. They feed on grasses, willows, alder tips, and kelp, and when driven down by snow, they come to the tidewater to browse on beach grass and kelp. The weather controls both the activities of the deer and the deerhunter's access to the area. Our party was two days late in getting to the hunt area near Akhiok. The previous party had beautiful hunting weather until five days of high winds and snow forced them to bed down at the local school of eleven students where they were fed by the villagers and entertained by the town dance group one night. While stranded there, the hunters held a Career Day at the school. Had they been there another week, they might have been inducted into the tribe.

This feeding black-tailed doe on the beach passed within 15 yards of the author. Although it was within easy range, the author decided that with plenty of good-eating deer back home in Georgia he would forego shooting a doe on the other side of the continent.

During our stay, winds to 70 miles per hour, waist-deep snow, alders, and eager rifle-toting companions conspired against my success with the crossbow. My best opportunity came on the third day of our hunt. The *Spirit* had been repositioned on Moser Bay after we had hunted Alitak, Sulua, and Deadman Bays. Snow had been falling for three days, and a stiff wind was blasting the exposed hills.

Four of us were put on the beach, and I immediately saw two deer break out of the alders and slowly make their way up the steep slope to the second beach ridge. Ed Foster shot the leading buck with a rifle. The buck diverted its course and crashed into an adjacent alder- and snow-choked gulley. Deer were still in the alder thicket as we approached, and I readied the crossbow and stalked into the snow after them. I could plainly see the deer but could not shoot them through the thick brush. Fighting through the alders and brush, I made my way closer to them as they broke into the clear. Raising my crossbow to shoot, I sighted on a buck standing in the snow 40 yards away. The wind was blowing about 30 miles per hour, and as I was considering the amount

Roger Kicklighter with a Fred Bear crossbow and a Kodiak Island black-tail. While the author was sighting in on this deer in preparation for a shot, fellow hunter Roger Kicklighter nailed it with a rifle from 200 yards away. Because the deer was still struggling, the author finished it off with the crossbow. The lesson he learned that day is that if you are going to hunt with a crossbow, don't hunt in the near vicinity of rifle hunters.

of wind deflection, the deer dropped in its tracks. Without seeing us or knowing that we were stalking the deer, Roger Kicklighter had shot it from about 200 yards away. The deer was down but not dead. I approached the buck and finished it with a crossbow arrow through both lungs. At a range of a few yards, this arrow completely penetrated the deer.

Later that day, I tried to stalk a good-size doe through the snow and brush but could not catch up with it. After three days of serious tromping through the alders, devil's club, vines, and snow, my crossbow remained functional. A part of the crossbow seemed to get hung up on something about every third step, but the arrows remained solidly locked in the quiver and the compound wheels and trigger system never froze up although I did have to periodically stop to blow snow off the crossbow. Once, when I was attempting to stalk the doe, the wind blew the arrow off the crossbow's deck. Most of the time the arrows were carried in the quiver, where they were firmly retained, so firmly in fact that it was difficult to extract one with the near-frozen fingers of my gloved hand.

If I had had my crossbow with me, I could have taken five deer while duck shooting on the beach one day. The deer, all does and small bucks, walked behind me and fed from 10 to 20 yards away, but armed only with a muzzleloading shotgun and duck shot, I made no attempt to shoot them. I knew I already had deer meat at home and would take more deer, which would be considerably less expensive to transport, while on other hunts that season.

By the end of the trip, all of the rifle hunters in our group took one or two nice bucks. Crossbow hunting is certainly possible on Kodiak, but it is a tough environment for both the hunter and his crossbow. Although my hunt was unsuccessful, I and my Fred Bear crossbow had a memorable adventure with good friends, and I experienced a part of the Great Land that even someone who had once lived in Alaska for twelve years had never seen.

On a final note about this trip, after W. C. Copeland and Jim Hopf cleaned a deer and drug it about 300 yards through the snow, a large brown bear found the gut pile. The bruin was content with its free meal and did not follow the hunters. Other brownies were spotted from the air on the trip out. I had already met my share of brown bear at close range, and I did not need to have another such experience, but another hunter on the boat had a brown-bear tag and took a nice 9-foot bear with his rifle. All told, I believe that everyone was satisfied that they had sufficient exposure to the huge bear.

DEER WITH A PRIMITIVE CROSSBOW

To achieve one of my objectives for this book, I wanted to take a deer with a replica of a fourteenth-century crossbow made by David Watson of Austin, Texas. My primitive crossbow was fitted with a 150-pound prod and without modification was a fine, reliable shooting instrument. At the same time I ordered mine, Bill Throubridge ordered a different model with a 170-pound prod. I suppose that I had put a bit of a bug in his ear to experience this old-fashioned technology, and as a crossbow maker, he could not refuse. He even ordered one for his friend Dan Miller.

As the deadline for finishing the book loomed closer, I could not get a deer, of any sort, to stand 20 yards or closer to me with my crossbow. It was not that I had my chances and missed; I just never got to release an arrow at a deer despite taking the bow out more than a dozen times. I had imposed the short range on myself because the crossbow delivered a very limited energy of only 16.78 foot-pounds. With his stronger prod, Bill was getting what he ironically described as "an astonishing 25 foot-pounds of energy."

Both of us started hunting with our primitive crossbows at about the same time, and we both experienced the same problems. The crossbows with their wooden and bone parts did not respond well to being wet, and once wetted, the wood swelled to the point where the releasing nut would not rotate or move at all. Only disassembling the crossbow and drying the components for several days would restore it to functionality.

Choosing points for the crossbow also presented its own challenges. I tried two-bladed broadheads by Fred Bear, Zwickey, and Magnus and found the best flying one of the trio used on Watson's wooden-shafted arrows was the ventilated Fred Bear broadhead. Bill Throubridge took a different approach and used a modern 20-inch carbon arrow and Magnus two-bladed point and steel broadhead adapter with the point oriented parallel to the crossbow's deck. We each noted the very different trajectory characteristics of these crossbows. At 10 yards, I had to aim 10 inches low to hit the point of aim; at 20 yards, the amount of hold-under had increased to 24 inches; and at 40 yards, the crossbow actually shot to about the point of aim. A 5-yard error in range estimation could easily result in the arrow striking 5 inches too low or too high on the target, enough disparity to move it out of the sure-kill area of a deer. The absence of a rear sight did not pose as serious a problem as either of us had expected. Sighting along the shaft provided more than sufficient accuracy to hit within a couple of inches of the point of aim at 20 yards.

Bill's first opportunity to take a deer came when a young buck approached within 15 yards, but because his cameraman could not see it, he did not shoot. He knew he could only take one buck a year in his Canadian province, and he wanted to maximize this experience. After a number of unsuccessful trips, he saw a doe stop about 20 yards in front of his blind. Deciding it was time to make meat and move on to something else, he took aim and shot. He was surprised that the arrow completely penetrated the chest cavity of the 80-pound animal and resulted in a quick kill. Bill's quest to take a deer with his replica crossbow was over, but mine continues.

BIGGER MEMBERS OF THE DEER FAMILY

Lee Zimmerman and his son Mark took their Horton crossbows to Colorado to hunt for Rocky Mountain elk. The hunt took place in October during the bugling season before the snow started to fall and the aspen were just starting to turn in the high country of the Three-Forks Ranch. When the Zimmermans' guide Allen Morris bugled, he received an answering call from across the valley, and he told Lee Zimmerman to get ready because "this bull is going to come."

Cow and calf elk at the water hole. During rut, a bull elk very likely would be close by, providing a nearly ideal setup for a crossbow hunter to establish a blind.

Responding to Morris's enticing cow call, the bull trotted down the slope in search of the elusive cow. Morris called again, using a cow elk silhouette head to mask his face. The bull crossed the bottom and climbed up into the aspen thicket, interrupting his progress once to bugle. That pause gave Lee Zimmerman time to take his shot. He fired his crossbow, but he was so excited that he was not sure of the hit. The guide, who viewed the shot from a different angle, saw the arrow go completely through the elk. Blood sprayed from the wound, and the bull left a good blood trail over an adjoining ridge. A relieved and proud Lee Zimmerman tracked the downed elk.

The next day was Mark's turn. A herd of elk had been located, and again Morris attracted the herd bull. Mark took aim, released the arrow from his Horton Hunter, and made a good hit through the lungs. The animal expired quickly and was recovered some 150 yards away.

Both the Zimmermans used 175-pound pull Horton crossbows and Rocky Mountain Assassin 100-grain mechanical heads. During a later interview, Lee remarked that the mechanical points had performed well as his arrow went completely through the elk and embedded in a log behind it. "I had rather use a point that flies true from my bow than a less accurate fixed point for anything smaller than the big bear or African species," he related. "On deer and elk, the mechanical points work just fine as we demonstrated on that hunt."

The Zimmermans' success marked the first time in Morris's 10 years of guiding that he had seen crossbows take game. Impressed, he expressed a wish that all of the elk his clients shot were as decisively killed and as easy to recover as the Zimmermans' animals. He attributed their good results to precise, close-range shooting with an effective hunting instrument.

11

HOG HUNTING WITH A CROSSBOW

The average North American hunter is aware that feral, or wild, hogs are an increasing problem in the lower forty-eight states and Hawaii. They forage in family groups, root up planted fields, and destroy understory habitats to the extent that the woods appear to be plowed. In extreme cases, not a green thing will be seen growing on the forest floor where wild hogs live. These feral hogs reproduce as fast as their domestic kin, and they sometimes look exactly like them.

More savvy hog hunters have learned that some strains of wild European stock are present in hogs in North Carolina, Tennessee, and California. These primitive hogs are jet black, have good teeth, and grow to weight more than 500 pounds. When allowed to freely interbreed, hogs tend to revert to their original wild appearance to become black, brown, or reddish Arkansas razorbacks, which have larger shoulders than hips.

The largest known American hog taken with a rifle was given the moniker "Hogzilla" as this huge hog was first said to weigh more than 1,000 pounds and measure 12 feet long. After exhuming the hog to verify these measurements, the National Geographic estimated its size at 800 pounds and 10 feet long. This enormous old boar, which was taken by Chris Griffin in June of 2004 on River Oak Plantation near Alphaha, Georgia, attracted worldwide attention.

Residents in the Southwest have their own hoglike beastie, the javelina or peccary. Javelinas look like small pigs and have much the same feeding habits, but they are an entirely different animal native to the Americas. They have a musk gland at the root of their tail and a unique tooth structure. Not only does their meat have a distinctive taste, but javelinas provide the "pig skin" commonly made into golfing and driving gloves.

The author took this Arizona javelina in the Catalina mountains north of Tucson in the late 1970s. Javelinas, which are not true pigs, are native to the Americas.

Anyone who has visited the southern part of Africa has met the warthog. These true hogs have very big teeth and a face so ugly that it's cute. Almost any hunt in that part of the country will include warthogs on the license, and some are often taken for camp meat since they are so tasty.

Africa is home to the giant forest hog, which inhabits the more wooded parts of the continent, and the bushpig, which lives in grassland habitats. The giant forest hog, with its 6-inch-diameter snout and huge rounded warts under its eyes, is one of the largest species of hog and as such has the heaviest teeth. These "chompers" are solid tools often close to $1^1/_2$ inches in diameter, but many times they are broken and not as attractive as the smaller, longer teeth of warthog. Much larger than warthogs, forest hogs have a local reputation for ferocity equal to Europe's wild boar.

Bushpigs have a distinctive wedge-shaped profile from their shoulders to their snout and a bristly white-colored ridge of hair extending from the head to halfway down the back. This crest of hair is erected when bushpigs are excited or irritated. Like other members of the hog family, they also have cutters, but these are not nearly so prominent as the warthog's. Bushpigs are mostly nocturnal and are often hunted with lights at night.

To complete the collection of the world's wild hogs, the bearded pig is native to Borneo and Malaysia, the pygmy hog is found in India, and the four-tusked babirusa lives on the island of Sulawesi, part of the

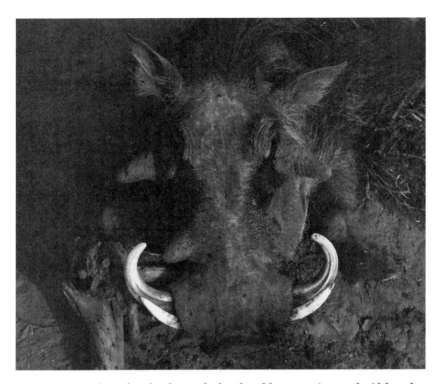

Boar warthogs have four knobs on the head and long curving teeth. Although their ivories are not the heaviest known to members of the pig family, they certainly are among the most handsome.

Indonesian archipelago. The babirusa has four tusks rising from the top of its snout with the central pair crossing over its nose to make an X. Because of destruction of habitat and overhunting, this species is in danger of extinction.

Hog hunting is available on all the continents located within the temperate and tropical zones, and almost any crossbow hunting trip can involve a side excursion for wild hogs. Like any game, hogs are not equally distributed, so be sure to ask your outfitter about the pig-hunting potential of a particular area. Groups of hogs roam from food source to food source, unless localized by topography, so it may be necessary to make inquires to discover the areas the hogs are using at the moment.

If you are hunting in a Muslim country, be aware that Muhammadans will have nothing to do with pigs. Therefore, if you want something done with your wild hog, you are going to have to do it yourself. So go prepared to salvage the trophy and take the meat you want to cook. Once the meat is in a container, it's usually OK. It is putting their hands on the pig or the raw meat that Muslims find objectionable.

HOW TO SHOOT HOGS WITH CROSSBOWS

Hogs, particularly huge hogs of any species, are powerful animals and take time to kill. Even with a crossbow arrow through the lungs, a hog may take some minutes to die. During this time a hog can easily rip or kill a man. Big wild boars are protected not only by their massive bulk, but by a gristle plate over their shoulders. This plate slows down the crossbow arrow, which does not penetrate as well as it would on a thin-skinned animal. In addition, a head-on shot is likely to strike the animal's sloping forehead and be deflected rather than penetrate into the brain.

If at all possible, you want to shoot at a hog that is not aware of your presence. In wet weather, hogs can sometimes be stalked close enough to take with close-range hunting tools such as bows, crossbows, and muzzleloading pistols. The preferred shot placement with an arrow is in back of the front shoulder ranging forward toward the off-side leg because this will ventilate both lungs and avoid the shoulder bone.

A 400-pound feral Australian hog shot by Kath Throubridge with an Excalibur ExoMax crossbow. A hunter can go almost anywhere in the world to shoot some variety of hog, but these versatile animals happily live in tropical and temperate climates, including on most of the Pacific islands.

Rather than facing the hog on the ground, try to shoot it from a tree stand. If the stand is situated within range of a forest trail, bait station (where legal), or wallow, you may be able to anchor your hog with one good shot. Just remember to shoot high enough so that the arrow penetrates both lungs and not just one. If the arrow hits only one lung, the hog will eventually die, but it may go to an area where you cannot find it. Even if hit with a pass-through shot, hogs do not bleed well, and they are difficult to find in the heavy cover they prefer to inhabit. Arrows do not offer much knockdown power, similar to a .22 long rifle, so you cannot expect to slow a charging hog, assuming that you even could reload your crossbow in time.

In some parts of the world, hog hunting is done with dogs. The dogs bring the hog to bay, and the hunter goes in with his knife or spear. When he sees an opening, he thrusts and kills the hog. At least, that is the theory. I remember reading about a medieval noble who complained that he could not keep his young squires alive long enough to train them to be knights. They loved to hunt wild boars, and the boars were killing off his squires at a rate faster than he could replace them with worthy candidates. Even if the crossbowman can get his arrow into the boar from a longer distance, he must be prepared to elude the charging animal if it manages to break away from the dogs. The boar knows very well who hurt it, and it wants a piece of him. The crossbow, no matter how powerful, is not going to stop a charge.

One style of hunting still done in Germany uses a spear called a "boar feather." Once a hog is located and brought to bay, a group of hunters will surround the hog and imbed the butts of their heavy pike-like spears into the ground. When the hog charges, it runs onto one of the spears and impailes himself in the chest. A crosspiece attached about a foot down from the point keeps the hog a "safe" distance from the hunter. Once the hog is impaled by the first spear, the other hunters help finish it.

In Argentina, hogs are hunted from horseback. After the hog is again brought to bay with dogs, the hunters dismount and attempt to close in on the hog. When a hunter sees an opportunity, he will thrust his knife into the hog behind its shoulder. Upon being stuck, big hogs often break away from the dogs and are brought to bay again whereupon the process is repeated until the hog is dead. This method takes brave hunters and brave dogs.

Wild hogs are such pestiferous animals that they are often trapped or shot over bait such as corn, spoiled fruit, produce, or even a gut pile. When shooting from a blind over bait, the hunter knows the distance to the target and can surprise a hog that is noisily eating and not likely to take notice of any slight movement or noise that the hunter might take. Is it sporting? Well, that is up to the shooter. Because they are so destructive, I will shoot hogs over bait, take one as a "target of opportunity," or hunt them specifically as the occasion demands.

The South contains many groups of young men who catch wild hogs. The hogs are bayed with dogs, caught in hand or with ropes, then tied up and taken away in cages on the back of pickup trucks. These fellows are prudent enough to only take on hogs that are 150 pounds and smaller and to either shoot the big old boars or let them walk.

When the British had such things as lancers in service in Africa (as there were until the turn of the twentieth century), it was considered sporting to go pig sticking with lances on horseback. Warthogs, which generally inhabited open country, were prime targets.

How does this information relate to hunting hogs with crossbows? If you are going to hunt hogs, it is best to do it from a tree stand. If you are hunting from the ground, you better have someone else available with a firearm who is able to deliver a quick finishing shot if it is needed. Otherwise, you must have a good climbing tree handy and be mentally and physically agile enough to climb it. Although you may be able to carry a heavy caliber handgun, something like a .44 Remington magnum, to finish off a hog, you are not likely to have time to draw and shoot it before the hog is on you. Have some bandages and tape with you. A clean T-shirt and some duct tape may work to staunch the bleeding until you can get yourself to the hospital or sew up the dogs and treat their rips.

Once, while on the Nail Ranch in Texas, I shot a 350-pound boar hog with a single-shot .50-caliber muzzleloading Thompson/Center Encore pistol. The boar was sparring with a smaller hog, and I was able to approach within 30 yards. From a sitting position, I launched a .370-grain Thompson/ Center MaxiBall powered by 100 grains of Pyrodex pellets, which is a stout pistol load with killing power in excess of the .44 Remington magnum. The boar ran 30 yards and went down. On receiving the hit, which penetrated 27 inches of tough hog to the off-side shoulder and lodged just beneath the gristle plate, the hog ran in the direction it was facing. Standing beside me during this encounter was a guide armed with a .270 Winchester rifle. He was good insurance as I could not hope to reload the muzzleloader in time to stop a charge.

A SOUTHERN HOG HUNT
Fellow writer and friend John Trussell took two hogs in three days from a Georgia wildlife management area. He knew the area well because his son Trent had taken his first deer there when he was 11 years old. On

this excursion, John was alone because Trent was away at college. This is the story John related to me:

> I had a relatively new hunting implement in my hands—a superb shooting TenPoint QX-4 crossbow with a 175-pound draw weight that hurled an arrow at 313 fps. The arrow was so quick that it seemed to disappear into the target as soon as it was released. I was shooting a 2219 aluminum shaft that weighed 420 grains with a Muzzy 100-grain three-bladed broadhead.
>
> As I eased down the creek bottom with the wind in my face, I hoped to intercept a deer or hog that heavily used this area for the white acorns that dropped from the trees and cool water that bubbled from the ground. This fall had been especially dry, and I knew the water was a particularly effective attractant.
>
> I stopped on a low rise for a few minutes, and as I watched the woods around me, I noticed a patch of black fur moving very slowly about 60 yards away. Was it a wild pig or a black bear? Both were common in these woods and just a glimpse of dark fur was not sufficient for a definitive identification. Through my binoculars, I saw one wild pig and then another, each probably weighing 125 pounds, which makes for excellent eating.
>
> Observing that the hogs were going to cross below me, I decided to close the distance. I quickly took a new position as the wild pigs moved to within 40 yards to eagerly feed on the acorns. Easing the TenPoint crossbow to my shoulder, I put the middle dot of my red-dot scope on the closest pig's shoulder and slid off the safety. After I squeezed the trigger, the crossbow's thump seemed instantaneous with the arrow's smacking the wild pig. The hit was solid, and I saw the arrow exit the hog's body and slide into the leaves behind him. After waiting a few minutes for the pig to expire, I followed a heavy blood trail to my soon-to-be barbequed pig. This was the second wild pig that I had taken from this spot in three days.

John's first pig was a 150-pound boar, but the hunt for this animal did not go quite as smoothly. His first arrow deflected from a twig, and the hog ran off. Fortunately, he spotted the hog again some 300 yards away and quietly sneaked through the damp area to close within 30 yards of the feeding hog. When he was about 20 yards away, he shot another arrow. This time the hit looked good, and he waited a few minutes before following a faint blood trail. Within fifteen minutes, he found the hog again, but it was not quite dead. He finished it with a second arrow.

John's experiences hunting wild hogs are typical. The brushy and palmetto-choked areas inhabited by the South's hogs make shot placement difficult and deflected arrows are common. It is not unusual to follow a faint blood trail and find a live, but mad, hog at the end of it. Southern hogs typically range over a wide area, but they often return to favored feeding and watering spots. John knew this spot with its bubbling spring and heavy crop of white oak acorns could be depended upon to draw game decade after decade.

In the South, hogs also can be taken as "targets of opportunity" while deer hunting. Either species is an acceptable result for most southern hunters. Even if hunters don't want the hogs for eating, taking these pesky animals helps to control their numbers and reduce damage to food plots.

JAVELINA

When I lived in Arizona, the spring javelina hunt was an annual event that I always looked forward to. When rifle hunting, I usually would sit on a good vantage point and use a glass to locate animals, and then I would stalk close enough for a 100-yard shot with my .308 Winchester rifle. Getting within archery range was considerably more difficult and required slow, careful stalking during which I paid particular attention to the wind. Several times when attempting to stalk pigs with a bow, the wind gave me away. Like true hogs, javelinas don't see particularly well, but they have an excellent sense of smell, and the variable desert winds are not the hunter's friend.

A Mexican javelina shot by the Throubridges with an Excalibur crossbow. This javelina was taken while feeding on corn scattered down a sendero, which is a cleared dozer track pushed through the thick brush and cactus.

In Mexico, javelinas are hunted in a different manner. Because it is difficult to sneak quietly through the thick brushy and thorny bottoms to get close enough to a hog for a shot, a dozer track is pushed through the mesquite brush and corn is placed in a long strip, piles, or a strip leading to a pile. When the javelinas come out into the open to feed on the corn, a crossbow hunter has an opportunity to take them as they feed.

Bill and Kath Throubridge were hunting Mexican javelina with their crossbows when they positioned themselves along a sendero and waited. Javelinas were spotted a couple hundred yards away, and they debated whether to move closer or wait for the animals to feed toward them. With two hunters, a guide, and a cameraman, they were not as mobile as an individual hunter. Ultimately, they did a bit of both: They relocated farther up the road and waited for the javelina to feed down to them. Kath shot the first hog with an Excalibur Exocet 175-pound pull crossbow using carbon arrows and a 100-grain Wasp Boss broadhead. After the shot, the herd scattered but did not go far. Bill walked a few feet into the brush and took a fleeting shot at a rapidly moving animal. He made a good hit, and both animals were soon recovered.

Of all the world's piglike animals, the javelina are among the smallest, and a 150-pound pull crossbow has ample power to bring one down. As always, the shot needs to be correctly placed. Because the crossbow is relatively silent and the animals usually are found in heavy cover, a shot javelina will often stay relatively close, making it possible to get a shot at a second animal while the herd reorganizes. Once you shoot, reload immediately and look around carefully as you search for your downed javelina. Another pig may be only a few feet away. If cornered, javelina will charge in an attempt to escape, but in general, they are relatively inoffensive animals. They like to hold up in caves and abandoned mining tunnels when the heat is intense and feed during the mornings and afternoons. When the temperature turns moderate during the winter months, they feed later in the day. During rainy weather, they will come out to take advantage of wet ground and relatively easy rooting. In higher elevations, they feed on acorns when available, and sometimes they may be encountered while deer hunting. The little javelina is worth putting on your "to hunt someday" list.

AFRICAN BUSHPIG

When Whitetail University's Wade Noland had the opportunity to hunt bushpigs in the Limpopo Province of South Africa, he used TenPoint's ProElite crossbow with 185 pounds of pull and a 100-grain three-bladed broadhead with a cutting point. To hunt bushpigs, he shot from a tree blind when the animals came to bait, a method similar to what he used

Warthog mother and offspring enjoying fresh grass in South Africa. Both sows and boars have long teeth.

to hunt leopard. Instead of a fresh kill for bait, a mixture of fermented beer and corn was put out for the pigs.

This high-tech set-up included a light controlled by a rheostat positioned directly over the bait and a sensitive microphone hung nearby. The hunt plan was to wait until the hunters could hear the hogs feeding and then to slowly turn up the light until the crossbowmen had sufficient visibility to shoot the pigs. The first night's wait brought honey badgers and porcupines but no bushpigs. Near midnight on the second night, the bushpigs came in to eat in the pitch-black dark. After the hogs were feeding, the light was turned up and one hog at the bait presented a broadside shot. The shot was taken and the hog ran off.

This experience comes as close to a classic leopard hunt as can be done without actually shooting a leopard, especially since the guide commonly baited leopard from this same blind. The dicey part of this trip came when the guide and Noland followed the wounded pig into the bush. The pig had been well hit, but finding it in the dark in an area frequented by leopards brought its own challenge. The guide with the gun led the way, and Noland followed with a light. The crossbow was left at the tree. This adventure had a happy ending as the bushpig was found dead some 30 yards away. For Noland, the hunt provided all the excitement of a leopard hunt at much less costs, and the result was a worthy animal not frequently harvested by visiting hunters.

If you go to Africa, be sure to inquire as to what hogs might be available in the hunt area. The warthog, the giant forest hog, or the bushpig all provide ample amounts of excitement, while also giving you a memorable hunt, an exotic trophy, and some good camp meat.

12

Bear Hunting with a Crossbow

Black bear are the third most common big-game animals sought by North American hunters. Only white-tailed deer and hogs are more popular. Black bear populations are stable or increasing in traditional bear states such as Alaska and Maine, and their numbers are steadily rising in eastern states, including New Jersey and even where I live in central Georgia. Ironically, the same week I went on a Canadian bear hunt, a black bear visited my hometown and caused considerable commotion for half a day before he was tranquilized and carted off.

Just as grizzly and brown bear are regularly taken by conventional archers, crossbowmen have taken them, too. Although most of us will not have a chance to confront these "superbear," hunting a black bear is an experience guaranteed to get your heart thumping.

BEAR HUNTING IN QUEBEC

When Bill Troubridge had a cancellation on a bear hunt in Quebec and asked if I would like to come and try Excalibur's new Exocet 200 crossbow, I did not take long to consider my reply. I sent a packet of electrons from my computer asking when and where. I would be attending a writers' conference in Madison, Wisconsin, and from there, it would be a short flight to Toronto.

While in Madison, I called to confirm my flight and was informed that I would need an original copy of my birth certificate or a passport to get into Canada and return. Drat! Years ago when I lived in Alaska, I crossed into Canada many times with only a state driver's license, so I did not think about needing a passport. My only option was to leave Wisconsin and drive all night to get to Georgia and extract my passport from my safety-deposit box and then fly from Atlanta to Toronto. Either that, or forget the hunt.

Black bear, such as this 200-pound specimen, are increasing in numbers throughout North America and are becoming a popular pursuit of crossbow hunters. Not only are these animals exciting to hunt, but their meat is excellent to eat, especially when they have been feeding on a diet of fruit, nuts, and vegetation.

On the flight to Canada, I reviewed the information that had been sent to me about the hunt, which would take place in the Reserve Papineau-Labelle approximately 90 miles north of Ottawa. The hunt would be conducted by Bernard "Ben" Arsenault, president of ACI Expeditions. We would be staying in cabins and taking our meals at the Riviere La Lievre Lodge. The literature stressed that we would need a good bug suit as mosquitoes and black flies would be plentiful.

Each day would begin with breakfast at 9 A.M., after which the guides freshened the baits. Hunters could fish, rest, or shoot their crossbows until 2 P.M. when lunch was served. All hunters were on their stands by 4 P.M. where they remained until the guides picked them up between 9:30 and midnight. When everyone was back in camp, we had supper.

After arriving, I sighted in the Exocet 200 and found that I could cock it easily with the rope cocking aid. The crossbow fit me well, and I had no problem adjusting the Vari Zone scope. This scope adjusts the cross-hairs for velocities of between 250 and 350 feet per second to allow the lower crosshair lines in the scope's reticle to be approximately on target at 20, 30, 40, and 50 yards, thus eliminating the need for hold-over at longer ranges. A few downward clicks and I was dead-on at 20 yards.

I was told that all of the stands would be 20 yards or closer to the baits. Ideally, when the bear would come to the bait, it would pass next to some drums or barrels to allow the hunter to judge its size and ultimately offer a broadside shot. The lungs of a bear are large and extend through the front quarter of the animal. The ideal bear-hunt game plan went something like this: A shot behind the shoulder blade would pass through both lungs and quickly kill the bear. Once down, a black bear would utter its "death moans" as it expired and give the hunter a final fix on where it was.

First day out, bear were spotted by two hunters, but they came out too late to be seen clearly and did not offer shots. Because the weather was in the high 80s and low 90s, the bear were not inclined to move. The second day was the ladies' day as two of them killed their first bears. Sheila Foulkrod, wife of well-known archer and hunter Bob Foulkrod, took a 260-pound black bear while her husband filmed the encounter, and Christine Kinsey scored with a 164-pound bear.

Sheila Foulkrod's First Bear

The whispered interchange between a wife who was doing the shooting and a husband who was doing the filming went something like the following:

> "Sheila, there is a bear."
> "Can I shoot?"
> "He's going into the woods to circle the bait. Wait."
> About 45 minutes pass.
> "There he is at the bait. Can I shoot now?"
> "Wait."
> "He's next to the bucket. Can I shoot?"
> "Wait."
> "I've got a good shot."
> "Wait."
> "But. . . ."
> "Wait."
> "How about now?"
> "OK. Behind the shoulder."
> "Now?"
> "Yes. Now."

Sheila fires the shot, the crossbow arrow hits behind the shoulder, and the bear runs off. Shortly later, a death moan is heard.

"Congratulations. It was a good shot, and he did not go far."

"Why didn't you let me shoot?"

"I needed to get some film for the show."

"But he was right there. I was afraid that he was going to just go off into the woods again, and we would lose him."

"He came back, didn't he?"

"Yes, but you should have let me shoot him."

"I don't care if I ever shoot another bear, but I had to have some film on your first bear for the video. Otherwise, we might as well not have come."

They got their film, and it will be aired on a video produced by Bob Foulkrod. When Foulkrod, a well-known archer, was asked how he was introduced to the crossbow, an interesting story emerged. Foulkrod explained that he was as anti-crossbow as any bowhunter when the first attempts were made to introduce crossbows in his native state of Pennsylvania.

"I even wrote that I would do all in my power to resist the introduction of crossbows during deer season, but if the state adopted it, I would not fight it anymore," he related. "As it turned out, this was a knee-jerk reaction on my part, and when I had a chance to really think about it, I completely changed my mind. In particular, the crossbow allowed me to hunt for three years with my 87-year-old father before he died. Later, when Sheila was struggling so much with a bow, she switched to the crossbow and is now able to accompany me on archery hunts.

"Who, after thinking about it, would deny people like this the chance to get into the woods with their loved ones and hunt? When my grandchildren want to go hunting with grandpa, it is likely that their first big game hunts will be with a crossbow."

Sheila remarked that Bob's father's success with the crossbow caused her to think, "If he can do it, I can too." And so she has. She said that the crossbow put an effective hunting instrument in her hands and gave her confidence. This was her first bear, but she had already taken wild hogs and several deer with her crossbow.

Christine Kinsey's Bear

Most often when bear are shot over bait by a solitary hunter, the hunter must first make sure that the bear is legal (sows with cubs may not be shot). Then he must size it up, make a killing shot, and do the best he can to mark the direction of the bear's departure. Christine Kinsey did all of this when she killed her bear.

"I had seen a bear the day before," she said. "When this one came into the bait, I waited until it was beside a bucket so that I could see how big it was. It was taller than a 5-gallon pail, so I knew it was a shooter. Although it was getting darker by the second, I could still see the cross-hairs settle right behind the shoulder. When I shot, the bear ran. I marked the direction, so we could find it later."

Guide Yannick Martel remarked that he wished that all of his gun hunters had done as well. "Sometimes they don't know where, or if, they hit the bear or what direction it went. Mrs. Kinsey did it right." With the help of her safety harness, the two of them drug the 164-pound bear out of the woods and into the truck. With the time taken to recover the two bears that night, it was near midnight before we returned to the lodge.

The Hunt Resumes

By the start of the third day, none of the guys had scored even though bear visited all of the baits each night. The third and fourth days were a repeat of day one. Bears were seen, but they were either too small or came too late to shoot. I was moved to another bait and on the third day of the hunt glimpsed a very large bear, but he spotted me in the stand and moved off into the woods. The last day of the five-day hunt, the guides relocated my stand to another tree.

On this day, only three hunters went out. I was at my stand where I had seen bear but had no shot opportunity the previous two days. Bill Throubridge was filming his friend Dan Miller, and a rifle hunter who was not with our group was also hunting over bait.

Like always, Yannick sweetened the bait, this time with vanilla, before he left. I started up my ThermaCell to help keep the bugs off me and prepared to wait. It was hotter than the previous day, and I did not know what my chances would be. Little game appeared to be moving when we came in. The day before when it was slightly cooler, we had seen grouse feeding on the roadside. Today, they apparently were in the treetops being cooled by the slight breezes that gently rocked the limbs.

I had sat from 5:30 to 8 P.M., when looking over my shoulder, I saw a bear coming through the thick stand of firs. Even if I could have stood and turned without the bear detecting me, the crossbow limbs would not have cleared the tree. Turning my head, I could see him pass directly behind me at about 30 yards. This distance would have offered a good pistol shot, which is illegal in Canada, but there was nothing I could do with a crossbow. Reversing direction, the bear retraced his steps and decided to come into the bait from my right.

This time I had enough light to see well. I raised the crossbow, took off the safety, and prepared for the shot. When I shot, the bear was perhaps

Christine Kinsey took this 165-pound black bear with an Excaliber crossbow.
According to her guide, she did everything right: choosing a good bear,
knowing where it exited the bait area, listening for the death moan, and
having a safety harness to drag the bear out of the woods.

15 yards away, and the arrow hit the animal behind the shoulder. The bear
ran in the direction it was pointed, and a few seconds later I heard the first
of three death moans delivered in rapid succession. I had taken my first
crossbow bear, which turned out to be 200 pounds. Each of the three hunters that went out that night took bear. Dan Miller's bear, the largest at
over 250 pounds, traveled about 130 yards and was a hard pull for three
men to get out of the woods. The rifle hunter also took a 150-pounder.

How the Crossbows Performed

When asked what he thought of crossbows, Ben Arsenault, president of ACI Expeditions, said that he was impressed both by their performance as hunting instruments and by the quality of the hunters who used them. In the previous two years, nine hunters had taken shots at bear with crossbows. Of these, eight killed their bears with one arrow, and each bear had been recovered. The other hunter had missed his shot when the arrow passed between the bear's legs.

"At first I did not know what to expect [with crossbows], but they kill good, and the people who come here know how to shoot them," Arsenault concluded. Was this simply an elite group of shooters? Some were, but certainly not all. I would not put myself in that category, and this was the ladies' first crossbow hunt for bear. No doubt, experience helped, particularly in attempting to gauge the size of the bears, but even average to inexperienced shooters had performed well.

As this was an Excalibur-sponsored hunt, the company's crossbows were used. Among those that killed bear were a 150-pound draw Vixen and 175-pound and 200-pound draw Exocets. Only the Vixen, which was used on the largest bear, failed to penetrate completely as it struck and broke on the right leg bone of the big bear. The other four Gold Tip carbon arrows and 100-grain Wasp Boss three-bladed fixed points passed completely through the bears. Arrow placement was good on all the shots, which led to quick kills.

How would the crossbows perform against a really big bear, such as the Alaskan brown bear with its heavy coat of fur? Bill Throubridge recommends the same 100-grain Wasp Boss head and a 2219 arrow shot from a 200- to 225-pound pull weight crossbow. He personally uses the company's 225-pound draw ExoMax, although he said that a 200-pound draw crossbow would perform well on the big but comparatively thin-skinned bear. Bill's ExoMax would be considered the crossbow equivalent of the 375 Holland and Holland magnum, a caliber generally considered appropriate for the huge Alaskan bear.

Hunts at the Papineau Labelle Reserve may be arranged through ACI Outfitters by contacting Bernard Arsenault at 4225 Lac Corbeau, St-Damien, Quebec, Canada J0K 2E0 or by e-mail at bernard.arsenault@sympatico.ca.

STALKING AND STAND HUNTING FOR BEAR

Not all bear hunting is done over bait. In many parts of the western United States and Canada, black bear are so numerous that they may be stalked or stand hunted. The best approach is either to find a natural food source that the bear are using and sit over it or slowly move through a

The steep slopes along Idaho's Salmon River contain scattered cultivated fields on the river bottoms and fruit orchards on the slopes of the small tributaries. Besides black bears, this excellent hunting country has healthy populations of elk, white-tailed deer, and wild turkeys.

feeding area looking and listening for bears. In much of the more open country, bear can be spotted moving from one ridge to the next. With considerable luck, a crossbow hunter or archer will be able to intersect a bear's travel path and ambush it at close range.

I once went on a muzzleloader hunt near Riggins, Idaho, a steep, moderately forested land that during the past century had been extensively planted with fruit trees to supply nearby mining camps. These trees and their wild descendants grew thickly up the steep slopes and provided fine eating for the local, and very large, bear population. All of this property had been in private hands since the late 1800s, and this two-day hunt was on a ranch located along a small tributary of the Salmon River.

As the hunt was sponsored by PowerBelt Bullets, I was expected to use this product fired from a Winchester Apex .50-caliber muzzleloading rifle. After arriving by plane in Boise, I was to go on a factory tour before driving to the hunt area to sight in the gun and hunt for two days. On such hunts, a participant has little choice but to shoot the ani-

Bear droppings with yellow plum pits, a sure sign that bears were feeding here not long ago. Within a few hundred yards of this pile of droppings, the author shot his bear.

mal he is shown and there is no time for scouting, which should be a strong component of anyone's hunt. Because the ranch owner would be guiding the hunters, we had a good opportunity of finding bear in a hurry. The day before I arrived, fourteen bear had been seen along with a good number of elk and a few white-tailed deer.

Bear sign was everywhere. We took four-wheelers to where we could spot bears coming into clearings, and we slowly walked the steep access roads listening for the sound of breaking branches as the bears fed. The first day I saw a lot of beautiful country but only two small bear. The second day I was to sit over a trail junction at the head of a draw thickly covered in plumb bushes. Sooner or later a bear would expose itself, and I would take it with the rifle. On the rock overlook, I was downwind of the intersection of the road, two creeks, and a small open grassy creek bottom, a fine setup that any bow, pistol, or crossbow hunter would enjoy.

Wayne Hungate and his son Drake glassing for bear. Drake's .22 is for mountain grouse. Most of the shot opportunities on this spot-and-stalk hunt occurred from 30 to 300 yards. In this brushy, dry country, it is difficult to stalk within crossbow range.

As it turned out, we heard the sound of a feeding bear and walked up the road to spot him some 30 yards away. I quickly took him with the muzzleloader, which ended my hunt. That night I cut up the bear, froze and packaged the meat, and prepared for the flight home. That fruit-fed bear made for excellent eating.

13

HUNTING IN AFRICA

Africa was, and remains, the greatest big-game hunting continent on earth. Nowhere else can a hunter expect to see up to 20 different species of big-game animals a day. A first-time hunter out for plains game can expect to find at least one animal that he wants to shoot every day. Very often an inexpensive five-species game hunting package enables a hunter to shoot a kudu, zebra, wildebeest, warthog, and impala over five days for about $5,000. This fee includes trophy fees, the equivalent of four-star lodging and meals, skinning, airport pickup and delivery, and a large number of intangible, but no less valuable, personal experiences that will remain with the hunter for the rest of his life.

Each year, the number of restrictions on transporting rifles and ammunition out of the United States and back seems to increase, but the good news is that, in almost every case, you will encounter no problems flying with your archery equipment as regular baggage stowed in the cargo hole. While the gun hunters will have to stand in endless lines and pay extra money to have their paperwork processed, the crossbow hunter can take his anciently derived hunting implements anywhere he wants to go.

Depending on the African country that you are hunting, you should start planning at least six months ahead by selecting an outfitter that caters to archery hunters and can offer the beasties that you wish to take. One of your first decisions about a trip is what particular species you want to hunt. High on almost everyone's first-time-hunt list are some of Africa's really handsome animals, such as kudu, oryx, impala, and zebra, with a warthog and one of the smaller antelope species thrown in for good measure. Not all outfitters will have all these species available.

On later trips, you may want to try other species such as Cape buffalo, so look for outfitters that have good populations in their hunting

Buffalo will be commonly seen but not necessarily shot during a safari. Safari hunting is most often a question of what the hunter can afford, and four or five species of plains game typically may be taken for the price of one buffalo.

areas and compare prices and the success rates of their archers. Buffalo hunts are longer, typically a minimum of fourteen days, but they also allow taking some species of plains game.

Some challenging but seldom hunted crossbow species are giraffe, hippopotamus, and crocodile. Not only are they large animals, but the environments where they live make them difficult to take with a crossbow. Nearly 4 inches of hide protect the giraffe's lungs, and because hippo and crocodiles are mostly aquatic, hunting them means many hours of sitting in a blind at near dark waiting for one to come up on shore. Keep in mind that a mature hippo will outweigh a rhino, and hippos kill more people in Africa than any other game animals.

Successful crossbow hunters in Africa will hunt over waterholes or bait or watch game trails. True, you may ride in a safari car and attempt to stalk, but because you are armed with something as clumsy as a crossbow, your success rate will be low. Stalking is also difficult in the typically dry weather that prevails during most of the hunting season. With good fortune, a gun hunter may get within 100 yards, but this is much too far for a crossbow shot.

African animals often are found in herds, which may contain several hundred, or even several thousand, individual animals. For the North American deer hunter accustomed to seeing one or a few animals at a

Access to the hunt area is usually by safari car. On a safari, game is so plentiful that it is commonly spotted from the road. Often a vehicle is used to go from waterhole to waterhole in hopes of finding fresh tracks of a large buffalo or elephant.

time, hunting a herd takes some getting used to. Not only must he pick out such trophy animals as the zebra stallion or blue wildebeest bull, but he must have a clear shot so that the arrow does not pass through one animal and hit another behind it. Even if it is a superficial or accidental hit, the hunter pays for each animal from which blood is drawn.

Selecting a trophy-size specimen of each of these numerous game animals is often a visiting hunter's biggest challenge. An enormous Eland may weigh 3,000 pounds but only have 8-inch horns. It is easy to pick out the largest of a group of animals, but is it of trophy size? This is where the professional hunter who accompanies you on a hunt will earn his keep. He knows the game and what trophy animals look like. Still, the decision to shoot or not depends on the hunter who ultimately pays for all game hit.

In addition to shooting practice, the hunter who plans to go to Africa should look at photos or, better yet, real trophies of the different African species so that he can better judge the size of animals that he wants to take. This is another reason for deciding beforehand what species you want to hunt. After all, this is your safari, and you will be the one who pulls the trigger. The professional hunter and tracker can help you out in the field, but the final choice of what to shoot, when to shoot, and even if you should shoot will be yours. Just like when hunting North American whitetails, Africa will have some areas that will produce better trophies than others.

On the continent of Africa, climates vary from tropical rainforest to desert, and each has its own distinctive game animals. The political climate may change radically as well. Each year since World War II, armed conflict has occurred in some part of Africa. Countries may also radically change their game-hunting regulations, including closing their country to hunting, anytime they see fit. Among the most stable and hunter-friendly countries at the moment is the Republic of South Africa.

Almost all hunting in South Africa occurs on privately owned game ranches, many of which are bordered by 12-foot electric fences. Within the fences are huge areas containing tens of thousands of acres that are preserved in as wild a condition as possible to provide sufficient water and food for maintaining their game populations. On these ranches, large populations of the various antelopes, wildebeest, elephants, giraffes, buffalo, monkeys, baboons, and predators such as lions, leopards, smaller cats, hyenas, and native African wild dogs roam. These ranches have done much to ensure the survival of the white rhino and are actively working to foster repatriation of the black rhino.

THE HUNTING DAY

A typical day on an African safari begins with wake-up at about 5:30 A.M. followed by a breakfast of coffee and homemade bread or rolls at 6. Then the professional hunter and you load up in the safari car and travel to where you will sit for most of the morning, most often either a permanent or temporary blind set up at a waterhole, feed station, or trail crossing. The parade of animals will start almost immediately. First, warthogs will arrive, followed by any of the twenty-odd different species of game that will pass that day. Of all of these animals, there may be one that you want to take and you may, or may not, be given a shot opportunity. The animals may be facing you or other animals may be too close to take a shot. Through all of this, you must be quiet and move slowly.

African animals know that they are venerable when they are at water so even when a herd drinks, it does not hang around long. After drinking, the animals typically move away from the water and return to the comparative safety of the surrounding forest or scrublands.

While sitting in the blind, you should have your crossbow cocked and an arrow placed in it ready to shoot. Sometimes you will be able to

This leopard-killed impala had been drug to the road by a mother leopard. She and her half-grown offspring ran when we approached by vehicle. This kill was made within 100 yards of the safari camp. Africa is still a wild place, but as long as they find an abundant supply of game animals, even predators such as leopards and lions will leave man alone.

shoot from a rest, but most of the time the crossbow will be shot off-hand through a window in the blind. If you're lucky, you may be able to take the animal while it is drinking and standing still. Or perhaps the only opportunity you may have is a quartering shot when it is turning to leave. Choose your shot opportunity carefully and make sure on a quartering shot that you aim far enough back of the shoulder that the arrow can drive through the lungs toward the off-side shoulder.

With good hits through the lungs, the wounded animals will not go far. Most are recovered within 30 yards, but a few may travel four times that distance. Warthogs, which are comparatively small and typically do not leave heavy blood trails, are often the hardest to find. They may go down aardvark holes or head into heavy brush before they expire. Always allow at least twenty minutes to pass before going after any African game. When approaching an animal, have an arrow in your cocked crossbow ready to shoot in case the animal is not dead.

Your trophy will most likely be retrieved with a winch mounted on the safari car. If the car can approach close enough to the animal, you will be able to pull the animal onto the back of the vehicle for transport back to camp. Once there, the game will be skinned and put into a cooler. Outside of what meat may be used in camp and for bait, the remainder of the animal is usually sold to the local butcher. Nothing is wasted; even the bones are ground into bone meal.

After returning to camp and chowing down on a combination of breakfast and lunch, you will probably have a few free hours in the middle of the day to nap, ride around the hunt area, go to town, or do whatever you wish to do. You might even want to take a swim in the camp's swimming pool. Later in the day, preparations are made for the afternoon hunt. You might return to the same area, if that looked promising, or be moved to a new area where the next species of game on your list might be more abundant. If you have taken your kudu on the first day, as I did, your professional hunter will ask what animal you want to try for next and put you in a blind near where these animals pass by fairly often. To build confidence, try shooting the smaller animals on your list first and then go for the larger ones. In any event, you should be prepared to take any critter on your list if it offers you a high-percentage shot and is big enough.

I have always advocated using a laser rangefinder on crossbow hunts since, when looking at new species, you may find it difficult to use the size of the animal as a rough approximation of range. Rangefinders can eliminate this ambiguity. Even when shooting from a blind, it is convenient to know with certainty, for example, that a particular stump is at 40 yards and a distinctive rock at 20.

For me, the best part of the day comes after everyone arrives back at camp, and we sit around a campfire, reliving the day's activities over a delicious meal that may feature the game you shot. This time of day is known as storytelling time, and I am pleased to say that it's a well-practiced art in Africa. The professional hunter will tell you about some of his interesting experiences with game and clients, and you will have a chance to relate some of your most interesting hunts. Rather than a recitation of what animals you have taken and where, the most interesting stories will be about success snatched from the jaws of catastrophic failure or interesting people you have met.

WHAT TO TAKE

When going to a far-off country to hunt with an instrument as uncommonly used as a crossbow, it pays to take two of them, even if one is of considerably lesser quality than your principal hunting crossbow. Baggage may be lost or a piece on one of the crossbows may be broken in transit. Safari time is too costly and hunting opportunities too infrequent to lose time making trips to one of the larger cities in an attempt to find repair parts or replace a crossbow. Sure, the professional hunter probably has a gun he can loan or rent to you, but if you were going to Africa for a crossbow hunt, using a firearm defeats the purpose.

Thinking about killing animals that weigh between 1,000 and 2,000 pounds can cause any rational person to wonder whether he and his equipment are up to the task. Plains Indians hunted buffalo from horseback by galloping up alongside the bison and shooting an arrow into its flank at point-blank range while both horseman and buffalo were moving over the prairie at break-neck speed. The weapons they used were short selfbows and, by modern standards, had low pull weights of 40 to 55 pounds.

Arrows from these bows killed buffalo, eventually, but the Indian hunter didn't care if the buffalo died quickly or sometime the next day. He knew it would ultimately be recovered. The modern hunting ethic requires that the game be killed as quickly as possible. The crossbow arrow must not only penetrate such things as caked-on mud, a 2- to 3-inch layer of tangled fur, and a hide, but it must find a way between the ribs and then penetrate as deep as possible into the enormous chest cavity. Because you need a crossbow with a minimum draw weight of 175 pounds, you may want to think about purchasing a crossbow with a pull of 200 to 225 pounds.

I suggest taking two crossbows and packing them in different pieces of luggage. Pack fewer clothes since they can be laundered daily. Although it may get into the 90s during the day, it cools off quickly after dark. I suggest taking a warm sweater, a light jacket, three shirts, and two pairs of hunting trousers. If you are going to purchase a set of African bush clothes, choose a darker color if you will be hunting in wooded areas and a light tan or sandstone if you will be hunting in a more desertlike environment.

American green-gray-toned camos and patterns designed for the desert Southwest are excellent choices for Africa. Since you will be hunting mostly from blinds, almost any color will do as long as it is not white, but it is usually better to go with darker tones than light ones. Most African countries do not require hunters to wear international orange, and some may have restrictions on wearing what might be considered military-style camouflage because of ongoing problems with insurgents or separatist groups. Your outfitter will be your best guide for clothing selection. One set each of boots and shoes and two pairs of socks for each is usually all that is needed.

A typical professional hunter will wear shorts, tennis shoes, and a safari shirt or jacket. Since Africa contains many things that scratch, bite, or sting, visiting hunters are well advised to wear long pants and more clothes in general. Almost every morning my professional hunter complained of the cold, but since he was wearing nothing much heavier than underwear, I can't say I was surprised. Extra layers of clothing can be taken off as temperatures climb later in the day.

Since the sun is bright in Africa, a hat or cap and sunglasses are necessary. Most North Americans do not get much sun at home so suntan lotion may save considerable discomfort. Because you may be scratched by thorn bushes, a small tube of antiseptic ointment and some band aids will probably be useful. South Africa is not washcloth country, so if you want one, take one with you. The same applies to some food products —if you need to use an artificial sweetener, for example, take a supply with you. Also, make sure you take an adequate supply of prescription medicines.

Many hunt camps have swimming pools, so be sure to take along a swimsuit or pair of swimming trunks as nude swimming is not an accustomed activity in polite South African society.

If you use any type of tobacco products, you better take them with you or buy them at the airport when you arrive. Like in the United States, fewer South Africans smoke cigarettes. A few crusty old "professional white hunters" may still cling to their pipes, but cigarette smoking is uncommon in the hunt camps.

Local beer, South African wines, and soft drinks will be provided at the camp, but if you have any special brands you like, buy them at the duty-free shop as you leave the United States and take them with you.

Do not plan on having access to a town so take whatever you think you might need with you. I always carry my own flashlight with batteries and use it to help get out of the blind with all of my gear after dark. A flashlight also comes in handy at camp. I keep it beside my bed and use it whenever I leave the room at night. I also pack a small folding saw, which I may need to move or make a blind or to trim an offending piece of thorn bush.

WHAT TO LEAVE BEHIND

When going on an African safari hunt, you will not need to take binoculars, hunting knives, a game field-dressing kit, game-dragging gear, meat-packaging materials, or game-dressing gloves. All the game will be retrieved, processed, and butchered by the outfitter staff. In fact, they are so efficient that you should be sure to take all the photos you want of your trophy game immediately. If you wait, you may be left with shots of a butchered carcass hanging in the meat house. Remember that no meat may be brought back into the United States, and this includes biltong, which is made from wild game and sold at the airport.

A lightweight rain jacket may be useful and can serve double duty as a windbreaker on top of a sweater on cool mornings. However, you

Skinning the author's kudu. Although skinning could have occurred at the kill site, it is more efficiently done back at camp, where the meat receives proper care and management. No meat is wasted. Because the hunter may not bring any meat back into the United States, it is sold on the South African market.

will not need a heavy rain suit. If hunting for buffalo, a set of calf-high rubber boots that have already been broken in and two pairs of matching socks may be helpful. The alternative is to wear tennis shoes and hunt with wet feet.

When flying to Africa, you are allowed two checked bags, one piece of carry-on luggage, and one smaller bag. Keep in mind that the maximum free weight allowance, which is 70 pounds when flying from the United States to Africa, drops to 22 pounds per person within Africa itself, although the number of free pieces of allowable luggage remains the same.

ABOUT SPOUSES

All safari companies have day rates for nonhunting spouses or other family members who accompany you to Africa, and most safari camps provide separate bungalows for hunters traveling with their families. Although the accommodations and the food are excellent, there is really not much for nonhunters to do. A day certainly could be spent driving around and looking for game, or perhaps a trip to town or a nearby park could be arranged. These activities must be specified when the hunt is booked so that arrangements can be made, tickets purchased, and any other advance planning completed to ensure that accompanying members also have an enjoyable African trip.

On my South African trip, I would not hesitate to take my wife.

COSTS

An African hunt is expensive, but the costs will probably never be cheaper than they are now. When booking a hunt, find out if the trophy fees are included and what other fees would have to be paid. A hunt can be priced very inexpensively, but the hunter may be in for sticker shock when he learns that the buffalo that he is about to shoot carries a trophy fee of $8,000 in addition to the $350-a-day rate that he is paying. E-mail makes it fairly easy to correspond with your safari company, and organizations such as the Safari Club hold annual banquets, which allow prospective hunters to meet their potential outfitters face-to-face. This alone is worth the costs of joining the club.

For my last hunt in 2004, the package for five species of plains game cost $5,300, which included the trophy fees for taking a kudu, zebra, blue wildebeest, warthog, and impala. Round-trip air fare was $1,300, and with tips and advanced processing of the gun-importing paperwork (an additional $150), this part of the costs rounded out to $6,800. The price rises to $7,800 when you add a $500 dipping fee for the trophies, a $100 crating fee, a $250 air shipment charge to the United States, and $300 for a bonded agent in New York to receive and process the animal. Next, add on taxidermy costs. A nice zebra rug will cost between $10 and $40 a square foot, and a head and shoulder mounted kudu runs around $700.

Payment for the trip to and from Africa to hunt does not end a hunter's financial obligations. Treating and transporting the trophies requires payment months after the safari is done, and the U.S. receiving agent must be paid before the taxidermist ever receives the trophies eight to twelve months after the hunt is over.

If you mounted all of your trophies, the costs of the trip quickly exceeds $10,000. By having only bleached skulls mounted and just the backskins tanned, rather than mounted into rugs, the total cost of the trip can be brought in at slightly less than $10,000.

When I heard the prices, I was tempted to stack the skulls and horns with firewood and ceremoniously return them to the soil of Africa from whence they came rather than pay this series of outrageously accumulating fees. None of this is the safari operator's fault but rather the middlemen who take an unjustified cut. An alternative is to have the trophies finished in South Africa and then sent home. The problem with this is that if something goes wrong, you can't pound on your taxidermist's door, since he is half a world away in South Africa.

Is the price of an African hunt worth it? When comparing it to the cost of a hunting trip to Alaska or a hunt for trophy elk in the Rocky Mountain states, an African hunt will produce a greater variety of game in a shorter period of time and at less costs than anything comparable in North America. Hunting in an exotic place where lions walk and you are surrounded by the ghosts of fabled hunters of centuries past is an experience all its own. In the final analysis, the experience of the hunt itself, and not the game bagged, is the most valuable and lasts the longest. Your first African trip will be one of the crowning experiences of your life.

Africa is a huge continent, and the Republic of South Africa is only one country. Other countries offer other game than can be shot with crossbows and different hunting tools, but at the present time, a South African hunt is among the least expensive, safest, and most productive destinations for an initial safari.

14

OTHER HUNTING AND BOWFISHING OPPORTUNITIES

Although crossbows are mostly thought of as deer-gathering tools, they also have use for small-game hunting, turkey hunting, and bowfishing. With appropriate arrows and points, crossbows may take on these tasks even though they have their own difficulties when it comes to harvesting game and taking fish. Years ago when crossbows were prominent hunting instruments, a variety of points and shafts, along with multiple stones (usually baked clay) or single bullets, were designed for small game and waterfowl. Projectiles included arrows with baskets on the front designed to contain "stones"—a dangerous design since the shaft was attached to the crossbow and would rebound back at the shooter—or tumbling arrows, which were used to break the necks and wings of waterfowl.

I know of one person in modern times who lost an eye while trying to use a stone-throwing crossbow; therefore, I will confine the following discussion to arrows and points. Outside of using loose shot in a slurbow, which has a barrel, I don't know of any design that could reliably prevent an errant stone from striking the sight or bowstave and bouncing back at the shooter. Stonebows shown in period prints have sharply swaybacked shooting decks, and the front sight usually consisted of a large rectangular bridge with a pin on top that was supposed to allow unobstructed passage of the shot. These crossbows also had short throws so that the shot would experience minimal dispersion as it left the crossbow.

SMALL-GAME HUNTING

The concept was simple. I was going to take my Horton Hawk crossbow, file some field points flat to make 125-grain blunts, and go shoot squirrels. I always had taken three to five squirrels a trip with my muz-

Author with a Horton Hawk crossbow and the Georgia turkey he took over a food plot at about 20 yards. He used a 125-grain judo point with clipped extensions to transmit maximum shock to the turkey and penetrate deep enough for the shot to be fatal, yet remain in the bird to prevent it from taking flight. In practice, the turkey was violently attempting to beat its wings when the author approached it. He thinks it would have escaped if he had not reached it quickly.

zleloading shotguns and rifles, so I figured that bagging five squirrels with a crossbow should be no great feat.

Boy, was I wrong. As my supply of available arrows rapidly diminished, I came to several realizations: 1) Only ground shots were permissible. 2) Even if a squirrel was just a few feet up a tree, if I didn't have immediate access to a ladder I did not have a shot. 3) The blunt points drove so deep into trees that the arrows had to be screwed off the points. 4) Any contact with brush would spoil the shot. And most importantly, 5) Blunts perforated squirrels but did not kill them. Unless they were pinned to the ground or trees, the squirrels could still wiggle off the arrows.

The first squirrel I killed was easy. I was sitting in my tree stand when I spied a large gray squirrel foraging for acorns some 20 feet from

A Zwickey Scorpio driven almost to the fletching after most of the arrow had passed through a squirrel.

the base of the tree. After changing to a field-pointed arrow, I waited until the back of the squirrel presented a straightaway shot (to compensate for any trajectory changes), aimed at the midpoint of the squirrel, and shot. The arrow struck the squirrel through the spine and stuck it to the ground. As the squirrel struggled, I climbed down the tree and finished it off by breaking its neck.

"Nothing to it," I thought. "I will just make up some blunts and shoot squirrels."

When I told Excalibur's Bill Throubridge what I had in mind he replied, "Small-game hunting with a crossbow is a losing proposition unless you have a source of really inexpensive arrows. You lose so many buried in the ground and snow, that it's not really worthwhile."

With Bill's admonishment in mind, I bought two four-packs of Zwickey Scorpios. These stainless-steel spring assemblies with projecting arms that slide along an arrow shaft to keep the arrow from completely penetrating turkeys and small game are available in various shaft diameters, and I purchased some $^{22}/_{64}$ths to fit my Horton and Barnett shafts.

To match the weight of the 100-grain mechanical points that I was using in the Horton, I filed the field points down until the combined weight of the point and Scorpio equaled the weight of my deer-hunting point. My game plan was to quietly take a few squirrels as the opportunity arose when I was in my deer stand or walking from it.

About twenty-five shots later, I had lost four arrows and damaged the fletching on another four with the Scorpios, but had only bagged three squirrels and hit but lost another after it pulled itself off the arrow. I might have had a higher score if I had been shooting tame squirrels in a city park, rather than my frequently hunted wild population of busheytails.

After eight to ten trips and twenty-five shots, my crossbow squirrel stew was still awfully thin, until I took a nice doe to add to the pot. I shot the deer with a Barnett crossbow while attempting to take some squirrels with a 155-grain Judo point, which incorporates a Scorpio in its design. The advantage here is that Judo points have a broad blunt point to give more shock to the animal and the Scorpios keep the points from burying themselves in the soil. Also, since the Scorpio is fixed near the point, it does not ride up the shaft to mangle the fletching. The big disadvantage is that you have to resight your bow for these heavier points (about 155 grains) or hold off various amounts at different ranges to hit the squirrels. Swapping arrows back and forth while simultaneously hunting squirrels and deer can be difficult and less productive than focusing on one animal or the other.

Nonetheless, I persisted in my plan to hunt deer and take crossbow squirrels as incidental game. By season's end, I had accumulated five squirrels for my stew. The stew was good, and I did not have to worry about picking shot out of the meat, but I would have to rate my squirrel-hunting experience as being possible but not very practical. Certainly, however, some other interesting styles of small-game points might have provided better success. I had not yet exhausted the small-game killing ability of the crossbow.

TURKEY HUNTING

Turkey hunters who use crossbows would seem to have an advantage over conventional archers because much less movement is needed to get a crossbow ready to shoot. While the bowhunter must draw his bow, the crossbowman must only move his safety forward and pull the trigger. Either way, archery turkey hunting is usually most successful when done from a blind or a location where the hunter is well hid in deep shade.

One season, after taking one tom with an antique muzzleloading shotgun, I decided to use my crossbow to try to collect the second of the three toms that Georgia allots to each hunter. Turkey hunting is always a "sometimes" event, and I fully expected to take the remaining month of the season to find success.

First, I had to design a point that I thought would work in providing shock to the turkey, penetrate deep enough to be deadly, and remain in the bird rather that blasting through it. By clipping the wires on the Judo small-game point, I had such a point. I just needed to get a turkey close enough to shoot. My brother-in-law and I had been hunting a tom that took one of three paths through a stand of planted pines and it seemed that whichever of the three parallel walkways that we set up on, this turkey always took an alternate route. As these same pathways were also used by deer, three elevated box blinds were situated on each of them. Five times I had sought this particular bird. Sometimes he would gobble and walk in response to my calls. Other times, I would hear nothing at all.

On the sixth attempt, I was sitting in the middle box blind after an early morning rain, with some mist rising from the ground, when I struck

Turkey point and feathers, the first result of using a judo point with clipped extensions. Unfortunately, the point only grazed the turkey's back cutting off a group of feathers and did not penetrate the bird. The turkey hopped once and then walked away--surprised, but no worse for the experience.

the call. The gobbler responded. As usual he was walking along a different path. This time, however, he was coming to the hen call. After he passed around the rear of the blind where I did not have a shot, I called softly again, and he retraced his steps. Stepping into the food plot itself, he walked up to my decoy and presented me with a quartering shot. When I shot, feathers flew and the turkey jumped to one side, shook himself, and walked off. My arrow had clipped a groove of feathers from the turkey's back but had not done him any other harm.

Later that season, using the same crossbow and arrow, I had the opportunity to take a turkey that was walking through the rye on the edge of one of my food plots. This time the hit was good, and the turkey went down and flopped. I quickly approached the bird and stood on his neck to keep him from running. The point did as planned and went about halfway through the 16-pound tom, although not sufficiently deep enough to kill him quickly.

I have heard good reports of archers using expanding points with wide blades to achieve more rapid kills on turkeys. Another approach is for the point to be open as it leaves the crossbow so that it cuts off the bird's head. If successful, this shot would make for a dead, but not very photogenic, fowl.

One thing I learned as a result of shooting turkeys with muzzle-loading rifles is not to take a shot at a bird coming at me head-on. Because turkeys stagger a bit as they walk, turning slightly left and right with each step, an arrow could penetrate one side of the breast but not hit the vitals, and the bird could fly off. Instead, wait until the turkey turns broadside and then shoot, most preferably when the bird is standing still. Because my back-scrapped turkey was still moving when I shot, my arrow passed harmlessly through the feathers on its back, instead of hitting more forward on the bird and penetrating the lungs.

BOWFISHING

Since my book *Practical Bowfishing* was published, I am frequently asked, "Can I bowfish with my crossbow?"

My usual reply is, "Yes, you can use your crossbow for bowfishing if state laws permit it, but many do not. If you shoot from a tub, rather that attaching a reel, you can shoot fish without having to modify your crossbow or buy a reel. However, if you can physically use a bow, you will find that any long bow, compound or recurve, that has a pull of 35 pounds or more will do better for ordinary bowfishing. Only for alligators and big fish are crossbows of any real use."

One of the best ways to rig a crossbow for bowfishing is to shorten a typical fiberglass shaft and screw a Retriever Safety Slide and stop bolt into the rear of the arrow. The Safety Slide keeps the crossbow string forward and prevents the bowfishing line from looping around the string or cables of the crossbow. If this happens, the crossbow arrow may reverse direction and strike the user in the eye or forehead with deadly results. At least one bowfisherman using a compound bow has been killed and another blinded in one eye by arrow reversals.

When shooting in shallow water, you will find that arrows from a 150-pound crossbow imbed themselves deeply in the bottom and are often difficult to pull out. Lighter crossbow arrows require a high-starting velocity to produce enough penetration to force the points into a heavily scaled fish such as a gar. After each shot, the line must be carefully reeled back into the bottle on the Retriever reel or stacked back into the line tub, the crossbow must be recocked, and everything must be made ready for another opportunity.

Reels offer great mobility. I like the Retriever "no-drag" reel, which holds the line in a bottle, rather than on a spool, and provides nearly frictionless feed, hence its name. A disadvantage of this design is that

A bowfishing arrow and tub can be successfully used with a crossbow. Advantages of this bowfishing technique include that the crossbow does not have to be modified to mount a reel and that any weight line, including this 600-pound gator cord, may be used.

the user is not able to exert any significant force on the line when retrieving the fish, and the fish has to be recovered by pulling in the line by hand.

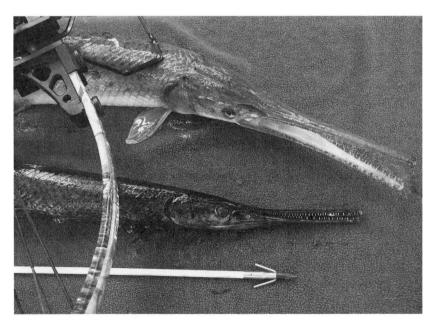

This Georgia longnose gar was taken with a crossbow and Muzzy bowfishing point.

Other difficulties of crossbowfishing include holding the heavy crossbow at the ready for extended periods, choosing an appropriate sighting system, and exclusively dedicating a crossbow, with its special arrows and points, for bowfishing. A typical recurve bow is lighter, faster to put into service, and easier to shoot.

As for potential sights, red-dot sights flair out in the dark and are too faint when it is bright. Telescopic sights, while better, are usually too high-powered for close-range shots. The best sight for bowfishing would be a 2X telescope with a center-ring reticle with coarse crosshairs pointing to, but not touching, the ring. In addition to light-gathering potential, such a sight would leave the center of the target clear for viewing a fish, require no electrical components, and be relatively fast. Unfortunately, I know of no such scope for crossbows, although some shotgun scopes might be useful substitutes. The best readily available sight for crossbowfishing is the ring-and-pin sight that has a large sighting hole.

If you really want to use a crossbow for bowfishing, here is how to set up one. Purchase a white fiberglass bowfishing arrow already rigged with a safety slide and a Muzzy bowfishing point. Measure the length of your crossbow deck and cut the fiberglass arrow a sufficient distance back of the point so that the point extends just past the deck of the crossbow. If your crossbow uses a flat-nocked arrow, trim the rear of the arrow square. If it takes a half-moon nock, use a chainsaw file to produce a nock that matches the diameter of the bowstring and has the same orientation as the point's barbs. Once this is done, the position of the stop for the Retriever Safety Slide must be determined. If the arrow-retaining spring has sufficient clearance, a $7/64$-inch hole may be drilled for the stop at least $1/4$ inch from the rear of the arrow. This hole should be at ninety degrees to the axis of the nock and orientation of the point. The screw and stop are then installed. The screw will cut its own threads in fiberglass shafts, so to prevent stripping the threads or splitting the shaft, do not overtighten the screw or use a smaller diameter hole.

Hunting the Black Gar

My bowfishing buddy Paul Presley and I had seen and missed a fish we dubbed "Black Gar" on a previous trip to one of our favorite bowfishing spots. Unlike the usual spotted long-nosed gar, Black Gar appeared to be jet black from the tips of its tail to its nose. The only thing white about him was his formidable set of needle-sharp teeth and some lighter scales on its belly. We had spotted him when bowfishing from a boat in the river and had decided that if we ever got him, we would have this unusual fish mounted.

Paul Presley with one of two all-black gars taken from Georgia's Oconee River. This gar shows an uncommon color phase of the normally grey-speckled fish.

Paul had been periodically checking the area when he informed me that he had discovered how the fish were acting. During high water, they hung close to the bank and fed on schools of shad minnows that hugged the edge. When they wanted a fish, they simply reached out and took one. Armed with this information, we agreed to meet at the river's edge one afternoon and give crossbowfishing a try.

I took with me a Fred Bear 150-pound crossbow with peep-and-pin sights that I was getting ready to use on an alligator hunt. I had already tried a couple of bowfishing arrows in it and even had one rigged and ready to go. It was already sighted in for a range of 10 yards, and I figured that this would be a good time to test the technology.

Paul was right; the gar were there. When we arrived, we quickly counted eight or nine within easy range, but by the time I cocked my crossbow and rigged it out, their numbers had diminished. Some of these gar had been shot at before, and when they spotted people on the bank, they must have realized that we probably did not have good intentions. Our strategy on this trip was to hold out for a big gar, one with a length of between 5 and 6 feet and weighing more than 20 pounds. We only saw gar between 3 and 4 feet long, certainly a respectable size if we were shooting for meat, but today we were after trophies.

The gar that were there were not stationary, and it was impossible for me to follow their movements and view them through the peep sights at the same time. We did not see the trophy-size fish that we were after, but we did spot a black gar that was smaller than the fish we had originally seen. When it swam by me, I tried for it and missed. The fish hesitated a bit too long in front of Paul, who took careful aim with his compound bow and nailed it through the body. It was only a 24-inch fish but was nonetheless a handsome specimen, dark greenish black on its back with lighter tones of white on its belly.

Our shooting had disturbed the fish, and they had either relocated or finished feeding. Not very mobile with my setup, I went up the bank to see if I could locate some more fish. Paul spotted the tail of a gar protruding from behind a rock and tried for it but missed. When I walked in the other direction, I saw a fish hugging the bank almost beneath my feet. I loaded the crossbow and prepared to shoot, but when I leaned out to take the fish, it saw me and moved. Then it made the mistake of returning to its former position, and I pulled the trigger. The line, tub, and all shot off the bank as the fish attempted to escape.

Not knowing how well the gar was hit, I carefully pulled in the line. The crossbow arrow had passed through the fish until stopped by the Retriever slide. The barbs held in the tough scales. I was able to bring in the fish and hoist it up the bank over the rocks. My Fred Bear crossbow had taken its fish, and the tub-shooting technology that I had developed for conventional bows certainly worked.

A reality check came when I asked about the costs of having the fish mounted. At $9 an inch, the cost prohibited me from getting the entire fish mounted. Instead I took a century-old weathered plank that I had pulled from the bottom of the river and mounted the head and short body sections of the black and longnose gar that Paul and I had taken. This started my collection of North American gars, and I figured I could add other species as I caught them. In this manner, I could preserve the memory of Black Gar.

Running line back into a tub is a time-consuming aspect of crossbow fishing. Using a wind-up reel such as the Zebco 808 close-faced model considerably speeds up the process.

My crossbowfishing experience left me pleased with my success, but nothing about it convinced me that crossbows were desirable tools for the able-bodied bowfisherman. If I had been using my regular recurve bow, I believe I would have been able to take several fish with much less difficulty.

Two problems—the poor sight picture and the heavy weight of the crossbow—caused me most of my difficulties. A lighter-weight Ranger crossbow with a scope sight, which I had already sighted in for possible use on an Alaskan hunt for black-tailed deer, may have been a good option, but I did not want to resight it for bowfishing. This scope had multiple aiming points and perhaps one of these would work.

I thought that the Ranger could target the bowfishing arrow to the point of aim if I used an aiming point immediately below the scope's crosshairs, and I planned to make at least one more crossbowfishing trip to see if I could achieve better results with the lighter-weight crossbow. When I did, I discovered that the Ranger was less powerful and shot an ordinary arrow at 205 fps instead of the 247 fps of the Fred Bear crossbow. The Ranger's arrow failed to penetrate a gar of similar size, and the arrow pulled out of the fish.

For crossbowfishing, you will obtain best results with a 150- to 185-pound pull crossbow with open sights, an 80- to 100-pound line, and a Retriever reel mounted on the crossbow. Tub crossbowfishing is a low-cost alternative but is slow and troublesome unless you are taking shots at a few big fish from a fixed position.

15

CLASSIC CROSSBOW HUNTS—NORTH AMERICA

A variety of North American game species not normally taken with crossbows is available to hunters looking for a different hunting experience. These opportunities range from alligator hunting in the southeastern United States to musk ox hunting in the Canadian Arctic.

AMERICAN ALLIGATOR

Once endangered, the American alligator is another conservation success story. Today, Florida has an estimated population of 14,000,000 alligators, about one for each resident. In Georgia, where I reside, the population is smaller, ranging between 200,000 and 250,000. These large reptiles aggressively compete among themselves, and occasionally with man, for food, water rights, and sunning places. Bigger alligators attack and eat smaller members of their own species, and frequently a "Boss Gator" will claim a territory and drive off any competitors. Only during breeding season are these oversize males sociable. Every year, Florida has one or two alligator attacks on people, sometimes with fatal results.

Large alligators are powerful. They can outrun a man on a straightaway and close their heavy jaw muscles with sufficient force to break bones. Their peglike teeth are designed not for ripping, but for holding while they turn and twist off a limb or break the neck of their prey. Often an alligator will lie just beneath the surface of a small pond waiting for some animal to come and drink. Then the alligator lunges forward, grabs its prize, and drags it in. Favorite meals are fish, turtles, deer, hogs, dogs, and small domestic animals. If it kills a large animal, the gator will hide it and let it decompose until it can rip it apart with its relatively primitive teeth.

A well-fed gator at his favorite sunning spot inside the Okefenokee National Wildlife Refuge in Georgia. To help control alligator populations outside of refuge areas, Georgia has initiated an annual alligator season, joining Texas, Louisiana, and Florida, which all allow closely controlled sport hunting of alligators.

Alligators are killed for various reasons: to keep their numbers in check, to provide attractive leather, and to make an excellent meal. The so-called "gator tail" consists of meat from the animal's tail as well as else-where on the body. The alligator's heavy jowls contain several pounds of tasty meat, and its ribs are also quite good. The meat from the legs is just as good, but it is reddish and not sold as a commercial product. Recipes for alligator meat are given in chapter 21.

Currently, Florida, Georgia, Louisiana, and Texas have alligator seasons, and other southern states are discussing opening brief seasons. In all cases, the harvest is closely controlled, and each animal is tagged and registered. The tags are attached to the hide and follow it through-out the tanning process until the hide is made into boots, watchbands, pocketbooks, and other leather goods. Florida has the largest take of alligators, followed by Louisiana, Texas, and Georgia.

I have hunted alligators in Florida and Georgia, and the states' laws are similar. Archery equipment, both bows and crossbows, may be used to attach a line to the alligator. If small, the reptile is pulled to the vessel, killed at the side of the boat, and after its jaws are secured with electrical tape loaded aboard. The alligator must be a minimum of 4 feet long, and since it is impossible to determine the sex of a floating alligator, both males and females may be taken. Mature bull alligators tend to be larger than females, which have a length of 6 to 10 feet, but any alligator 9 feet or longer is considered trophy size. As alligators grow, often reaching sizes between 9 and 16 feet, they progressively add more body mass until they weigh more than 800 pounds. An alligator that is 12 feet long and weighs about 400 pounds is commonly considered "big."

Getting Ready for the Hunt

One approach to alligator hunting is to hire a guide and use his boat to take gators. Instead, I had been accumulating the necessary equipment to do the job, including a 15-foot by 48-inch semi-V, welded aluminum boat with a 40-horsepower engine rigged for night running and a 12-volt lighting system that Georgia permits its hunters to use. The boat was ready and tested, and all it needed was an alligator in front of it. My friends Roger Kicklighter and Ed Foster and I were ready to try it out.

After looking at several crossbows, I decided to use a Horton Hawk because it is a sufficiently powerful 150-pound crossbow and was

A Horton Hawk crossbow with arrow, Muzzy gator-getter point, knife, and pistol, all used to take this 6-foot alligator.

already rigged with the peep-and-pin sights that I prefer for bowfishing. I just had to make arrows with suitable shafts and Muzzy gator points and pick up some 600-pound gator cord, harpoon, and snares. To restrain the alligator and pull it to the boat, we decided to use an arrow, snares, and a large gaff that Foster built from a hook once used to move cotton bales. Without hurting the alligator much, these tools would enable us to secure the alligator, tire it out from dragging a float, and allow it to be brought to the boat for a killing shot to the brain or spine.

Georgia allows a handgun to be used (Florida requires a bang stick), and I had a stainless .44-caliber Ruger Old Army that was up to the task. As black-powder handguns go, the Ruger is not particularly potent, but it would sufficiently shoot an alligator at a range of a few feet. To kill the gator, we knew it would have to be shot through the ear, through the bony flat behind the eyes (if shooting at a high angle to avoid ricochets), or directly behind the skull into the brain or spine. Shots into the body of the alligator are not quick killers and may result in a lost gator. For the alligator to be eligible for the American Bowfishing Association's Dangerous Game Category, it would have to be finished off with hand tools, and we could do this with a kill arrow in the brain or a drive stake through the top of the skull.

Florida requires sport hunting of alligators to be done at night. Although Georgia allows either day or night hunting, night hunting is the better choice since alligators are more active after dark, and the red reflection of their eyes makes alligators easy to be spot. To judge the size of an alligator, measure the distance from its eyes to its snout, as this measurement in inches provides a rough estimate of the gator's length in feet. Thus, a distance of 8 inches between the eyes and snout indicates an 8-foot alligator. Keep in mind that all of the alligator may not, in fact, be there. Some alligators lose the ends of their tails, or a limb, to other alligators, and occasionally a hide may be so scarred from fighting as to not have any commercial value.

Prehunt scouting is crucial for determining where the big alligators pull out on shore and where they make their home. Unless disturbed, a large alligator will tend to range in a "home" area where it has abundant food and cover. If the hunter sees a number of smaller alligators and then sees none, a Boss Gator may be residing nearby. Look for the gator to raise up its head once it feels the vibration of the boat. On quiet nights, you may be able to even call alligators. Like bull elk, they will come looking for a fight, so the crew must be ready to take the alligator or flee. Each alligator hunting season brings at least one boat back to the dock with teeth marks on it.

A typical view of an alligator in the water. Alligators, which can be hunted during the day and night, sometimes approach very close to boats, making them ideal targets for the crossbow.

Once the alligator has been killed, you must lash it to the boat or bring it inside, as dead alligators sink. However, first use a few wraps of electrical tape to secure its mouth in the closed position. "Dead" alligators sometimes have the nasty habit of reviving once they are handled or inside the boat. As insurance against this, fish and game officers recommend that you sever the animal's spine with a stout knife before loading the animal into a boat.

In a small boat, only allow one person with a crossbow to shoot at a time. Once the hunter is in position, an arrow can be loaded into the crossbow. The designated hunter has the tasks of shooting the alligator, putting a second arrow into it, finishing it off, and taping its mouth. After putting it into the boat, take a strong-bladed knife and push it between the gator's vertebrae to cut the spinal cord. Even then, after the head is detached from the body and the "dead" gator is considered safely dead, the jaws can still close on a hand. You will need at least two other participants to train the light on the alligator, visually follow the float, steer the boat, handle the lines, fight the alligator to tire it out, and help pull

Smaller boats, such as this 14-foot fiberglass variety, may be used to hunt relatively small alligators. To hunt alligators 10 feet or longer that weigh well over 300 pounds, a larger aluminum-hulled boat is recommended. Huge alligators have been known to take bites out of small boats and disable them.

the alligator into the boat. One trophy-size alligator a night is usually about all that most people can handle. Besides, it takes a big boat to hold a couple of 300-pound gators and three adults.

During our prehunt meeting, state wildlife officers explained that Georgia's population of alligators, while certainly large enough to sustain harvest, was not as large as Florida's. "You will not see as many alligators, and they will generally be more difficult to approach," they remarked. "You will have to hunt to get a trophy-size male."

The two officers who had removed many nuisance alligators over the years typically took them by a combination of calling and snagging them with rods and reels equipped with lead-weighted snagging hooks with ¾- to 1-inch gaps. When the alligators were brought close to the boat, the officers attached snares until the alligators were exhausted, then taped their mouths, and removed them live for relocation. In our case, when we got them close to the boat, we would put an arrow or bullet into their brains and haul them into the boat. The officers had several other useful tips such as filling a jug with expandable foam so that it would not sink if bit by the alligator. They also told us that an alligator could stay underwater for an hour and a half on one breath of air and that the previous year, when coastal hurricanes shortened the season, only about thirty percent of alligator hunters had been successful.

Designing a Gator Arrow

Ideally, an arrow that can take an alligator must be heavy, have a detachable head (so that the shaft will not provide leverage to pull the point from the alligator when it rolls), and be rigged with strong line that is attached forward of the crossbow's string and cables. The Muzzy Gator-Getter head has a hole back of the point, which is designed to be a slip fit onto the shaft, for attaching the 600-pound test braided line.

I purchased some 3/8-inch stainless rod from a hardware store and cut a pair of 19-inch shafts, but these proved to be too heavy compared to the relatively light point. I obtained a better result from a solid fiberglass shaft onto which I filled a half-moon nock with a chainsaw file. The point itself was attached to the shaft with melted beeswax to provide an easily breakable seal and hold the point on the arrow. (Dipping the arrow shaft and point into melted wax, sticking them together, and allowing them to cool sufficiently attaches the point.) One end of the line is run through the hole in the rear of the shaft and attached to the point with a bowfisherman's nonslip loop knot. The other end of the line is passed through a hole drilled in the rear of the shaft about an inch from the nock and run forward to the point where it is lightly secured to the shaft with a scrap of electrical tape. The purpose of this tape, which should not be wrapped around the shaft or pasted on tightly, is to hold the line forward on the shaft to the point where the arrow leaves the crossbow. Then the tape detaches with as little friction as possible, leaving the arrow stabilized by the trailing line just as is done with a typical bowfishing arrow.

With the line held in a tub on the ground, the crossbow was targeted in to be dead-on at 5 yards, and the fiberglass arrow was found to drop 6 inches at 10 yards, the maximum range that we intended to shoot. When shooting from the tub, we had to make sure that the line exited freely and was dropped loosely into the top-center of the tub so it wouldn't tangle. I also found, after shooting beneath several gators, that the tub should be placed high in the boat so that the line does not drag against the boat's gunnels as it leaves the boat.

Drop the 600-pound test line loosely into the top center of the tub to feed it without tangling.

Scouting

On previous duck-hunting trips, I had become somewhat knowledgeable about the lower Altamaha River, which drains much of central Georgia. Where it discharged on the coast were several distributaries with large low islands between them, almost all of which housed pre-Civil War rice plantations. Some of Butler and Rett Islands' rice paddies had been maintained for waterfowl, and while deer hunting on Butler Island, I had seen a 12-foot alligator in one of the canals, so I knew they were certainly there.

Roger, Ed, and I drove down to the launch area with the purpose of scouting Rett Island. When we launched, we were told by some locals that alligators were always hanging around. The hot weather and high tides apparently kept them out of sight the day we were there, because, although we circumnavigated the island, we did not see any. What we did discover was that we had only two hour's running time on a tank of gas and that the area contained a large number of crab traps that we would have to avoid.

Strong tides around the islands prevented me from keeping the boat on station. If gators were in the impoundments in the interior of Rett

Island, we would have to tow a smaller boat over and use it to run the perimeter canals. We were informed that a large number of gators lived on Rett, so we chose to employ this two-boat method for our initial hunt.

First Crossbow Hunt

The day of our hunt, Roger and Ed pulled up with Weldo trailer and Bondo boat, two experienced veterans of a cross-country bowfishing trip and numerous other multistate travels, behind their vehicle. The trailer, a rusted relic, lost its fenders recently on Montana's rough roads. A fiberglass Ganeau-type vessel, Bondo boat is stable enough to carry two people and can even allow one to stand and shoot. Neither looked like much, and Roger expressed concern that they could even make it the 120 miles to the coast and back. I assured him that despite their looks—I could leave this outfit at any launching site in North America and expect it to be there when I returned—they were accustomed to being driven 500 to 800 miles a day.

My larger boat, a 15-foot by 48-inch welded Aluminocraft with a 40-horsepower Tahotsu engine, had never had previous problems, but it chose this hunt to act up. Immediately after leaving the dock, the fuel line came out of the gas tank. Completely unknown to me, the threads had apparently been stripped on the plastic gas tank, and the plastic hose connection pulled out. As we approached what looked to be a likely pullout spot on the island, Roger looked back at the engine and saw two smoking electrical wires, which he quickly pulled from the battery to allow them to cool. Apparently the wires had been crimped by the utility door on the back of the boat and shorted out. Fortunately, this occurred on the other side from the gas tank, which shared space with the battery in the utility well. When the wires were cooled and rewrapped, we pulled up to the dike, hauled Bondo boat on top, and proceeded with our hunt.

Because of unusually high tides, which were pushed ashore by Hurricane Ophelia, we could pull Bondo boat directly over the top of the dike. Two hunting methods suggested themselves. The first was to walk the dike and hunt from shore with different people carrying the crossbow, harpoon, pistol, and recovery line. The second was for two of us to hunt from the boat while one remained behind. Thick vegetation prevented much travel along that portion of the dike, so the boat option remained the most viable. Roger, who was licensed for this area, chose to use the harpoon while Ed ran the trolling motor. I remained behind keeping guard over the part of the canal I could see with the crossbow. Darkness fell and out came the mosquitoes. Fortunately a bug suit and a

ThermaCell at my feet helped alleviate what would have been an unbearable situation.

The falling tide left the boat stranded on the mud, and we would not be able to leave until the next high tide. Roger and Ed returned empty-handed. They had approached several alligators, but when they were nearly within throwing range of the harpoon, the gators sank and did not give them a chance. The trolling motor had drawn down the battery, and the other battery, which I had fully charged and reconnected to the trolling motor on my boat, had somehow leaked enough voltage to be completely discharged. We had nearly 150 pounds of wet-cell batteries, all of them dead.

Paddles work, and Roger volunteered to paddle me around to where they had spied twenty-five gators to see if I could get a shot with the crossbow. The only illumination we had was from our headlights and a sealed-beam spotlight powered by an internal battery. After removing the now-excess trolling motor and battery from Bondo boat, we launched.

We found a corner of the flooded paddy that had a good alligator population. Most were small, but a few were as long as 8 feet. I tried for one from the front of the boat with the tub sitting on the floor between my feet but missed by shooting below the gator. I then passed the crossbow to Roger and placed the tub in the middle of the boat on the top of the dry well. After all our setbacks, we were determined to have an alligator in the boat before we left. We spotted one that appeared to be a bit larger than the rest, and Roger raised the crossbow, but when he put the stock to his shoulder and attempted to sight on the gator, the beam from his light was cast off the target and he could no longer see it. He tried moving his light on his cap, but after the lost time and noise, the gator sank out of sight.

We approached two more alligators but could not get close enough until finally, one cooperated and Roger shot. The splash was in the head area, and both he and I thought that he had missed. However, when I started pulling in the line, something was on it. Once at the side of the boat, the alligator started thrashing. After bringing it up for the third time, Roger stuck a harpoon tip into its neck, which generated more thrashing. Now we had a rope attached to the alligator, and after more thrashing, I was able to bring him up by the snout and Roger shot him behind the head with a 38-special. The gator went limp, and I clamped his jaws shut with one hand while Roger put several wraps of electrical tape around it. Once we got it in the boat, we severed the alligator's spine by plunging a Buck Bowie knife blade between the vertebrae.

We saw that the crossbow arrow had struck the alligator between the jaws and passed completely through them. Half of the arrow shaft was sticking out the other side, and even after the alligator was pulled in, the shaft remained fixed in the animal. When measured, the alligator was 6 feet 3 inches and weighed about 70 pounds, certainly not the biggest alligator in Georgia, but large enough to prove the effectiveness of our technology and to help us perfect our alligator-hunting techniques.

I shot at three more alligators with the crossbow and missed low each time. After returning to the launching area, I realized that the drag on the line rubbing against the gunnel of the boat had slowed the arrow to the extent that it was striking low on the target. I would have to place the tub on the foredeck of Bondo boat to reduce the friction.

A Trophy Gator

Scouting of the next hunt area to the south, where Ed had his permit, took us to a good-size creek that appeared to have alligators. The next weekend found us on another hunt. We launched in midafternoon and headed downstream against the rising tide. Our intention was to return and hunt the upper tributaries after the full 9-foot tide filled the channels. We hunted from 3 P.M. to 3 A.M., and although we saw a total of nineteen, we had no gator in the boat. Ed was just pulling the trigger on a 10-footer when the gator went to the bottom. Ugh! Well, that's hunting.

After a few hours' sleep in a motel, we arose, ate breakfast, and returned to my area with the idea of scouting another part of Altamaha estuary. We launched and headed out toward the ocean into the salt marsh. The sun was hot, the temperature easily reaching 92 degrees by midafternoon, and the twisting channels in the marsh were confusing. Ultimately, I saw a small wooded hammock sticking out of the marsh, and we took a channel that appeared to snake by a small island. As we rounded a bend, I spotted the largest alligator that we had yet seen on the bank. We motored by it with the intention of paddling back to get close enough for a shot.

For once the tide was favorable, and I got the crossbow ready as we approached. I made sure the tape was properly attached to the arrow and the tub containing the line was on the upper deck of the boat. When we were 15 yards away, the gator either heard or saw us because it rose on its legs and turned to offer a broadside shot. Then, like a streak of reptilian lightning, it made for the water. I was already sighted on the gator for a chest shot, and when the alligator started its run, I pulled the trigger. By the time the crossbow arrow and the gator connected, the reptile had covered enough ground that the Muzzy point struck the alligator in the right rear leg, not an optimum shot. But the first thing an alligator hunter must do is attach a line to the gator, and this shot accomplished that objective.

Line shot off the front of the boat, and the float followed. We could see the float being drug up the channel. Ed had the job of gently pulling up the line so that we could get the alligator close enough to the surface to jab a harpoon head into its hide. I tried twice, but the harpoon would not penetrate the reptile's armored back. Reloading the crossbow, I took a shot at the animal's flank the next time it approached the surface. This time the arrow penetrated the chest cavity, and almost the entire shaft disappeared into the alligator. Now, with two 600-pound test lines attached, we had our gator, although it was still full of fight. After another quarter hour, we got it close again, and I managed to plant the harpoon head into the soft skin of its neck.

Still far from dead, the alligator rose several times snapping at the boat and at us. I fed it the boat broom while trying to manhandle it into an appropriate position so that I could make a kill shot to the brain with the Ruger Old Army .44-caliber percussion revolver. This gun had a relatively low-velocity bullet that would penetrate sufficiently to blow up the animal's brain without destroying the skull or sending bullet and bone fragments into the boat or me. The alligator offered an ideal shot from the middle of the boat, but I was in the bow. Then when I moved to midboat, it surfaced at the front. Roger was trying to keep the boat in the middle of the channel with the paddle, but the alligator kept pulling us toward the marsh. Once in the edge of the grass 5 yards in front of the boat, the beast raised its head sufficiently to give me a shot at the flat of its skull. I took the shot, put the pistol back into its box, and pulled the boat to the alligator. Quickly clamping its jaws shut with one hand, I wrapped 5 yards of electrical tape around the deadly jaws.

We had to use the boat motor to pull the alligator out of the weeds. As it was still more than a little lively, we decided to take the animal to shore and finish killing it. Once the reptile was partly pulled up on shore, I took a Buck Bowie knife and rammed it behind the head up to the hilt severing the spine. Despite being arrowed, harpooned, broomed, taped, shot, and knifed, the alligator took another 15 minutes to quiet down sufficiently that we could pull, push, and shove it into the boat. We used this time to take photos and to straighten out the lines and rope and recover our equipment. The alligator, which was 10 feet 2 inches long and weighed more than 250 pounds, was estimated by the processor to be approximately 70 years old. This old beast had certainly provided us with one of the most exciting hunts that North America offers.

CANADIAN MUSK OX

The musk ox, the shaggy beast of the Arctic, is a large cowlike mammal with pendulant brown fur that is more nearly related to sheep and goats than oxen. What could be more different from hunting alligators in 90-plus degrees Fahrenheit in Georgia swamps than hunting musk ox in blowing snow in temperatures below 0 degrees on the barren grounds of the Canadian Arctic. Notwithstanding, the modern crossbow is capable of functioning in both environments. In the following description, Bill Throubridge of Excalibur Crossbows demonstrates the crossbow's worth in a hunt for musk ox.

Wild musk oxen are found in Alaska, Canada, and Greenland, but you may have a more accessible look at the animals at the Musk Ox Farm adjacent to the University of Alaska's college campus a few miles west of Fairbanks. There, the animals are managed for their yield of meat, milk, and the soft underfur called qiviut, which may be spun to yield lightweight woolen garments.

Throubridge's quest for this large furry animal took him to Victoria Island where he hunted out of Nunavut on Cambridge Bay. In May, spring temperatures range from about zero degrees during the day to 20 below at night. Throubridge had some concerns about how his crossbow would respond in this harsh environment on the rugged hunt. For starters, he had to sight in his crossbow under approximately similar weather conditions. Then, his bow had to go on a bouncing ride on a sled pulled

Home sweet home in the frozen north while on a spring musk ox hunt. Even during the Arctic spring, the weather may be so severe that it is not unusual for hunters to be weathered in for days at a time during a hunt.

The shaggy musk oxen are well adapted for life in the wind-blown Arctic. Wind blows snow off grass patches so that these animals can feed during the winter months.

behind a snowmobile. Finally, he would have to cock his crossbow while dressed in enough clothes to make him look something like the Pillsbury Dough Boy. For such a hunt, he selected a 175-pound pull Exocet with a peep-and-pin sighting system, instead of his usual scope-mounted 225-pound ExoMax. He figured the combination would be easier to cock while he was dressed in heavy clothes and the sights would be more reliable after a rough-and-tumble trip. At home, he waited for an appropriately cold morning and sighted in the crossbow at minus 20 degrees. The crossbow worked fine, and he was now ready for an Arctic adventure.

In Arctic regions of the world where weather dominates man's activities, natives scoff at carefully laid plains and tight schedules. The climate is harsh, unforgiving, and deadly even during the relatively balmy month of May, which heralds the arrival of spring. The Inuit people know this well and plan hunts around existing weather conditions, not calendar days. For much of one day during the hunt, Throubridge, three other hunters, and their guide, Kevin Evetalegak, huddled in plywood shacks 50 miles from the airport while waiting for whiteout conditions to abate so that they could actually see the animals and find their way to hunt.

Bad-weather days in hunt camp can be grim. You can tell your favorite stories, talk about your equipment, read (if you had the foresight to bring a thick novel), eat, and sleep. You have a lot of time to talk and a lot of time to think. Always in your mind, whether spoken or unspoken, is the question, "When is the weather going to break?" The wind may be howling and the snow blowing, but daylight had arrived in the Arctic. Once the wind abated, they knew they would be able to hunt from 4 A.M. to 10 P.M.

Evetalegak assured the group that the musk ox were feeding on the coarse grass and willows of the windswept hills. In fact, the wind was vital to the animal's survival because it exposed feeding areas as first one area, then another, was blown clean of snow. This information, along with his tales of truly epic storms that blew for days, was little consolation to the visiting hunters.

Then, one day, something was different. At first, it took the newcomers a minute to figure out that the wind, which had been steadily blasting the walls of the plywood shacks and pelting the metal stove pipe with an unrelenting blast of ice crystals, had slacked, become hesitant, and then quit. With eight hours of daylight remaining, the hunt was on!

Dressing hurriedly, the hunters piled on layers of underwear, trousers, overtrousers, and top coatings and topped them with heavy parkas. On the feet went oversize felt shoepacks designed to offer maximum

Musk oxen circle when facing danger. The largest bulls and cows form a circle on the outside, keeping the younger individuals safe inside the ring of sharply hooked horns.

Bill Throubridge with the musk ox he took with a 175-pound draw Excalibur Exocet crossbow. Because of the severe climate and below-zero temperatures he was hunting in, Throubridge used the more rugged ring-and-pin sight system instead of a scope.

protection in the cold but dry environment. Quickly dressed and out of the shack before the clothing became wet with sweat, the hunters, upon their first exposure to the cold, felt the effects of the many cups of sweet warm tea and took quick action to relieve themselves before they went bouncing along on a sled pulled over rocky ground at high speed.

The day he arrived, Throubridge had managed to get out briefly to look for musk ox, but by the time he spotted a group of brown blobs on a distant hill, the weather was closing in, and it was too late to hunt. Today promised a better result.

Shaking the snow off the caribou-hide robes in the plywood sled or "komatik," Throubridge covered his exposed skin and prepared for the bone-grinding trip as the snowmobile towed him from hill to hill in an attempt to relocate their target animals. The brown musk ox against the white snow were not hard to spot, but they were hard to approach. Several stalks were attempted, but the hunters walking in the snow in heavy clothes were easy to spot, and the musk ox would move away, well out of range of the crossbow. There was nothing to do but return to the snowmobile, get closer, and try again.

Time was, when approached by something they sensed as dangerous, the musk ox would circle their young and place the old bulls and cows on the outside. This maneuver worked against wolves but not with hunters with rifles. Although they still used this defensive posture, the ox would move that way only after being progressively approached. Ultimately, the herd formed a circle, and Throubridge and his guide moved closer.

One impressive bull separated a bit from the group and turned broadside. Taking advantage of the 30-yard shot opportunity, Throubridge quickly brought the pin to a point at the crease of the shoulder and pulled the trigger. Despite some hours of pounding in the sled, the crossbow released its arrow, which disappeared in the ox's mat of long hair. At the noise of the shot, the herd ran, but the stricken bull fell behind, slowed, and collapsed. The crossbow had performed well: The animal had been taken with a single shot. Now the skinning and recovery of the meat could begin. In the Inuit tradition, a small portion of the meat would be consumed in camp, but most would be divided among villagers.

16

CLASSIC CROSSBOW HUNTS—AFRICA

Africa, with its large number of game animals and diversity of hunting opportunities, is a destination often hunted by representatives of crossbow manufacturing companies. They go to test their crossbows and arrows as well as enjoy the hunting. It should come as no surprise that Bernard Horton, an avid hunter and founder of the crossbow-making company that carries his name, now lives in Botswana. Companies such as TenPoint and Excalibur also make regular trips with their crossbows to the continent of Africa, and the following relates some of their experiences taking African game with their products.

EXCALIBUR HUNTS
Bill and Kath Throubridge have made four trips to Africa with their crossbows and have had fairly typical hunting experiences. From talking to them and seeing the footage they have shot, I believe that their experiences reflect an average South African hunt. The hunt described below took place with Johan Kruger of Lumbata Safaris in the old Northern, now Limpopo, Province of South Africa. On previous hunts they had attempted some stalks on plains game, which they found to be interesting but not particularly successful. On this hunt, a full two weeks long, they had resigned themselves to the fact that if they were going to film the animals they wanted to, they would have to shoot from blinds.

As Kruger explained to them when they arrived, "You will be shooting from blinds. Some will be on the ground, some elevated, and some sunken. You may see as many as twenty different species of game a day as they come to water. Your shots will be at close range, and I have no doubt that your new crossbows will do very well."

This semiarid area of South Africa looks much like the dry, hilly parts of the southwestern United States. When I was there, I had to keep reminding myself that I was really in Africa and not west Texas or Arizona. The shrubs and trees, although acacia and marula rather than mesquite and oaks, even looked similar to home. Only the lion tracks, piles of elephant dung, rhino sightings, and a leopard-killed impala just 100 yards from the camp gate served as reminders that this was not Texas.

Hunting in South Africa begins in May and lasts through the summer months when the weather is typically dry and hot. The topography and brush might be conducive to sneaking up on something, but the noisy vegetation and the constant presence of thornbushes alert the game long before you can get in crossbow range.

The first thing Bill and Kath did was make sure that their crossbows had survived the eighteen-hour flight to South Africa and were still in shooting condition. Each of them took crossbows to increase the chance that at least one would arrive in working condition. As a side note for anyone taking their crossbows on an airplane, if your suitcase is sufficiently large, you may be able to pack your crossbow, with its risers and prods removed, among your clothes to save some expense. Otherwise, invest in a hard case for your crossbow. A crossbow packed in a soft case does not have much of a chance of survival.

Bill Throubridge took this cape buffalo with 38-inch horns with his 225-pound draw weight Exomax and twin-bladed magnus arrows.

On this trip, Kath was shooting an Exocet 200 and Bill was using an ExoMax, which at 225-pull is the highest weight pull crossbow that Excalibur makes. When asked about these choices, Bill replied, "For the general run of plains game, the Exocet 200 was adequate, as Kath demonstrated. The only reason that I carried the ExoMax was that it was a new crossbow and I wanted to find out how it shot and handled."

Kath and Bill certainly get full marks for producing crossbows that are "made by hunters for hunters." Each season finds them in the field hunting with their crossbows, and they have accumulated a respectable number of fine trophies along the way.

On this trip, they usually did two "sits" a day, sometimes occupying the same blind and sometimes not. At the start of the hunt, Bill could have taken a nice size kudu, but because it was early in the hunt he passed on it in hopes of seeing a better bull.

"We saw everything," Bill recalled. "We had big kudu, small kudu, warthogs, monkeys, guinea fowl, and impala coming to the water all morning. I was tempted by the kudu but was going to wait for a larger one."

Kath took one of the first animals of the trip, a large red hartebeest, which was shot as it drank at a range of about 20 yards from the blind. At the shot, the animal got up and ran a short distance before it went down almost within sight of the blind. The heart and lungs of African game are found predominately in the front quarter of the animal, and as instructed Kath placed the arrow sufficiently forward to cut both lungs.

Kath was so excited that she could hardly compose herself. She was quite impressed with how quietly the animals came in to water. The blind, which muffles interior noise, also prevents the hunter from hearing approaching game so if you hope to be successful, don't nap in the blind and expect to be awakened by the sounds of the animals coming in.

A similarly quiet encounter occurred when Kath shot her gemsbok or oryx. Hidden among a group that had earlier approached the water, drank, and left was a large female with good horns (they have longer horns than the males). Around dark, this female returned alone and was taken. It ran 15 yards, then stood and dropped its head before, obviously mortally hit, it walked off. Rather than attempt to follow it in the near-dark conditions, the hunting party left the animal until the next morning.

Kruger explained, "A wounded oryx with its long, very sharp horns is particularly dangerous. I was sure that we would find it the next day and we did." They recovered the oryx about 300 yards away from where it was shot.

In the meantime, Bill was also busy shooting. He had bagged a warthog, an unusual impala with a twisted horn, kudu, and zebra. Both

Wildebeest in the meat house. No game meat is wasted in Africa. When the animal is killed near towns, it is sold to local butcher shops, and when it is taken in the bush, its meat is dried and processed into biltong.

Bill and Kath were particularly proud of their zebras since these animals, which do not have to water daily, had given them difficulties on previous trips.

At the end of the hunt, Bill concluded, "Shooting over water may not seem to be particularly sporting, but this is not a 'gimme' situation. Some of these animals may go twenty days without visiting a waterhole."

Some days the Throubridges sat in their blinds and never had a shot. After rain when water was abundant, it was difficult to judge which waterholes a group of animals might use. At those times, hunting was a bit slow. The hunt providers want their guests to be able to take their allotted species of game, and they will do everything necessary to ensure that these opportunities exist. The hunter, for his part, has to shoot swiftly and accurately when the occasion demands. The crossbow with its short range and slow reloading does add additional difficulties, and not every hunt will be successful.

Over their fourteen days, Bill and Kath each shot kudu, zebra, oryx, and warthog, and a single hartebeest and blesbok were also taken. For Bill, the highlight of the trip was taking a nice kudu. "I had tried for three years to get a really good one. This trip I did it," he said. "Will I go back? You bet. This time I will go somewhere else to hunt something else. For Africa, once is never enough."

At the end of the hunt, Johan Kruger of Lumbata Safaris shot a warthog with a crossbow. "The crossbow and those behind it had killed their game as well as they could have with a gun," he concluded. "I know that I am going to have good experiences with this crossbow that you are leaving behind."

TENPOINT HUNTS

Well-known bowhunter Wade Noland also hunted for plains game in the Limpopo Province. His hunt took place with Dries Visser Safaris on property, a portion of which is exclusively managed for bowhunting, 220 miles north of Johannesburg and about 10 miles south of the Botswana border.

When the hunting party arrived, Dries Visser explained, "To have a successful bowhunting property, you must have a large number of game animals, and the animals must not be spooky. Because we own our properties, we limit the harvest so we will always have some good animals to shoot. We hunt for the most part from sunken blinds, which

Although some African hunts employ tent camps as home base, comfortable lodges like this one are more typically used to house visiting hunters.

provide good scent control. We have enough blinds that no hunter will hunt in a blind more than two days. As a result, our animals are not spooky."

Because last year was so dry, Visser said that to keep his animals healthy he was still feeding them a ton of feed a day, something, he explained, that would probably not be done on leased properties where hunting rights could be sold to another party the following year.

For this hunt, Noland and his party were using TenPoint's ProElite crossbows, which have 185 pounds of draw weight and shoot at about 313 fps. The arrow used a 100-grain fixed broadhead with ventilated blades and a cutting point. Noland noted that the crossbow "packs a tremendous amount of kinetic energy and has pinpoint accuracy. Most of the time the arrows went straight through and were found 40 to 50 yards beyond the animal. Every animal was recovered at a distance of 50 to 60 yards, and some were closer."

After seeing a variety of game the first two days of the hunt, Noland watched a trophy gemsbok come in with an eland on the third day. After he shot the gemsbok, it traveled 60 to 70 yards but was only on its feet for five to seven seconds after the hit. Earlier in the hunt, his son took a warthog. In the filmed sequence, his guide told him to aim 5 inches back of the shoulder for a quartering shot. He made the shot correctly, and the warthog quickly expired.

Aiming far enough back on quartering shots is important to prevent the arrow from only penetrating a portion of one lung or, in an extreme case, only the muscles of the foreleg and not pass through the body cavity. In the excitement of shooting an animal, it could be easy not to think about the interior path the arrow takes through the vital organs.

On his trip, Noland also took blesbok, impala, and wildebeest. His favorite hunt was sitting up for two nights in a tree blind waiting for a bushpig, which is hunted at night over bait. The hunters are positioned in a tree blind, and bait is placed in a pile 20 yards away, with a microphone and light placed over the bait. When feeding sounds warn the hunters that a pig is on the bait, the rheostat is slowly turned up until the hunter has sufficient light to aim at his pig. The first night, Noland only saw porcupines and a honey badger. At about midnight on the second night, the pigs came in, and Noland successfully shot one with his TenPoint crossbow.

Summing up his experiences, Noland reiterated that he thought the crossbow was powerful and accurate and killed well.

HORTON HUNTS
Bernard Horton, an avid hunter all his life, relocated to his current home in Botswana so that he would have a chance to live, and hunt, among

some of the world's greatest game animals. Over the years he has taken a variety of plains game with his crossbow as well as with native bows and spears. His most memorable hunt was a safari after lion, leopard, and buffalo.

For equipment selection, he advises, "Changing bows, arrows, and broadheads for different game is a recipe for disaster as no two setups will shoot the same. Under the excitement and vigor of a dangerous game hunt, there is no room, or time, for concerns or errors in one's equipment. I have learned to trust the setup that works for me in just about every situation."

Horton uses a Horton Hunter with a 185-pound draw front end, aluminum 2219 arrows with feather fletching, and a Zwickey two-bladed broadhead. His arrow weighed 650 grains and with a speed of 245 fps gave slightly more than 86 foot-pounds of energy. Since 1989 when this hunt took place, more powerful crossbows and better broadheads have become available.

He also settled on a 2.5-power scoped sight, which is about the optimum magnification required for big game at close range. More magnification at a range of just a few yards makes it difficult to determine where you are aiming and can do more harm than good in the split seconds when the animal turns for an optimum shot.

Horton's biggest problem was convincing Professional Hunter (PH) Mike Heath that he needed to approach his game alone to get close enough for a shot and that he had to choose the time for his shot. Heath's hushed "Shoot now, shoot now, SHOOT NOW!" instructions once caused Horton to rush a shot and spoil a chance at a huge sable. Only after he successfully took a puku and a warthog with his crossbow were the PH and his trackers more confident in the ability of this "bow thing" to actually kill something. Still, when the opportunity came to take a lion and Heath encouraged him to use a heavy rifle, Horton assured his not-too-confident PH that the crossbow would do just fine.

They discovered the lion when buzzards attracted the hunters to a small elephant that had apparently died as a result of a poacher's bullet. As they approached, a lion ran off from the carcass. Although they didn't see the lion, they knew from the tracks that it appeared to be a big male. They decided to leave it until the afternoon. When they returned, they parked a mile away and walked in as silently as possible. "The lion heard us as we got close, and it moved off growling his displeasure at being disturbed a second time. It was huge!"

After squatting down in the scant cover of a termite mound and a small bush, they waited for the lion's return. When it did, it offered a per-

A group of eland head toward water. The largest member of the antelope family, the eland has modest horns compared to the kudu, but it is a tremendously powerful animal. Among the animals considered plains game, only the 4,000-pound bull giraffe is heavier.

fect broadside shot at 20 yards, and Horton placed his crosshairs low on the body behind the front leg. The arrow passed through the lion and kicked up dust when it hit the ground on the other side. "The lion did not flinch, blink, or move in any way at all," said Horton. "He looked at me again, took three steps, and sunk to the ground."

The PH saw the dust fly and was certain that Horton missed the shot. Horton insisted that the shot had been right through the top of the heart and that the lion was lying dead just a few yards away. "You can see him," Horton said. "No, I bloody well can't," Heath replied. The guide insisted that they wait, but darkness came quickly. When other lions came to the carcass and moved within 10 yards of the hunters, Horton and the trackers backed off as quietly as possible and returned with the truck. Even after a rifle shot, the other lions were reluctant to move. Horton's lion was so big, over 500 pounds, that they had to use a winch to load it into the safari wagon. Full mounted, the lion stands in Horton's trophy room today.

This old male, although a magnificent animal, had been driven out of his pride. Without its protection, it ultimately would have been pulled

Water buffalo should always be regarded with caution regardless of the weapon you carry. Crossbow arrows may ultimately kill buffalo, but they will not stop them during a charge. A killing shot must pass behind the massive shoulder bone into the lungs from the back.

Bernard Horton with a large lion he took as it was preparing to feed on a dead elephant. This lion was taken with a single arrow, which completely penetrated the lion's body after passing through both lungs.

down by hyenas and eaten alive. Horton gave it a quick, clean death that would have never occurred in the natural environment.

A leopard was next on Horton's list, and after setting out baits they finally attracted one. A four-sided bush blind was built on the spot. The leopard came in, and the shot looked good. Unfortunately, the arrow hit a twig near the bait and was deflected over the top of the animal. Typically leopards that have been shot at do not return to baits, but Horton insisted that they hunt the bait again the following night, and, although somewhat later than the night before, the leopard did return. This time no brush intervened with the shot, and the arrow flew true. The leopard bounded off the limb and disappeared in the inky darkness.

Again not confident that the leopard had been hit, Heath insisted that they retire for the night and look for the leopard in the morning. When they returned, this time with guns, they quickly found the leopard 30 yards away. The enormous tom leopard, which weighed nearly 180 pounds, was mounted as Horton first saw him, lying across a branch, now locked in immortality.

Finding buffalo in Africa is not difficult to do, but finding a trophy buffalo is. After a long crawl through the brush, Horton was in the

Bernard Horton and his wife pose with the leopard he shot at night from a blind. On his first attempt at the large cat, the arrow struck a branch and was deflected. Horton returned the following night and shot the leopard from the branch of a tree.

Bernard Horton with a cape buffalo, Africa's big black and ugly. In an
unusually productive safari, Horton took a lion, a leopard, and a buffalo on
the same trip.

direct travel path of a herd of buffalo, but he could not find a shootable
bull among them. This time the PH was well back of him, and Horton
was completely exposed on a burned-off plain. To keep from being
trampled, he stood up, raised his crossbow over his head, and danced
around and shouted. This had the desired effect, and the buffalo moved
away from what they probably thought was a "madman in their front
yard."

After days of checking waterholes in the hope of finding the tracks
of a big, lone buff that had come to water, they found evidence of their
buffalo on the last day. They followed the tracks for hours, and when
fresh dung indicated that they were closing in on a pair of buffalo, they
paused to rest. Suddenly, only 35 yards away, the buffalo got up. Horton quickly aimed and shot. His arrow imbedded in the chest of the
largest animal, and Horton quickly reloaded. The buffalo, which did
not know it had been hit, turned and offered another shot. This time the
arrow hit a bit high in the spine, and the huge animal dropped. Horton
reloaded again and moved around for a finishing shot. Although the
buffalo could not get up, it was angry and pulling itself along toward
the hunter. Horton shot again, but the buffalo swung its head and the

arrow struck ineffectively high on its nose. Before Horton could reload again, the buffalo died.

On this single hunt, Horton had taken three of Africa's big five with a crossbow. In each case, when the hits were good, the crossbow had sufficient power to drive the arrow deep enough into the vitals of the animal to result in a quick demise. Was there an element of danger in these hunts? Yes, there was. It certainly adds to the excitement of the hunt when issues of life and death to both the hunter and the hunted come into doubt. Luck also played a part in that Horton had stumbled across such outstanding animals as the lion and leopard. The odds were swayed in Horton's direction because he chose an outfitter with a reputation for providing good trophies even though Heath was not, at that time, experienced in guiding crossbowmen or bowhunters.

Horton's active, energetic nature usually prevents him from being patient enough to sit for hours in a blind waiting for game, but as this was necessary on the leopard hunt, he surprised himself by adapting to the circumstances. The experience was intense enough to absorb Horton's complete attention while waiting for the big cat to appear and even walk around the blind before going to the bait.

17

CLASSIC CROSSBOW
HUNTS—AUSTRALIA

If Africa is a long way away, Australia is even farther with a 24-hour flight required to get to the nearest part of the "great southern continent." Most Americans and Europeans don't appreciate Australia's size or diversity. Its central desert is many times larger than South Africa's Kalahari, and its more densely populated areas are close to the coasts. The northern coast around Darwin quickly gives way to vast seasonally watered ranchlands inhabited not only by indigenous marsupials and reptiles, but also by introduced species.

From childhood on, nearly everyone has likely been fascinated by Australia's kangaroos and other unique animals, but it is the introduced species, such as exotic deer, pigs, bush cows, and water buffalo, that are usually the focus of visiting hunters. Nearby New Zealand also has numerous species of horned game (red deer, white-tailed deer, and elk), but to find large numbers of the world's biggest and "baddest" Asiatic water buffalo you have to go to northern Australia. These animals outweigh the African buffalo by a considerable amount, and their wide arclike horns can become scythes of death for unwary hunters. As their name implies, they prefer to feed in well-watered grasslands and are quite comfortable in swamps and flooded savannahs, although they will also graze in dry areas.

Although taking so many horned deer species at once is not probable, a visiting hunter could, between Australia and New Zealand, take elk, red deer, fallow deer, sambar deer, axis deer, and several other deer species as well as such exotics as camels, thar, and wild goats. We haven't even mentioned bird shooting, pig hunting, and fishing. Unfortunately, bush cows and buffalo in the northern part of the country must be taken during the dry season when most of the deer species are not available, because their antlers have been shed or are growing. Bush

Bill Throubridge with an Asiatic water buffalo taken with a 700-grain heavy carbon arrow two-blade cut on impact point and 225-pound pull weight Excalibur Exomax crossbow.

bulls are also available in the south during deer-hunting season, but water buffalo are, by far, most abundant in the north.

Water buffalo were introduced from Indonesia in 1820 as a source of meat. Not only did they thrive, but they have caused what some call, "major environmental damage to native flora" by making large wallows. This has led to large-scale culling operations, including shooting the animals from helicopters. More recent investigations have indicated that perhaps the environmental damage was overstated. Indeed, studies have shown that buffalo fed on low-quality forage yield a better meat than cows. When millions are starving in Africa, one would hope that a better use could be found for these animals than shooting them and letting them rot.

Bush bulls are cows of various appearances and colors that were missed for several years in the annual "musters" and have become too wild to round up. Harvesting these animals by shooting them is the only effective tool for controlling their numbers and keeping them from undesirable interbreeding with domestic cattle. Wild camels, which are frequently found on the fringes of the desert, are challenging to hunt in the barren country in which they inhabit.

J. Y. Jones, a hunter I know, had considerable trouble in the 2004-2005 season getting his trophies out of Australia, apparently not because of paperwork, but due to lassitude on the part of his Australian expediter, Kuehne and Nagel PTY Ltd. in Sidney. To have his trophies shipped to the United States cost Jones between $3,555 and $4,000. Almost a year later, he was still waiting for one to arrive. To make matters worse, the hides of those that he received were unusable because they had been improperly treated and packed.

Although Bill Throubridge could not recall exactly what it cost to get his and Kath's trophies back from Australia, he said, "It costs a fortune. I use to think that getting things back from Africa was bad, but this was worse. Much worse."

Faced with these kinds of problems, I think I would have taken good pictures, stacked the trophies with firewood, and returned them to the dusty land from which they came. Alternatively, the solution would be to prepare the trophies yourself, take the necessary import paperwork with you, have the outfitter get the export documents, and take your chances with working through the export-import procedures. One of the most experienced U.S. companies to receive your trophies is Fauna and Flora in New York. It will handle the U.S. import requirements and

Bill Throubridge with a scrub bull. A bull this size was taken by Kath Throubridge with a 100-gram Wasp Boss point, the same size point that she uses on deer-size game.

send your skulls, horns, and hides to the tanner or taxidermist you designate. Even if you only clean, boil, and take your pig tushes with you in your luggage, you will save considerable costs.

EXCALIBUR HUNT

The chance to hunt a buffalo that was one and a half times larger than the African species enticed the Throubridges to hunt in northern Australia. Australian buffalo range widely and prefer to live in herds, although, like the African buffalo, solitary aged bulls get pushed out of the herd and go off either with a couple of their buddies or by themselves. Each year, a few people are gored when they surprise a water buffalo (literally run into one after dark while walking home).

The Throubridges flew into Darwin and hunted one of the large nearby ranches. One of their first animals was a scrub bull that weighed about 1,500 pounds, which they spotted from the vehicle and stalked. Kath had the first shot at about 30 yards. She was using an ExoMax with a 225-pound pull, a gold-tip carbon arrow, and 100-grain Boss three-bladed point, the same arrow-point combination that she uses on almost all her other game. The shot was placed about one-third the way up the body over the front leg. The big bull absorbed the hit, then turned and trotted off a short distance before going down in sight of the hunters.

Wanting the deepest penetration possible, Bill elected to use a two-bladed cut-on-contact point made by Magnus with a carbon shaft and point weighing 700 grains. He shot his water buffalo at 30 yards. The arrow broke a rib, entered the chest cavity, and was stopped by a rib on the far side. The bull ran a distance of 50 yards, stopped, stood still, and then fell over. This bull was one of three they had spotted at a distance. Bill and his guide deduced what would be the most likely travel path of the group, then got into position behind some brush, and waited. When the best bull was close enough, Bill stood and shot.

Of the three bovines shot, two were killed with single arrows and the third required two, not a bad average on such huge animals. The Throubridges owe their success to careful shooting at an intimidating target. The shot must be placed between one-third and one-half of the way up the body over the front leg and below the heavy shoulder bone. An arrow would have a difficult time passing through both the shoulder and a rib before getting into the heart-lung area.

18

CROSSBOW ORGANIZATIONS AND PUBLICATIONS

Although it must have felt differently when various states were passing legislation to restrict or even prohibit the use of the crossbow, the crossbow hunter is no longer alone. Increasingly, the crossbow as a unique hunting tool is recognized by more national and international organizations, such as Safari Club International, which even has a separate category for trophies taken by crossbow hunters. In the United States, the National Wild Turkey Federation in support of the nation's disabled hunters recognizes that the crossbow is an appropriate hunting tool for those who lack the full use of their bodies. Perhaps one day even the archconservative Pope and Young Club will come to the realization that the crossbow will bring more hunters into conventional archery sports and extend the hunting lives of many older bowhunters, but as of this time the organization refuses to recognize crossbow trophies.

The near absence of written and visual materials about the crossbow is being rectified by publications such as this book, two regularly published magazines, two special-interest magazine editions in 2005–2006, and video and DVD productions available on national television and for purchase. In addition, states that permit crossbows during their regular archery seasons have included segments on the crossbow during their hunter-safety training.

In support of these efforts, the industry members of the American Crossbow Federation have taken pains to ensure that any public information released about the crossbow accurately reflects the advantages and limitations of this age-old hunting instrument. Many American makers include videos or DVDs with their crossbows that not only explain the characteristics of their particular crossbows, but also include information about their history and proper use. These productions also employ hunting episodes to give the buyer an accurate feel for using the crossbow under real-world conditions.

The American Crossbow Federation's official monthly publication, *Horizontal Bowhunter,* regularly features articles on the crossbow, related regulations, and other relevant subjects. The organization also arranges hunts designed to provide its members access to guides and hunt organizers at attractive prices. Articles in the magazine are penned by such authorities as Excalibur's Bill Throubridge, Horton's Otti Snyder, and others with extensive crossbow-hunting experience. In 2004, *Horizontal Bowhunter* announced that it would launch its own registry of big-game trophies taken with the crossbow as well as with bows and firearms.

Horizontal Bowhunter's editor, Daniel James Hendricks, runs what is basically a one-man shop and will happily respond to questions and take subscriptions directed to his Internet address at bowtwang@runestone.net.

A second magazine, *Crossbow Connection,* is published three times a year by Editor Leon A. Russo. This publication, which celebrated its fifth anniversary in 2005, features crossbow hunts, product reviews, and ads pertaining to crossbows and their accessories. The easiest way to subscribe is through the publication's website at www.crossbowconnection magazine.com.

Both publications are interested in stories about crossbow hunts, particularly those about young people, the disabled, women, families, and unusual game species. The articles should be brief, 600 to 800 words, and accompanied by good-quality film or high-resolution digital photographs. If you are thinking of submitting an article, please contact the editors. Brief letters to the editor discussing opinions, activities, equipment, or accomplishments are also accepted. These do not have to be accompanied by photography. All submissions may be edited and may or may not be used, depending on the space available in the publications. Because of a relatively small number of subscribers, both magazines presently are not able to pay for submittals.

Excalibur, Horton, and TenPoint regularly produce a variety of products, mostly in video or DVD format, that contain instructive materials and feature hunts with their crossbows. Almost invariably, the materials showcase hunters shooting top-of-the-line crossbows and rarely show use or explanation of lower-priced entries. Nonetheless, these well-produced, useful, and entertaining products will help those new to the sport to understand the uses and limitations of their crossbows.

More crossbow hunts are finding their way to the Outdoor Channel and other television markets. Most feature deer hunting, but hunts for a variety of other species and in other parts of the world also appear. As the standards for commercial television videos continue to rise, these are high-quality productions. Unlike the companies' packaged videos that are sold with their products, the television productions say comparatively little about the equipment being used, why a particular crossbow-arrow combination was selected, and how it performed. The emphasis is on the hunt, with little time spent on instructional content.

Independent video producers, such as Bob Foulkrod, also make crossbow-hunting episodes that are finding their way into hunting video sales markets. All or parts of these may be televised, but in general the independent video will be more extensive than the limited coverage allowed in a television show.

Increasing amounts of crossbow-related materials are also finding their way onto the web at such locations as the Sportsman's Guide and Cabela's websites. These sites also feature activities in the international market, such as crossbows now made in Russia and a new-departure design, the Swiss Twinbow II produced by Swiss Crossbow Makers GmbH. This crossbow, which may be seen at www.swisscrossbow.ch, has four limbs that are mounted parallel to, rather than ninety degrees from, the stock.

The Archery Trade Association has now included crossbow competition in every promotional archery shoot that it sponsors. For those with a competitive edge, you will find lists of crossbow shoots regularly published in *Crossbow Connection*. The majority of those currently listed are in the Northeast and Midwest.

One of the more active state crossbow associations is the New York State Crossbow Hunting Association, which ironically is located in a state where crossbow use for hunting purposes is presently restricted to only the most profoundly disabled individuals. If a hunter can wiggle a finger in New York, he is considered too able-bodied to qualify for a crossbow permit. For information about the association and its continuing battle with legislative committees, consult Bill Hilts, spokesman for the association, at penrodacre@aol.com, or write to him at 5115 Bear Road, Pen Rod Acres, Sanborn, NY 14132.

19

CLEANING AND PROCESSING WILD GAME

Most of today's hunters are at least two, and often as many as four, generations away from the days when domestic animals were regularly slaughtered and prepared for the table. The rich rural traditions of catching and killing a chicken for Sunday dinner or waiting for the weather to turn cold to slaughter a hog are mostly dim memories in stories handed down from previous generations.

To be sure, you can use commercial processors to produce nice packages of plastic-wrapped cubed steaks, roasts, specialty sausages, and other meats from your kill, but knowing how to clean game and prepare it yourself for cooking is a useful skill to have. The pride you will feel at not only taking an animal using your crossbow, but also personally cleaning it, packaging it, and cooking it for your family and guests will provide honor to you and to the animal that you killed.

What do I mean by "honor"? Like many Americans, I have a polyglot ancestry. I am nominally Caucasian of mixed Irish, English, Spanish, and Scotch ancestry with a dose of American Indian. All of these cultures have rich hunting traditions where the taking of game, the killing of a wild animal for food, is not just slaughter and butchery.

Old-time hunters would honor fallen game by placing a bloodied branch in its mouth as a last meal or playing a salute to it from a hunter's horn at the end of the day. The practice of marking a hunter's face with the blood of his first kill, which some of us still do, is about all that is left of the European-derived hunting traditions in the United States. The pragmatic colonists were more interested in getting the meat in the pot. In Native American cultures, the fallen animal was often honored in prayer, song, or dance in recognition that this animal died that we might live.

Have no doubt that you honor the animal that you killed by cleaning it yourself, rather than placing it in the hands of anonymous strangers in a meat-processing plant. Other advantages to doing it yourself are that you know without question that this is your deer, and not someone else's, and that the animal has been processed promptly, rather than hung in a cooler to age (rot) for days or weeks. I like to remove the guts from the game as soon as I can get to a relatively clean spot, skin the animal while it is still warm with body heat, and, if possible, cut it up, package it, and store it in the freezer within twenty-four hours of its death.

Oftentimes, beef fat is put in deer burger, but this does nothing but load up an almost fat-free meat with cholesterol-inducing saturated fats. True, deer burger is too dry to grill as you would a beef-derived hamburger, but other ways abound for cooking deer. To have your deer hamburgers, you will need to change your cooking technique to a moist cooking method, similar to the way Southerners cook sausage by first browning the meat and then putting water in the fry pan to boil the sausage until it is done. We'll cover cooking more completely in the following chapter, but for now we have to know what to do with the dead deer on the ground.

FIRST THINGS FIRST

After the animal falls, approach it carefully with an arrow in your crossbow ready to shoot. Before even thinking about touching the deer, make sure it is dead. The eyes should be dull and the animal unresponsive to the touch. On more than one occasion, a "dead" deer has revived, thrashed the hunter with horn and hooves, and run off. Spine hits are notorious for dropping a deer like a stone, only to have the animal get up and run off when approached. If you have any doubt, put another arrow through the lungs.

Recover your arrow and point. These points are sharp and are a hazard to you and other hunters who might happen to walk that way for years to come. Each year, several hunters step on or are jabbed in the leg by someone else's arrow.

Next, you must decide whether to gut the animal on the spot or take it to a better location before starting the gutting process. If it is a large animal and you can't move it by yourself or get help, your only choice is to start field dressing where the beastie lies. If you have a long drag in front of you, you can reduce the body weight by thirty percent by leaving the entrails on the ground, as long as you can legally do so. Some states and some hunts prohibit field dressing.

One of the best methods that I have found to move a dead animal, such as a deer, is to use a plastic sled. These are sold for $30 by the Sportsman's Guide mail-order house. The sled, which is about 6 feet long and has tie points for tying the animal's legs close to the body, is lightweight and works better than anything with wheels in snow or sand. It keeps the hide and carcass protected and is the easiest thing I have ever found to help pull an animal over logs and through timber.

Once you have the animal at a place where you can work, it is time to get started. If you can get the animal back to camp or home, chances are you have a place where you can use a pulley, gamble, and rope to hoist the deer up. If not, I have dressed many deer and hogs on the tailgate of my truck.

FIELD DRESSING

When I start working with a new hunter, the first thing we do is hunt squirrels and rabbits. The same techniques we use to clean these smaller animals are employed on deer. It is just a matter of scaling up the process. To butcher deer and hogs, you will need a saw to cut off the legs, split the pelvis, part the breastbone, and remove the ribs. A common hacksaw or any of a number of folding saws sold by several companies work well. Gerber sells a Change-A-Blade saw with a coarse blade for cutting wood and a fine-toothed blade for cutting bone. Some folding knives such as Buck's Crosslock series offer a saw-gut hook blade as an option, and Case has an XX-Changer with three interchangeable blades, including a saw, contained in a single leather case. Bigger animals require larger tools, and it is common to use a chainsaw lubed with vegetable oil to cut up such animals as bison and moose.

Huge knives are not necessary for deer, but you will need something with a reasonably heavy 6-inch blade for elk, moose, and the like. More important than length is that the blade is sharp and the hunter has a steel to retouch the blade when needed. I have dressed much game with a 3-inch pocketknife. Quality folding knives made by Bear Manufacturing, Benchmade, Buck, Camillus, Case, Emerson, and others will last for generations and can certainly clean every deer you will ever shoot.

To get started, lay the deer down on its side. Pull up the tail and cut around the anus pulling it out as far as possible and reaching in to cut the gut away from the body cavity. Take a rubber band or cord and tie off the anus as you later will pull it through the pelvis into the body cavity. Cut off the forelegs downward from the "elbow and knee" joints. I often give these to my dogs to keep them busy while I process the rest of the deer.

If you are going to hoist the deer, make holes in the triangle of skin above the "knee" on the rear legs, taking care not to cut the tendon. These holes provide places to put the gambol hooks or suspending ropes. After

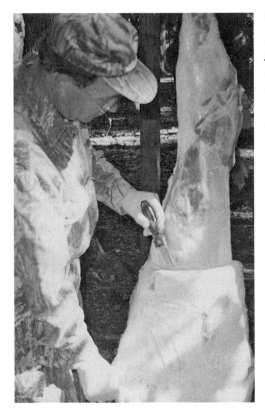

The author skinning a hog. Like bear, hogs have a lot of fat under their hides. Both animals provide excellent eating as long as they have been feeding on acorns, fruit, and vegetable matter.

the holes are made, skin that part of the leg. If hoisting the deer, pull up the deer in stages, skinning as you go. Do not open the body cavity until the deer is completely skinned. The neatest way to skin is to cut the inside of the legs, skin out the hams, cut off the tail, and make another cut on the midline of the animal all the way down the neck (provided that you are not going to have it mounted). If you want a shoulder mount on your deer, the best result is to "case skin" the deer starting 2 feet behind the shoulder and coming forward, peeling the skin off as if you were taking off a sock. The second best method (and the more costly to you because of the extra work needed to sew up the hide) is to make a cut along the top of the backbone starting at the base of the skull and to skin down from there. If the deer is going on the wall, a cut along the back will not show, but one up the front of the neck will be difficult to repair. Don't "bleed the deer" by slicing it across the throat. Believe me, if you have put an arrow in the chest cavity, the animal has already bled out.

When cleaning deer, hogs, or other animals, you always run the risk of being infected with a variety of blood-transmitted diseases. To prevent this, carry several pairs of rubber gloves and use them when work-

With the bear almost completely skinned, one person uses a knife while the other pulls the hide. It is good practice for only one person at a time to use a knife to work on a piece of game.

ing inside the body cavity or if you have a scratch or nick on your hands. If you tear a glove on a bone fragment, put on another. Not only are gloves a good alternative in an area where clean water for hand washing may be lacking, but they are a low-cost and reasonable way to protect your health.

If you happen to knick yourself and your hands are covered with animal blood, wash them in your own urine since this is the closest thing you have to a sterile, antiseptic solution. It may sound disgusting, but it is safer than possibly picking up bacteria from contaminated surface water.

If you are cleaning the deer on the ground or on a tailgate, gut the deer before the hide is removed, unless you are going to save the forward part of the hide for mounting. Tie off the anus as described earlier. Make a cut through the hide and abdominal wall, taking care not to puncture the intestines, which are probably already starting to expand with unpleasant-smelling digestive gases. Although a knife will work, a gut hook is the most effective means of opening the abdomen. The best way to keep from puncturing the gut is to run your finger inside the animal on top of the blade as you make a forward and downward cut through the abdominal wall and hide.

Keep cutting forward until you reach the solid bone of the sternum. You can use a knife to cut this bone on small and young animals, but a saw is better for mature animals. Cut and peel back some of the skin so that the saw can cut the bone and the teeth will not become matted with broken hairs to be drug into the chest cavity. If the animal was shot through the heart and lungs, blood will freely flow when you cut the diaphragm. I catch this in a 5-gallon bucket. Once the sternum is cut, spread the ribs. If it's a large animal, I sometimes will jam a freshly cut branch into the chest cavity to keep it open.

At this stage, the paunch and intestines will already be oozing from the body cavity. If the animal is lying on its side, work either from front to back or from back to front. If hanging, cut from the pelvis down. Reach in and cut the windpipe, diaphragm muscle, and heart loose. Put the heart aside. Now reach in behind the paunch and cut away the connective tissue from the back. Move the bucket as you go to catch the lungs, paunch, stomach, and intestines as they fall from the animal. Save the liver and put it aside. Once the major organs are removed, the large intestine and bladder will still be in the pelvis. Carefully take your knife and remove the bladder. Tie off its neck and place it to one side. (Buck or doe urine is a useful scent attractant as are the tarsal glands on the rear legs of a buck.) Then pull the intestine and tied-off anus free of the body.

With the guts removed, there is still blood inside the carcass. At this stage, I finish skinning the animal laying the hide back into the bed of the truck as I go. When it is time to skin the other half, I rotate the skinned portion back onto the flesh side of the hide and skin the remainder of the animal. I use a knife and saw to cut off the head just back of the skull. Then I drive the truck to a water source and wash out the carcass.

When cleaning a hanging deer, you will progress through the same steps. If you do it in camp, all of your hunting buddies will want to "show you how." If they are so inclined, step back and let them, but make sure only one person at a time works on the deer with a knife. If someone else approaches the deer with a knife, put yours away and hold the deer for him while he cuts. Follow this rule even if you are in a hurry or a storm is coming. You do not want you or your buddy to be stabbed or cut while cleaning a deer. Also, don't allow the drinking of anything alcoholic until the knives are cleaned and put away.

CUTTING, WRAPPING, AND GRINDING

Meat cutting is a respectable profession, but hunters do not have to be nearly so proficient to cut and package their own deer. One general rule is to store no meat with bones except for the ribs and neck roast, which are best if cooked within a month after the deer is killed. Among other good practices, throw away any bloodshot meat (or boil it for your dogs), and freeze muscle masses, rather than cut individual steaks, to reduce the amount of freezer burn. Cut up parts of the lower legs that have too many tendons to eat and grind this into hamburger along with any smaller hunks of meat near the bones. I also use the flanks and excess meat on the outside of the ribs for this purpose. I usually cut the backstraps, which are taken out as long thin muscle masses, into 12-inch sections, wrap them in both plastic and paper, and freeze them. The tenderloins on the underside of the rib cage should also be individually frozen.

Use your knife to remove the muscles from the bones, but you will still need a saw to cut through the pelvis so the hindquarters can be separated and taken inside for more careful processing. The pelvis with any meat sticking to it makes a good soup bone, as do the backbone segments. I also use the saw to cut the ribs loose and freeze them separately. I purposefully will leave some meat on the ribs, but I take most of the top layer of meat for hamburger. If you don't want to save the ribs, cut the meat from between them for ground meat. I cut off the neck, remove the gullet, and bake the neck as a pot roast with onions, celery, potatoes, and carrots.

If I have room in the freezer, I will boil some of the bones for my dogs and save them for Christmas treats. Any bloodshot meat or organ meat that I do not use is also boiled for them. Remember your pets are carnivores, and their heritage is to kill and eat game animals—hide, guts, bones, and all. I have no qualms about giving large adult dogs boiled deer bones and meat, but be careful with puppies. They should get only soft bones and gristle in small amounts that they can chew and process.

I wash the liver and heart and freeze them separately. Although I have cut the liver in slices and soaked it before freezing, I have found it is just as good if I freeze it whole and cut it immediately prior to use.

The rationale here is that if you are going to make meals of your deer all year long, as I do, meat such as butterfly steaks sliced from the backstraps and cubed steaks are best cut when the meat is still in a half-frozen state. Larger hunks of meat can be made into roasts or cut into smaller pieces for stews.

To process deer meat, I use a hand grinder mounted on a kitchen table into which I feed hunks of meat. When I am done, I put the ground meat into plastic bags I seal and, depending on how long I expect to keep the meat before use, either freeze directly or wrap again in paper.

Processed this way, the deer is available in an almost infinite variety of products, depending on your inclinations at the moment. You will note that I said nothing about marinating the meats, aging them, or doing fancy cuts prior to freezing. If you want any of this, you can do it at a later stage. For now, your chief objective is to get the meat in the freezer as quickly as possible.

When freezing deer, spread it out in the freezer. If you pack it in a single box or bag, the outside of the deer may be frozen quickly, but the interior packages may take days to freeze. When transporting deer, nothing beats dry ice. Ten pounds of dry ice, even in a large cooler, will hold a frozen deer for days and will complete the freezing process if the meat is only partly frozen. If declared, one kilogram (2.2 pounds) of ice may be taken onboard international flights, but none may be transported on domestic connections, under present flight rules. If contemplating a hunt where you will be bringing back meat by air, check with your carrier about how to transport your game.

If possible, pick up is a Styrofoam container packed inside a cardboard box, which has been used to transport medical supplies. These containers come in all sizes, including very large, and hospitals regularly throw them away. They make wonderful, disposable containers for flying your meat and/or hides home.

CLEANING FOWL

A real challenge for any hunter, but particularly the crossbow hunter, is to take a wild turkey. But if you do, these magnificent birds provide excellent eating, as long as they are properly cleaned and cooked. In today's rush-rush society, it is common to save the breast and maybe the leg quarters to cook and to throw away the remainder of the bird. Doing so is a disservice to the hunter and the turkey. Instead, I recommend giving your hard-won fowl a place of honor at the Christmas table. Cooking instructions will follow in the next chapter, but for now here is how to clean your bird.

First off, you will need a clear area outside where you do not mind having a few loose feathers, a couple of tall kitchen plastic bags, and enough time to do the job right. Leave the head and feet on the bird since they are handy for hanging and handling. Using garden shears, cut the wings at the first joint away from the body of the turkey. Save and dry the wing tips. They are useful for making turkey fly-down noises. Remove the beard and cut away the tail. If you want to put the tail and beard in a wooden holder to display your trophy, pin them to a cardboard sheet and coat them with borax and salt to dry.

As you hang or hold the bird by the neck, put the body of the turkey in a plastic bag, grab a pinch of feathers from the lower back, and jerk firmly. Drop the feathers in the bag and continue until all the feathers are removed. Plucking is easier if the bird is still warm. Turkeys have lice, and as you pluck the bird you will see the white, semitransparent insects, which are about a $1/4$ inch long. Do not touch your hair while you are plucking the bird. Although these lice are species specific and will not reproduce on people, you will not want them crawling around in your hair for a week or so. If it happens, a good disinfecting shampoo, which you can also use on your dog, will take care of them.

If the feathers are stubborn, scald the bird by dousing it up and down in a cast-iron wash pot full of boiling water or, although somewhat less effective, pouring boiling water over the bird. Some people singe the carcass with a piece of burning newspaper to remove any remaining hairlike feathers, but since I do not eat the skin, I seldom bother with singing.

Once the body and neck are plucked, remove the legs, saving the spurs, if desired. Slice the head from the neck, and cut the neck free of the body. Use your knife to remove the crop and windpipe from as far down in the body as you can reach. At the rear of the bird, you will see an oval of soft skin beneath the breastbone extending around to the back. Remove this skin, taking with it the anus. The intestines will now be exposed; reach in and pull them out. Once these are removed, recover the liver and gizzard and set them aside. Now take the knife and remove the diaphragm, then the lungs (at the top of the rib cage), the heart, and the windpipe. Feel along the inside and remove any tissue that remains. Thoroughly wash the bird inside and out taking care to scrub away any blood on the skin.

While you remove the skin and windpipe from the neck, allow the bird to drain; then wash the blood out of the heart, clean the liver, and split the gizzard. Once you cut into the gizzard you will see that it is filled with sand. Dump this out, and also remove the yellow protective membrane between the gizzard and the muscles. Once done, wash the gizzard again, and place it and the other giblets into a plastic bag to freeze inside the bird. These components will make good giblet gravy.

Wet the outside of the bird one more time, and place plastic grocery bags around both ends of the bird, tying them together. Wrap the turkey in freezer paper or aluminum foil and freeze. Preserved in this manner, the turkey will still be good by Christmas, even if taken during spring turkey season. You may also use this cleaning method on other large fowl, such as geese and swan.

CLEANING FISH AND ALLIGATORS

Everybody knows how to clean fish. Right? Well, what about large fish such as the various gars, which may range from 20 to over 200 pounds, stingrays, alligators, and other species taken while bowfishing. These critters have size, weight, teeth, and stingers and often do not have happy dispositions.

First off, make sure your catch is really dead. Alligators in particular may thrash around for some time even with their brains blown away. Several wraps of electrical tape around the snout is good insurance at any time, but remember that those powerful tails and claws can also cause significant damage to us relatively puny people.

Gars have the best-eating flesh of any freshwater fish. Contrary to the popular opinion that they are too bony to eat, they contain two strips of boneless meat on either side of the backbone, and this meat has a mild taste on the order of flounder or crappie. The meat of smaller gar may be cut into small chunks and cooked and served as one would scallops. Steaks for the grill can be cut from larger fish, while ground meat from the huge gar makes the best fish sandwiches ever.

Gars have very tough scales, and the bigger they are, the harder they are to penetrate. For gar weighing up to 30 pounds, I use a hatchet to chop the tails and tin snips to cut up the backbone. After making a downward cut back of the head, pull the skin down to reveal the "backstraps," which are removed exactly as they would from a deer. You do not have to open the body cavity of the fish. Also, avoid the gar's poisonous row. If an arrow passed through the egg sack, spilling some into the meat, cut away that section and discard it.

On big gar, I use a "gar ripper," which is a pole tool with a foot rest that I had made by Murray Carter, a master knife maker who, although Canadian, lived and worked in Japan. I use the foot piece to push the stiff short blade through the scales and the pole to rip open the fish by

The author uses a "gar ripper" to open up a big gar so that he can remove the boneless backstraps from either side of the backbone.

pulling upward with both hands on the handle. The Cajuns use a sharp hatchet to work up the backbone and chop around the tail and head. To keep the fish from moving, they put it into a wooden trough with a plank across the end to restrain the fish's snout and keep it from moving. The last time I was in Louisiana, dressed gar was selling for $8 a pound. Have no doubt that it is good stuff.

Members of the ray family also have a mild-tasting white meat, although its somewhat unusual texture resembles parallel strips of spaghetti. The wings are cut away from the body and skinned with the very thin edges removed. Next, use a long fillet knife to cut down until you reach a layer of cartilage. Cut along this layer and remove two tapered strips of meat from the top and bottom of the wings. To keep from overcooking the meat, I either cut the entire wing into strips of approximately uniform thickness, or on small rays split the upper wings horizontally to give six pieces of meat of approximately equal thickness from each ray.

Huge alligators are best processed commercially, but a 4-foot (the smallest legal size in Florida and Georgia) to 6-foot alligator can be dressed by you. The first task is to find a clean cool place to work. Wash down the outside of the alligator with a bleach solution to remove any salmonella or other bacteria. Starting from the tail, cut a line down each side of the back plate. Think of it as the lid of a sardine can that you are going to peel away. Once the side cuts are made, start rolling the back-skin forward toward the head. Cut off the back of the head, and remove the side skins from the tail and ribs.

The gator tail of commerce is any white meat from the alligator regardless of what part of the animal it is derived. Most of it comes from the powerful muscles of the tail, but significant meat can be found in the heavy jowls of the head and next to the backbone. The fat, which is white but with a slight yellow tinge, gives an off-taste to the meat and should be removed and thrown away. Once the muscles are removed, they can be cubed and shrink-wrapped.

The meat from the legs of the alligator is red, and although not sold commercially, it tastes as good as the white meat. I often grind this meat and mix it with a little egg white for gator burgers. I have made grilled alligator ribs and soup from the skinned alligator paws. Both are excellent, and an unusual departure from the usual fried alligator nuggets.

20

FOOLPROOF RECIPES
FOR WILD GAME

I buy almost no meat, fish, or fowl. Nearly all the animal protein I eat is taken with my black-powder guns, bows, or crossbows. In my freezer at the moment are two deer, one hog, four pheasants, fifteen quail, six squirrels, two carp, three gars, and one turkey. I usually would also have some geese and swan, but those were eaten over Thanksgiving and Christmas. I have also consumed all my alligator, but with luck I will draw a Georgia tag this year.

Not only does wild game save on my grocery bills, it provides healthier, low-fat meats that are free of additives and preservatives. Commercial red meat is not so bad, but store-bought turkeys are injected with up to ten percent water, butter, salt, and preservatives so that they will not require basting and keep longer in the store. At least I know that my wild meat is free from growth hormones and other potentially nasty chemical additives whose long-term effects on the body may take decades to appear.

We are all human, but our individual body chemistries react differently to chemical compounds, whether they are injected into the body or taken through the mouth. Some people are violently allergic to dairy products, while others may not safely eat peanuts or mushrooms. The bottom line is to take care about what you eat, regardless of whether it comes from natural sources or chemically "enhanced" commercial products. As a general but not universal rule, properly cooked wild game has less fat and contains fewer potential chemical toxins than commercially available products.

However, never assume that, just because they are "natural," all the parts of the game are safe. Some parts, such as the roe from gar and the liver of the polar bear, are poisonous. Carp and gar taken from polluted waters may be so loaded with mercury and organic toxins as to not be safe, although the same species taken from clean waters makes a nutritious meal. Potential blood-borne diseases and parasites may infect organs and even the muscles of some animals. Careful cleaning and thorough cooking will eliminate these. Like the small percentage of insect parts allowed in commercial flour, which you don't want to think about when eating bread, your animal meat may contain parasites, but once cooked it is safe to consume.

Many wild-game recipes call for wrapping the meat in bacon, adding animal fats, or using other techniques to cover the so-called "wild taste" of game. Most of this "wild taste" comes from meat that has become partly rotted as a result of overheating during the cleaning or transportation process. On many animals, particularly deer and antelope, the fat is the first thing to spoil and should always be discarded. Fat from hogs and bear can be melted, strained, and canned in sealed jars, where it becomes more stable and may be kept for some time. But once opened, the jars should be refrigerated. Bear fat makes excellent pastries, but as it is a saturated fat, it should be consumed in modest amounts.

I add little, if any, fat to the dishes that I cook. If I fry something, I do it in olive or canola oil, not only because these oils contain fewer saturated fats, but because their omega-3 fatty acids are vital to human health.

In this chapter, I have included a number of recipes for deer meat that are equally applicable to the meat of any member of the deer or antelope families. The meat from hogs is treated separately. The world's various hogs, although they look different, cook and taste similarly no matter if they are feral hogs from the United States, wild boars from Europe, or warthogs and bushpigs from Africa. The taste of wild pork depends on the animal's diet. I have shot small hogs in coastal marshes that I could not eat, but found that older hogs taken from the same island but eating a diet of acorns were fine. Bear is a somewhat fatty meat that is similar to pork, and the pork recipes, particularly barbeque, work reasonably well for the bruins.

A modern reality is that few gals and almost no guys are taught how to cook in their mothers' kitchens. My sister and I were active participants in getting our family meals ready, particularly around the holiday season when preparations for Christmas might start a week before the event.

In recognition of this increasing lack of kitchen training, the following recipes take the user step by step through the cooking process. I have not included fancy food preparation techniques or any ingredients that could not be purchased in any reasonably well-stocked major grocery store. If you are going to shoot game, you are going to want to eat it, and

Bear fat rendered and canned in jars will last almost indefinitely. This product may be used like lard to make pastries, grease pans, or aid with general-purpose cooking. Because it is a saturated fat, it should be used sparingly.

you are going to have to cook it. Don't be fearful. Start with something simple, and as you gain confidence proceed to more complex dishes. I am unapologetically a Southerner, but these dishes will do well on anyone's table.

A note of caution: resist the temptation to overseason wild game. The only reason food from tropical countries is so highly loaded with pepper is to hide the taste of spoiled meat. Likewise, don't use too much sugar, honey, or the like on wild meats. I have mixed feelings about marinades. Some work, but I tend to use them sparingly. The added sugar can turn your main meat dish into what is calorically a sugar-loaded dessert.

DEER

DEER BURGERS, ALL-DEER ALL THE TIME

1–2 pounds of ground deer meat with no fat added
1 medium Spanish onion, finely chopped
1 3-ounce can chopped mushrooms or 8 fresh mushrooms
$1/4$ bell pepper, finely chopped
$1/2$ teaspoon salt
$1/4$ teaspoon black pepper

Thaw ground deer meat. Be careful when thawing in a microwave, as a portion of the meat frequently starts cooking on the outside. If some meat has started to brown, remove and discard the discolored portion before making the hamburger patties. Chop the onion and bell pepper, mix them together, and set aside. Place the hamburger in a bowl, and add salt, pepper, and about three-quarters of the chopped onions and peppers. Mold into hamburger patties approximately 3 inches in diameter. Too many chopped onions and peppers will cause the burgers to split and fall apart. Spray grill with Pam or other nonsticking agent, or brush the surface of the grill lightly with olive oil before adding burgers. Put burgers on charcoal grill with mesquite chips, and grill on both sides until brown. Once browned but still only partly cooked, place burgers in fry pan in approximately $1/2$ inch of water. Heat and allow water to boil, then add remaining chopped vegetables and mushrooms. Once about half the water has boiled away, turn burgers. Add more water if necessary to complete the cooking process. When done, the burgers will have shrunk approximately half an inch in diameter. Remove from pan and cover the burgers with the peppers, mushrooms, and onions before serving. Alternatively, the burgers may be topped with a low-fat cheese, placed on whole-wheat buns, and served with mustard, catsup, lettuce, and sliced tomato. Yet another variant is to eat as a hamburger steak with Hines 57 sauce. Always serve hot out of the pan, and eat immediately. A frosted mug of draft beer goes well with these burgers.

FAT-REDUCED LOW-SUGAR MEATLOAF

2 pounds ground deer meat
1 3-ounce can tomato paste
2 slices of toasted and crumbled wheat bread
1 medium onion, finely chopped
$1/2$ bell pepper, finely chopped
5 tablespoons mild salsa
3 tablespoons mustard
1 teaspoon horseradish
$1/2$ teaspoon salt
$1/2$ teaspoon olive oil

Preheat oven to 350 degrees. Thaw ground meat and place in a large bowl. Add all ingredients except the salsa, which is placed in a small bowl and refrigerated. Mix well with the hands. Wipe the bottom and sides of a 12-inch cast-iron frying pan with olive oil. Mold the meatloaf in the bottom of the fry pan, making a loaf that stands between 2 and 3 inches high and has steep sides. Cook in oven for approximately fifty minutes. The meatloaf is done when the fluids from the loaf have evaporated from the bottom of the pan and the edges of the meat have turned dark brown. Take a metal spatula and run around the sides of the fry pan and under the bottom of the meatloaf. With two spatulas, lift gently and place on a platter. Cut and serve while warm. The meatloaf will tend to tear. Add 1 or 2 tablespoons of salsa to each slice, and serve with mashed potatoes and butter. I like a semidry rose wine with this dish.

WORLD'S BEST SPAGHETTI SAUCE

2 pounds thawed ground deer meat
2 15-ounce cans of stewed tomatoes
2 cups water
3 Roma tomatoes, medium chopped
4 bay leaves
1 large Spanish onion, medium chopped
12 ripe olives, diced with pits removed
1 tablespoon olive oil
$^1/_2$ bell pepper, medium chopped
$^1/_2$ teaspoon oregano
$^1/_2$ teaspoon powdered garlic
$^1/_2$ teaspoon black pepper
pinch of red pepper

Nothing makes a better spaghetti sauce than ground deer meat. Heat olive oil in the frying pan, then add onions and bell pepper, and brown the thawed deer meat, breaking up any lumps. When browned, remove from pan and place in a large cast-iron pot to which you add the other ingredients. Allow the sauce to come to a boil, and then simmer for a minimum of two hours, adding more water and stirring occasionally to keep from sticking. After two hours, put a sample on a point of dry white-bread toast and taste. It should taste distinctly salty. Add more spices as desired, and continue to simmer for another hour. If the taste is still too harsh, melt in 2 tablespoons of margarine immediately before serving. Serve over toasted French bread or on hot freshly drained spaghetti. Complement with a red Italian wine.

DEER PARMIGIANA

6 deer steaks about 2 $^1/_2$ by 3 $^1/_2$ inches and $^3/_8$ inch thick,
1 large Spanish onion, cut medium fine

1 cup water
$^3/_4$ cup plain white flour
$^3/_4$ cup grated Parmesan cheese
2 Roma tomatoes, medium chopped
1 tablespoon olive oil
1 teaspoon salt
$^1/_2$ teaspoon oregano
$^1/_2$ teaspoon black pepper

Cut partly thawed deer meat across the muscle grain into slices about $^3/_8$ inch thick. When these slices are more nearly thawed, pound both sides with a meat mallet or the bottom of a glass bottle. (Often 4 to 8 year olds make enthusiastic meat pounders, and the more active they are in preparing the meal, the more likely they are to eat it.) Mix flour and spices together in a plastic bag while heating olive oil in a frying pan. Shake steaks in flour mixture, and place in fry pan, browning quickly on both sides. Add chopped onion, and once it starts to turn transparent, add water. Turn down heat to medium and allow steaks to boil in liquid. (If you continued to simply fry the meat, you would have country-fried steaks, which are also quite good.) Add additional water, as necessary, so that the steaks do not cook dry. The steaks are done when no bloody fluids issue from the meat. While they are still in the pan, sprinkle the steaks with cheese. Serve hot. Parmesan cheeses may range in flavor from relatively mild to quite strong. The more strongly flavored the cheese, the heavier and dryer the red wine you should serve with the meal. Even harsh Chiantis can be served with a heavily flavored Parmesan cheese.

DILL DEER STEAKS

Dill weed, the same spice used to make dill pickles, goes well with deer meat. I often mix dill in browning flour when making deer stews or fried dishes. Deer meat cut into "nuggets" can be served hot or cold or as appetizers. When frying, I prefer canola oil, which will take more heat than olive oil.

6 cubed steaks
$^3/_4$ cup plain white flour
1 cup canola or olive oil
1 teaspoon salt
1 large brown paper bag

$^1/_2$ teaspoon dill weed
$^1/_2$ teaspoon black pepper

Heat the oil in a deep-walled pot to frying temperature. The oil is hot enough when a small piece of breaded meat dropped in it instantly starts to bubble. Mix together the dry ingredients in a plastic bag. Add deer steaks to bag and shake to coat all parts with the flour-seasoning mix. Use tongs to drop the deer steaks into the hot oil. Take care not to be burned by the splatter. Turn the steaks when they are medium brown on one side. Once browned on both sides, lift them with tongs and allow excess oil to drip back into pot. Place meat on a brown paper bag to drain. The deer steaks taste best warm but can be served at room temperature. They also keep and transport well. I like to take some dill steak nuggets in a plastic bag into the deer blind with me. Dill deer steaks have a mild taste, which goes well with a Riesling, rose, or light-red wine.

THE BEST-EVER DEER STEW

Of all the deer dishes I cook, I have more requests for deer stew than any other. It has been on the table at wedding receptions and Christmas dinners as well as less formal occasions. The stew can be made in a pressure cooker, which accelerates cooking speed, or a stove eye (stir often).

2 pounds deer meat, chopped into cubes from $^1/_2$- to 1-inch square,
    depending on preference.
2 cans stewed tomatoes
3 Irish baking potatoes
2 Roma tomatoes
1 large Spanish onion
1 teaspoon dill weed
2 cups canola oil
2 cups water
1 large brown paper bag
$^2/_3$ cup plain flour
$^1/_3$ cup chopped carrots
$^1/_2$ bell pepper
$^3/_4$ teaspoon salt
$^1/_2$ teaspoon black pepper
$^1/_2$ teaspoon tarragon
pinch red pepper

Heat oil in a deep-walled pot. Place the cut-up meat cubes in a plastic bag with flour, salt, dill, and black pepper and shake until the meat is well coated. Fry the meat in the hot oil until brown, then remove and drain on the paper bag. After oil in pot has cooled, pour off, leaving the brown residue in the bottom of the pot. (The discarded oil is perfectly safe to reuse. After it has cooled, pour into a glass jar and store in refrigerator. Although it may set and turn white, it will quickly reliquify when heated.) While the oil is cooling and the meat is draining, peel and cut up vegetables. Place chopped onions, bell pepper, and carrots into pot with brown residue, and heat while stirring with a metal spatula. Return meat to pot, and add potatoes and canned and chopped tomatoes along with pan-browned vegetables. Add enough water so that the stew is fluid but not soupy. As last ingredients, place tarragon and red pepper into the pot. Seal the pressure cooker, and once it reaches operating pressure, cook for fifteen minutes. Remove from heat, or unplug pressure cooker, and cool in a sink full of cold water. When pressure drops to a safe level, remove lid and taste. Depending on the amount of salt in the canned stewed tomatoes, it may be necessary to add a little more. If too acid, a pinch to $1/4$ teaspoon of baking soda will sweeten the stew, but be cautious—add slowly and taste as you go. Tarragon has a distinct odor and taste. Make some batches with it and some without and see which your family prefers. Do not use more carrots than the recipe states because excess carrots give a bitter taste to the stew. This stew is best served with eggbread, which is a baked cornbread (see page 260). I like Georgia's Fox Ridge Antebellum Rosé with the stew, but any slightly sweet rosé, Riesling, or light-red wine goes well with this dish. Another excellent candidate is Heart of the Desert's Pistachio Blush, a New Mexico wine.

HOG

STIR FRY

This recipe may be made with pork, deer, other wild game meat, or breast from fowl.

> 1 pound lean meat with gristle or tendons removed, cut into thin slices about $1/4$ inch thick and 1 inch long while still partly frozen. Backstraps or tenderloins are preferred, but any cuts may be used.
> 1 cup of pea pods whole
> 1 medium onion, medium chopped
> $1/2$ cup bean sprouts

Stir-fries may be made with deer, pork, bear, alligator, or the meat from gar fish. A stir-fry meal is rapid to prepare and an ideal choice for when a group of friends want to come over to try something a bit different.

$^1/_4$ cup sliced carrots
6 fresh pole beans, cut into 1-inch segments
2 tablespoons olive oil
4 tablespoons soy sauce
1 4-ounce can mushrooms
1 8-ounce can water chestnuts
1 8-ounce can bamboo shoots

Heat oil in wok or large fry pan. Add sliced carrots and cut pole beans. When these have begun to soften, add meat, onions, and drained water chestnuts and bamboo shoots. Stir continuously. As mixture starts to dry, splash with soy sauce. When carrots are soft, add remaining ingredients and additional soy sauce as necessary to keep moist. Just as mixture starts to stick in pan, remove and serve. Some salt may be added to taste, depending on the amount of sodium in the soy sauce. Eat as is or serve over rice or Chinese noodles. A light wine may be served with this dish, but I prefer the accompanying taste of a light beer or a pilsner.

BAKED HAM

1 ham (size will vary, depending on the size of the hog)
3 tablespoons sugar (or honey)
1 cup water
20 cloves

When preparing a fresh ham for baking, wash it thoroughly and trim excess fat to ¼ inch from exterior of ham. Rub sugar or honey into top of ham, and stud with cloves. Place ham with some water into a roaster lined with aluminum foil. Make a tent of aluminum foil over the ham, and crimp closed. Cooking time will vary according to size. An average size ham should take about two hours. The ham is done when it has pulled away from the bone and lost about fifteen percent of its volume. The trick to getting it thoroughly cooked is to make sure it is completely thawed before cooking. If necessary, cooking may be completed in a microwave oven after the ham is sliced, but this tends to dry out the meat. Before removing from oven, discard top layer of foil and allow ham to brown. Drizzle sugar and/or honey on the top of the meat for a traditional ham, but mustard may be substituted for a different, less sweet taste. Cloves may be used with sugar, mustard, and honey or mixtures of them, as in a honey-mustard glaze.

BARBEQUE

Hams, shoulders, muscles, ribs, or any other part of a hog or bear
Bed of hot coals from hickory, pecan, oak, or mesquite
Barbeque sauce
    salt
    vinegar
    catsup
    honey
    black pepper
    red pepper
    mustard

A Southern barbeque is the most free form of all cooking. It consists of cooking cuts of pork over a bed of hot hardwood coals overnight either in the ground or in a metal smoker. This all-night cookout usually involves several participants and a case or two of beer. The meat is cooked on a metal grill over the coals and turned and basted with bar-

Bear haunch on grill, the start of a tasty barbeque. Like pork, bear meat may also be made into roast and cooked either bone-in or deboned.

Barbequed ribs with a tomato-base sauce. These ribs could be derived from alligators, bears, deer, or hogs. The meat tastes slightly different from animal to animal, but all varieties are delicious.

beque sauce as needed. Continuous watch must be kept to keep the fat dripping from the pork from igniting and burning the meat. Barbeque sauces vary widely. In North Carolina, a vinegar-pepper sauce is used. In the Piedmont area of South Carolina and Georgia, a tomato-based pepper sauce is the standard, and a mustard-based sauce is traditional in parts of Alabama. Experiment until you find your own favorite. Honey is preferred over sugar, at least by me. Once the barbeque is cooked, it may be sliced or pulled and served either on a bun or a plate without bread, topped with additional sauce. Barbeque goes well with cole slaw, potato salad, and beer. Brunswick stew is a traditional accompaniment.

BRUNSWICK STEW

Traditionally, Brunswick stew was made from the edible parts of a hog's head, although my late wife, Thresa, claimed, "There are no eatable parts on the head of a hog!" In recent times, Brunswick stew is chicken based and cooked with tomatoes, corn, butter beans, and often such other meats as turtle and/or squirrel. Good Brunswick stew has a slight vinegar and pepper taste, but it is not hot. This recipe is for an animal that has a live weight of about 100 pounds. Scale up accordingly for bigger hogs or bear.

1 cleaned head of a hog or bear
1 pound deer or other meat
2 15-ounce cans cut corn (not cream style)
1 medium Spanish onion, finely chopped
1 6-ounce can tomato paste
4 tablespoons white vinegar
4 tablespoons Catalina salad dressing
1 teaspoon salt
1/2 teaspoon black pepper

Place skinned and washed head into a large pot and cover with water. Boil until meat is tender. Remove meat from skull and neck and chop finely. Discard membranes from tongue and anything else you deem too far out to eat. Let the boiled brains remain in the skull. Pour about half of the boiled water into a smaller pot, and add other ingredients except corn. Continue boiling until meat almost completely separates. Add corn about an hour before serving. The stew should be meaty and thick and may be eaten as is or served over toast or rice.

ROAST PORK (OR DEER) (POT ROAST)

Pork backstrap, ham, shoulder, or other muscle group
1 teaspoon salt
$1/2$ teaspoon black pepper
$1/2$ onion, coarsely chopped
$1/2$ bell pepper, coarsely chopped
1 cup water

Rub thawed pork with salt and pepper, and place in aluminum foil or pan with chopped onions and peppers. Add $1/2$ cup of water and seal foil. Roast in oven at 350 degrees. Check after one hour; add additional water and continue cooking, if necessary. Deer will lose almost half its volume, but pork will not shrink as much. Slice and serve while warm. A variant of this recipe uses pot roast. Cut up potatoes, carrots, and cabbage, if desired, and place into a large iron pot with the roast. Cook on a stove eye until done. The roast makes an easy one-pot meal for the deer camp.

TURKEY

CHRISTMAS TURKEY, WITH CORNBREAD DRESSING AND GIBLET GRAVY

Cooking the Christmas turkey dinner is a three-day process. Three days before the holiday, I cook eggbread, hoecake, and toast for the dressing. The day before Christmas, I cook the turkey, and on Christmas morning the dressing goes into the oven so that it is served warm. The following recipes are presented in order of recommended preparation.

EGGBREAD

$2^3/4$ cups yellow cornmeal (or yellow cornmeal bread mix)
1 teaspoon sugar
1 teaspoon baking powder (if using plain cornmeal)
1 teaspoon baking soda (if using plain cornmeal)
1 teaspoon black pepper
1 teaspoon salt
2 eggs
1 teaspoon olive oil
$1/4$–$1/2$ cup milk

In a large bowl, combine yellow cornmeal, flour, and 1 teaspoon each of salt, sugar, baking soda, and baking power (if using a cornmeal bread mix, add flour, but omit other ingredients). Melt one tablespoon of shortening and pour over mixed, dry ingredients. Add eggs and sufficient milk to make a thick liquid paste. It should be thin enough to pour freely. Coat fly pan with olive oil and pour in mix, shaking it to allow bubbles to rise. Cook in 350-degree oven for fifteen minutes until brown on top and bread starts to pull away slightly from edges of the frying pan. When done and cool, crumble into a large bowl. Eggbread is excellent when buttered and eaten warm or served with syrup and butter for breakfast.

HOECAKE

2 cups flour
3 tablespoons Crisco shortening
milk
1 teaspoon baking powder
1 teaspoon baking soda
1 tablespoon olive oil

This simple bread is made by combining 2 cups of flour with 3 tablespoons of Crisco shortening and sufficient milk to make a soft paste. If using self-rising flour, do not add baking powder. If using plain flour, add one teaspoon each of baking powder and baking soda. Use a spoon to layer the mix in the bottom of a thick cast-iron frying pan that has been whipped with Crisco or oil. Cook in 350-degree oven with eggbread. The hoecake will be white on top with lightly browned points when done. Crumble with eggbread into bowl, taking care to break the crust into fine particles.

ROASTED TURKEY

1 plucked wild turkey with giblets
butter
salt
1 large onion
3 stalks of celery
3 cups water

To thaw turkey, set it out on a counter the day before it is to be cooked. Once the surface is soft to the touch, move it to a cooler spot and continue the thawing process. Put it in refrigerator overnight. The next morning, place it in a sink of cold water. When possible, pull out the frozen bag of giblets and change the water. Place giblets in a 3-quart pot to boil, and wash turkey thoroughly inside and out with clear water. Line the bottom of a roaster with heavy-duty aluminum foil, leaving at least 2 inches protruding from the top of the roaster. Rub turkey breast with butter and salt. Cut up a large onion and three stalks of celery and place them inside the body cavity. Place turkey into foil-lined roaster. Wild turkeys have tall breasts, which may not allow the lid of a conventional turkey roaster to close. Add 3 cups of water. Place another sheet of foil over top of turkey crimping the edges. Cook turkey in oven preheated to 350 degrees. Cooking time will vary, depending on the size of the bird. Check the bird after three hours and add more water, if necessary. The turkey is done when the legs move freely and start to tear away from the body. Do not brown the bird, as this merely dries it out. When done, remove from oven, save "drippings" from pan, and place turkey on large platter to cool. When still warm, cover with a clean cotton towel and place in refrigerator. Once cold, slice immediately before serving.

DRESSING

Turkey drippings
Eggbread
Hoecake
3 slices wheat toast
2 teaspoons black pepper
6 eggs
3 stalks of celery
1 large onion
1 teaspoon sage (optional)

Dressing is cooked in a separate pan; stuffing is placed inside the bird. A vital component of dressing is the turkey "drippings" gathered from cooking the bird. The drippings are refrigerated overnight and used to make the dressing Christmas morning. (Sage is not used in stuffing and dressing in the Southern tradition. If your family has traditionally used it, it may be added, but sage is a strong spice and a teaspoon in a pan of dressing is sufficient.) Add three slices of crumbled wheat toast to crumbled eggbread and hoecake, and mix with 2 teaspoons of black pepper. Crack six eggs on top. Now add finely cut celery and onions. Reliquefy the turkey "drippings" by placing them in a boiler and heat-

Cornbread dressing with giblet gravy on the bottom and turkey soup are side dishes made from an oven-roasted wild turkey.

ing. Start pouring in the liquefied "drippings," mixing as you pour. The dressing mix should be moist but not a liquid. Reserve 1 heaping table-spoon of raw dressing to add to giblet gravy. Spoon into large greased pan in a layer not more than 1 inch thick. Cook excess, if necessary, in smaller fry pans. Smooth top of dressing in pans. There should be no free liquid, but all of the particles should be wetted. Place in oven at 350 degrees and cook approximately twenty minutes. When the dressing is browned at the edges and the celery is soft, it is done. When cut, it should still be slightly moist. Cut, place on platter, and serve warm.

GIBLET GRAVY

Neck of wild turkey
Giblets from wild turkey
Turkey drippings
1 boiled egg, peeled and chopped

Remove boiled liver, gizzard, heart, and neck from pot of boiling water, and allow organs to cool. Add remaining pan "drippings" from turkey to pot. Chop up one boiled egg and place in pot. Pick meat from neck and cut longer strings with scissors so that none is longer than $1/2$ inch. Cut up organ meat and add back to pot. Simmer for thirty minutes before serving. The gravy is quite lumpy and is best dipped with a ladle rather than poured.

Accessory dishes: To complete a Southern Christmas meal, you could serve a baked ham, rice, sweet potato soufflé, succotash (corn and butterbeans mixed), homemade rolls, and, for those not brought up in a rice-eating culture, potato salad. Condiments would include cranberry sauce, pickled peaches, celery stuffed with pimento-cheese, toasted salted pecans, and white-powdered sugar-coated dates stuffed with pecans. Dessert offerings could be a nut-filled fruitcake, pecan pie, coconut cake and ice cream, and Christmas cookies. No alcohol was served during Christmas dinner—only water or iced tea. After we ate, sherry and port were offered to adult guests.

Putting a meal like this together takes considerable work, but when served on old-family china with silver, this meal is a tangible link between all generations of the family, including those who are no longer with you.

FISH

GAR STEAKS, NUGGETS, AND SCALLOPS

2 pounds gar meat, cut into steaks, nuggets, or
    1-inch cubes for scallops
3 cups canola oil
1 cup flour
2 teaspoons salt
1 teaspoon black pepper
1 teaspoon dill weed
1 large brown paper bag

Heat oil. While oil is heating, mix dry ingredients in plastic bag and flour cut pieces of gar. Use tongs to drop gar into oil one at a time, taking care to avoid the splatter. Cook to golden brown and drain on brown paper bags. Serve while hot. Do not overcook, as this will toughen the meat. Gar is versatile. It may be used in stir frys, ground and made into patties, or battered in an egg-flour-milk mixture and deep-fried for an excellent fish sandwich. Serve with a semidry white wine, such as Italian Pescevino, which is particularly blended to complement fish.

BAKED CARP

1 carp, cleaned and scaled with head removed
1 medium onion, chopped
2 teaspoons margin
1 teaspoon salt
1 cup water

Wrap scaled, cleaned carp in aluminum foil. Add water and salt, and dot margin and sprinkle onion over top of fish. Bake at 350 degrees for about an hour. When slightly cooled, remove from foil, take off skin, and place fish on platter. Rub with 1 teaspoon of butter, and sprinkle with salt and lemon juice. Serve hot. Carp taken from clean waters makes an excellent baked fish. Remove the red medial line from the center of both sides of the fish before serving. Avoid cutting carp into sections, as this cuts through the small bones. Guests should use their forks to pull meat from one side of the fish, then turn the fish over, and pull from the other side. Uneaten baked carp can be mixed with mayonnaise, boiled egg, and sweet pickles to make a carp salad, which will keep under refrigeration for a couple of days. Serve with a semidry white wine.

INDEX

Page numbers in italics indicate illustrations.